CLASS

This engaging account traces the complex relationship between class, literature and culture from the medieval period to the present. It is the ideal guide for any reader seeking to understand this complex term and the ways in which it can inform literary and cultural analysis.

Gary Day guides readers through the complex strands of a relationship where literature represents class but also enables certain class formations to develop. As his survey enters the twentieth century, he looks beyond the written text to examine the ways in which cinema and television represent class. The author then uses his revised notion of class to tackle contemporary cultural theories head-on.

This is the perfect introduction to a concept which impacts not only on literary and cultural studies but also on daily life.

Gary Day is a principal lecturer in English at De Montfort University, Bedford. He is the author of *Re-reading Leavis: 'Culture' and Literary Criticism* and has edited a number of books on literature and culture.

THE NEW CRITICAL IDIOM

SERIES EDITOR: JOHN DRAKAKIS, UNIVERSITY OF STIRLING

The New Critical Idiom is an invaluable series of introductory guides to today's critical terminology. Each book:

- provides a handy, explanatory guide to the use (and abuse) of the term
- offers an original and distinctive overview by a leading literary and cultural critic
- relates the term to the larger field of cultural representation

With a strong emphasis on clarity, lively debate and the widest possible breadth of examples, *The New Critical Idiom* is an indispensable approach to key topics in literary studies.

Also available in this series:

CLASS

Gary Day

LONDON AND NEW YORK

First published 2001
by Routledge
11 New Fetter Lane, London EC4P 4EE

Simultaneously published in the USA and Canada
by Routledge
29 West 35th Street, New York, NY 10001

Routledge is an imprint of the Taylor & Francis Group

Typeset in Garamond by Taylor & Francis Books Ltd
Printed and bound in Great Britain by Clays Ltd, St Ives plc

British Library Cataloguing in Publication Data
A catalogue record for this book is available from the British Library

Library of Congress Cataloging in Publication Data
Day, Gary, 1956–
    Class/Gary Day.
      p.cm – (New critical idiom)
    Includes bibliographical references and index.
    1. Marxist criticism. 2. Criticism–Political aspects. 3. Canon
(Literature) 4. Social classes in literature. I. Title. II. Series.

PN98.C6 D36 2001
801'.95–dc21   00–65296

ISBN 0–415–18222–0 (hbk)
ISBN 0–415–18223–9 (pbk)

For Charlotte, who is in Mrs Mills' class
and for Deborah who is in one of her own

CONTENTS

SERIES EDITOR'S PREFACE

The New Critical Idiom is a series of introductory books which seeks to extend the lexicon of literary terms, in order to address the radical changes which have taken place in the study of literature during the last decades of the twentieth century. The aim is to provide clear, well-illustrated accounts of the full range of terminology currently in use, and to evolve histories of its changing usage.

The current state of the discipline of literary studies is one where there is considerable debate concerning basic questions of terminology. This involves, among other things, the boundaries which distinguish the literary from the non-literary; the position of literature within the larger sphere of culture; the relationship between literatures of different cultures; and questions concerning the relation of literary to other cultural forms within the context of interdisciplinary studies.

It is clear that the field of literary criticism and theory is a dynamic and heterogeneous one. The present need is for individual volumes on terms which combine clarity of exposition with an adventurousness of perspective and a breadth of application. Each volume will contain as part of its apparatus some indication of the direction in which the definition of particular terms is likely to move, as well as expanding the disciplinary boundaries within which some of these terms have been traditionally contained. This will involve some re-situation of terms within the larger field of cultural representation, and will introduce examples from the area of film and the modern media in addition to examples from a variety of literary texts.

ACKNOWLEDGEMENTS

I would like to thank my colleagues at De Montfort for taking the strain while I enjoyed the leisure of a sabbatical, particularly Nigel Wood and Alistair Walker. The scepticism of Kathy Bell and Dominic Fox sharpened many ideas as did the constant questions of Kevin Morris. Clive Bloom was, as ever, a useful source of information and an invaluable support as was Libby di Niro, who generously read much of the manuscript and educated me about the eighteenth century. Andy Mousley's sense of humour has sustained me while his expertise on the Renaissance and his work on humanism have helped shape this book. My biggest intellectual debt is to the general editor, John Drakakis, for his encyclopaedic knowledge, his tips and pointers, and his sharp eye for the weak link or the poor phrase. I am grateful to Margaret Griffith of De Montfort library for her advice and for her miraculous knack of knowing just where to look. Thanks to Joy Dye for the glossary and for her endless e-mails about life, the universe and everything. Finally, I owe thanks to Elizabeth Thompson at Routledge for all her encouragement, polite reminders and grace under pressure and to Sophie Richmond, the copy editor, for her eagle eyes.

INTRODUCTION

This book examines the relationship between 'class' and 'literature' from the late medieval period to the present. I put these terms in quotation marks because they are problematic and I will use quotation marks whenever I need to *emphasise* the problematic nature of such terms. I base this book on the conviction that class still has a role to play in understanding the nature of literary works. In particular I am concerned to show that there is a link between the economic form of capitalism and 'literary' representation. As such this book is different from the prevailing view in literary studies that it is not necessary to relate 'culture' back to some prior cause in order to understand it. I use Karl Marx's (1818–83) analysis of class but also look briefly at Max Weber's (1864–1920) view of the subject. These two thinkers are widely recognised as the most influential commentators on class and, as Stephen Edgell (1993) has noted, contemporary sociologists adopt and modify one or other of these paradigms.

We shall encounter a number of Marxist approaches to 'literature' in the following pages but some of the main ones can be mentioned here. First, there is Georg Lukács' claim that literature, particularly the novel, is able to penetrate the surface of society, highlighting hidden connections and identifying the underlying trends which may lead to its revolutionary transformation. A closely related view is Louis Althusser's assertion (1966 & 1996) that 'literature' can make us aware of the ideological nature of our conventional conception of 'reality'. Second, there is Lucien Goldmann's idea (1964 & 1975) that literature represents the world-view of a particular group. Finally, Etienne Balibar and Pierre Macherey (1978) argue that the education system reinforces economic divisions by restricting access to knowledge of the 'literary' canon. While these and other views are important, my approach is different. My focus is the relationship between 'literature' and exchange – basically the system of money, its meanings and its uses. My reason for adopting this approach is that it brings together 'literature' and economics in contrast to current postmodern thinking which insists on their separateness. The relevance of this for class is that the growth of exchange represents the triumph of bourgeois capitalism over aristocratic feudalism. In the following chapters I trace the rise of exchange and its connection with English literature because it was in England that the development of capitalism first took place and because Marx based his analysis of class on English society. This does not mean, however, that my observations cannot be applied to other literatures since we now live in a world of global capitalism. Before we discuss how the relationship between literature and class is manifest in exchange, it will be helpful to outline the main features of the argument and quickly review some of its main terms.

A BRIEF HISTORY OF 'CLASS'

'Class' is a notoriously difficult term to define because it occurs across a range of disciplines – sociology, politics, cultural studies and 'literary criticism' – all of which give it different meanings, weightings and explanatory values. In very broad terms, the word 'class' refers to divisions in society. The term did not exist in ancient Greece where the usual word for such division was *genos* meaning race, or *mere* meaning category. The city states of ancient Greece were divided into three main groups: citizens, *metics* (resident foreigners) and slaves. Citizens, the majority of whom were farmers, tradesmen or artisans, were distinguished from one another by how much land they owned or by which trade they followed. This, in turn, determined the amount of tax they should pay. Citizens were distinguished from *metics* and slaves by their entitlement to participate in the state. Aristotle distinguished between citizens and slaves by saying that the former were ruled by their minds and the latter by their bodies (1962: 33): a distinction that, in a modified form, has persisted to the present day. Tony Parsons characterises the working class as 'belch[ing] and fart[ing] their way through life' whereas the middle class 'read books [and] fill the theatres' (1994: 228, 238). The divisions between the various groups of ancient Greek society were based on birth and believed to be divinely ordained for the well-being of society. There was, then, no class structure in ancient Greece, but there were social divisions connected to categories of person, occupation and wealth. These divisions, moreover, were not seen as harmful but were viewed as the expression of a finely balanced society where everyone knew their place.

We get the word 'class' from the Latin *classis* (plural *classes*). According to Charlton Lewis and Charles Short, compilers of the *Standard Latin Dictionary*, this term is a variant of *calare*, meaning to 'call out, proclaim, or summon a religious assembly'. It had two main senses. The first referred to an armed gathering, either on land or water, while the second, and most important, referred to the divisions of the Roman people according to their estates and age. These divisions were instituted by Servius Tullius (578–534 BC) who sorted the Roman people into property classes in an attempt to break up the various 'clans' whose activities were threatening the stability of the state; and he followed this up by organising them into centuries or regiments for military purposes. The result of this division was the creation of two major groups in Roman society, the patricians or aristocrats, and the plebeians or commoners. The plebeians were often in conflict with the patricians over what they saw as the arbitrary way the law was applied – a situation that was eventually resolved by the codification of the law and the creation of tribunes, or representatives of the people, who won a veto over the action of patrician magistrates (494 BC). The codification of Roman law stipulated that while rich and poor were entitled to its protection, a slave was not. As in Greek society, there was a clear division between a free man and a slave. At its end, the Roman Empire consisted of four layers: nobles, other citizens, freedmen and slaves. The word used to describe these divisions was not classes but *ordo* which not only corresponds to the English order but also translates as 'rank' as in 'the ranks of the armed forces' (Calvert 1982: 41). The terms 'rank' and 'order' were to dominate ideas of the social structure until they were superseded, arguably only briefly (Cannadine 1998), by Karl Marx's concept of class.

With the conversion of Constantine the Great in AD 338, a new element appeared in the conception of social division, Christianity. St Augustine (AD 354–430) located the origin of social differentiation in the Fall. From that fateful event came the division of mankind into masters and servants, the institution of private property and its consequent inequalities, and the impossibility of ever realising a truly harmonious society without the need for laws. In addition, 'society was no longer stratified horizontally, between master and servant but vertically between ecclesiastic and layman' (Calvert 1982: 44). The Christian view of humanity underpinned the estates model of society, which dominated Europe from the Middle Ages to the Enlightenment. It consisted, in simple terms, of three layers: the nobles, the clergy and the common people, with each one being regarded as a necessary part of the whole, a conception expressed in the image of society as a body. There were, of course, divisions within each layer, and here the term 'rank' was important, particularly in respect of the nobility, but the word 'station' was the one more commonly employed to designate a person's place in society. According to Peter Calvert, the word 'station' referred to a person's employment as well as their specified location and it differed from 'class' in being 'a concept essential to the individual rather than the collectivity' (1982: 14). However, the more common word for referring to social divisions was 'order', which of course implied that any other form of social organisation was a species of 'disorder'.

Although Christianity stressed the inevitability of social division, it also contained within itself a more egalitarian view of human relations. The message of the Gospels was that all men were equal before God: a pronouncement which over-rode social and racial distinctions but not gender ones. This 'brotherhood of man' fuelled criticisms of the social hierarchy prior to the English Revolution as expressed in the popular refrain 'When Adam delved and Eve span / Who was then the Gentleman?' Simultaneously, Christianity also facilitated the growth of capitalism with commentators reminding readers that God 'hath instituted the use of negotiation, market and exchange for the mutual benefit of all' (cited in Hill 1993: 158). The seventeenth-century puritan Richard Baxter said Christian societies could not tolerate idleness and this stress on the necessity for hard work justified the division of society into rich and poor: wealth, in puritan doctrine, was God's reward for labour as well as a sign that a person was destined for heaven not hell. The mobilisation of Christian doctrine to legitimise the development of capitalism may have provided a critique of the divisions of feudalism but it was only to institute new ones based on money rather than land.

It was in the seventeenth century that the word 'class' entered the English language for the first time. Thomas Blount, a seventeenth-century Catholic, recorded it in his dictionary, *Glossographia* (1656), where it is defined as 'a ship, or Navy, an order or distribution of people according to their several Degrees. In Schools (wherein the word is most used), a Form or Lecture restrained to a certain company of Scholars' (cited in Calvert 1982: 12). The question arises as to why, at this point in English history, the term 'class' should start to displace the more common ones of 'order' or 'station'. One explanation is that the act of classification was becoming increasingly important to the natural sciences. Its success in ordering the variety of the plant and animal world promised a more comprehensive account of the social order. However, while in biology the word 'class' assumed an equality between the different types of, say, flowers this was not how it operated in social description where, grafted on to existing divisions, 'class' made them seem a law of nature rather than an accident of history. Another explanation for the entry of 'class' into the English language in the mid-seventeenth century is that this was a decisive moment in the development of capitalism. Simplifying greatly, the feudal economy was based on agriculture and characterised by a series of obligations between landlord and tenant, whereas the capitalist economy was based on manufacture and characterised by a purely monetary relation between employers and employees. The appearance of the word 'class', in other words, is linked to fundamental changes in the economy and to their effect on social relations. In brief, the older vocabulary of 'order' and 'station' projected an essentially harmonious view of society whereas the new idiom of class was an expression of social conflict.

MARX AND CLASS

Marx located the source of this conflict in the fact that one class owned the means of production, while the other class owned nothing but their labour power, which they were obliged to sell in order to survive. He therefore explained class in economic terms. The means of production were the land, factories and machinery necessary to produce goods, as well as the money to invest in new equipment, whereas labour power was simply the skills or strength of workers to undertake specific tasks. Marx called the class who owned the means of production the bourgeoisie and the class who sold their labour power the proletariat. According to Marx, the interests of these two classes were fundamentally opposed since the bourgeoisie, in order to make a profit, paid the workers the lowest possible wage while demanding that they attain the highest level of productivity. Marx used the term 'social relations of production' (1859 & 1968: 181) to describe the ownership and non-ownership of the means of production. He went on to say that the sum total of these relations constitutes the economic structure of society, 'the real foundation on which rises a legal and political superstructure and to which correspond definite forms of social consciousness' (ibid.). In other words, the nature of the economy determines a society's politics, laws, culture and education.

The precise role of the economy in respect of culture has excited a great deal of comment. Does the economy wholly determine the nature of culture? Is it merely the expression of the ideas of the ruling class? Does culture have its own autonomy in respect of the economic base or is it entirely independent of it? These questions will inform our discussion of 'literature' and so need not detain us here. What does need to be stressed is that Marx defined class in objective terms as a specific relation to production. Furthermore, he believed that class struggle was the motive force of history. The antagonism between the classes, based on their different relations to production, makes them conscious of themselves as classes and this leads to conflict and therefore change. However, Marx's concept of class struggle was based on his analysis of the bourgeoisie and proletariat in industrial society and we therefore have to be careful about applying it to earlier periods. There is also the problem that Marx's definition of class varies greatly and is ultimately inconclusive. Sometimes he says that society is composed of two classes and sometimes three, and he occasionally uses the term as a synonym for a faction or group without particular reference to its position in the mode of production. Marx did attempt a systematic analysis of class at the end of Volume 3 of *Capital* (1864) but died before completing it.

CLASS AND STATUS

Marx regarded the transition from capitalism to feudalism as crucial to his account of class. The ascendancy of the bourgeoisie showed that social position was no longer dependent on birth but effort. This change in the conception of the social order was captured by the appearance of the word 'class' which formed a dynamic contrast to the more static 'order' or 'station' derived from the Latin *stare*, to stand. However, it would be wrong to suppose that the use of the word 'class' entirely superseded older views of the hierarchical nature of society. The terms 'class' and 'status' – a variant of 'station' – existed side by side and are still linked in our understanding of the contemporary world, with some commentators emphasising class (Adonis and Pollard 1997) and others status (Brook 1997) in their respective accounts of the nature of English society. Raymond Williams has drawn attention to the confused labelling that arises from the proximity of these two terms, especially in our understanding of 'middle class' and 'working class'. These appellations must be distinguished from bourgeoisie and proletariat which describe a relation to production whereas 'middle' and 'working' class, while not excluding this relation are, particularly the former, more suggestive of the old hierarchical relationships in society. Williams claims that 'middle class' was 'a self-conscious interposition between persons of rank and the common people' and is therefore more appropriate to a hierarchical view of society (1988: 64). By contrast, he argues that 'working class' signifies a relationship to production and is therefore more applicable to a class view of society (ibid.). However, this distinction is not as clear as it first seems, for both the middle class and the working class saw themselves as the productive groups in society compared to the 'idle' and unproductive aristocracy (ibid.: 63–4). The picture becomes more complicated after 1830 as the middle class and the working class not only begin to oppose one another but also to divide internally, with the former separating into lower and upper sections and the latter into skilled, semi-skilled and labouring ones. These intra-class relationships were based on status considerations such as dress, attitudes and behaviour and they contrasted with inter-class relationships based on an opposition of economic interests. Moreover, these internal differences, at the upper end, were often based on an identification with the class above and this was particularly true of the nineteenth-century middle class who strove to enter the ranks of the aristocracy. In short, the internal relations of class existed in some tension with their external ones: the consciousness of belonging to a status group, we might say, inhibited the development of class consciousness.

Status and class are intimately related. As a term in English, status pre-dates class and is taken directly from the Latin *status* meaning 'standing', 'position' or 'condition'. It was originally a legal term designating any mark of distinction which placed an individual in a defined position in society in relation to others, for example marriage. However, it had also had a more general application because one of its meanings, 'condition', 'led to *state* and *estate*' (Williams 1988: 298), terms cognate with the hierarchical conception of medieval society whose most complete expression was the great chain of being. This was a metaphor for comprehending how all creation, from God to the smallest living creature, was linked together in an intricate, interdependent structure. More relevant for our purpose is that medieval society, as mentioned earlier, was divided into social groups: the nobility, clergy and commoners. Hence we can say that status, in so far as it was one of a complex of terms used to describe this society, differs from class in that it refers to *social* rather than *economic* groupings.

The German sociologist Max Weber was interested in the relationship between class and status. Although he did not agree with Marx, he did acknowledge that 'property and lack of property are the basic categories of all class situations' (1948 & 1993: 182). The emphasis in Weber's definition of class falls not on production but on the constraints operating on a person's ability to earn a high income, to purchase high quality goods and to enjoy enhanced 'personal life experiences' (ibid.: 181). In this sense, argued Weber, 'class situation is ultimately market situation' (ibid.: 182). Status, by contrast, is defined in terms of honour or prestige; hence it is perfectly possible for a profession to carry a high prestige factor, for example a priest, while at the same time having a low remuneration. In addition, status groups are defined in terms of communities in contrast to classes which Weber claims, rather cryptically, are not communities, merely 'bases for communal action' (ibid.: 181). Status groups share the same values and style of life and their strong sense of group membership ensures that contact with other groups is kept to a minimum. Traditionally the identity of status groups was expressed through 'the privilege of wearing special costumes, [or] of eating special dishes taboo to others' (ibid.: 191) and, while certain groups today also distinguish themselves by style of dress, status is more likely to be expressed through a whole range of activities and attitudes, making it synonymous with 'culture'. Summing up the differences between 'class' and 'status' groups, Weber writes that the former 'are stratified according to their relations to production and acquisition of goods' whereas the latter 'are stratified according to the principles of their consumption of goods as represented by special styles of life' (ibid.: 193). These 'styles of life' give status groups a stronger sense of their own identity in contrast to classes where one of the problems is how to understand class consciousness: how it arises and what forms it takes.

If we are to give an accurate account of the social structure, we need to examine it in terms of class and status. However, because we live in a consumer society, it is reasonable to assume that 'status' would be a more prominent term in social analysis than 'class'. In fact, however, the concept of status seems to have been overshadowed by that of 'culture'. This is understandable because the two terms do overlap since both are concerned with 'modes of living' (Weber 1948 & 1993: 182; Williams 1958: 311). Nevertheless, there are important differences between them, the main one being that status refers emphatically to the exclusiveness of group identities and how they are expressed, whereas culture refers to the struggle between dominant and subordinate groups over the construction and meaning of social experience. In short, the concept of status is premised on social stability, that of culture on social conflict. This highlights the fact that each has a different relationship to the idea of class. Status is associated more with a view of class as balance, culture with a view of class as struggle.

I have dwelt on 'class', 'status' and 'culture' because these will be important terms in the chapters which follow. Strictly speaking, we cannot apply the term 'class' to English society before the mid-seventeenth century; status is a more accurate description of social divisions before that period. This does not mean that economic divisions did not exist, only that we cannot understand them in terms of the Marxist conception of class, which centres on the antagonistic relations between the bourgeoisie and the proletariat. As Marx himself noted, the small-holding peasants of feudalism did not constitute a class because their 'mode of production', farming their own and their lord's land, 'isolate[d] them from one another instead of bringing them into mutual intercourse' (1852 & 1968: 170). And he continues, 'In so far as there is merely a local interconnection among these peasants, and the identity of their interest begets no community, no national bond, and no political organisation among them, they do not form a class' (ibid.: 171).

CLASS AND EXCHANGE

However, if we look at another aspect of class, notably its relation to exchange, it is possible to extend the notion back to at least the late fourteenth century. The term 'exchange' is short for the exchange relation which, along with production, is the 'foundation [on which] the bourgeoisie built itself up' (Marx and Engels 1848 & 1968: 40). In very basic terms, the bourgeoisie grew rich from trade and manufacture and thus became more powerful than the feudal lords. They pioneered a new economy based on money rather than land. According to Marx, the exchange relation, in its simplest form, is the process by which commodities are exchanged for money. Money provides a common measure by which commodities can be exchanged. It does so by representing commodities not as they are but by what they have in common, and what they have in common is the human labour that produced them. The difference in price between commodities expresses the different amounts of labour used to produce them. In order for money to represent what commodities have in common, it must ignore what is individual about them. Money, we might say, takes no account of the fact that one commodity is a car and another is a computer, it is simply a measure of the amount of labour time necessary to produce these different items. Money does not differentiate between different kinds of labour but views the variety of physical or mental work purely in terms of time. It is therefore an abstract system of representation dealing in quantities not qualities.

The calculation of labour in terms of time rather than kind brings us to Marx's theory of surplus value. At its most basic level, this states that the capitalist sells his or her product for more than he or she pays the workers who produce it. More specifically, the capitalist pays the worker for the time it takes for him or her to earn the minimum amount of money he or she needs in order to survive. If this time amounts to three hours a day, and the worker is employed for eight hours a day, that means the capitalist obtains five hours of free labour from the worker and this is the source of profit. The worker is therefore exploited by the capitalist since he or she does not receive the full remuneration for his or her labour. It is important to stress the fact of exploitation because it has been ignored in recent accounts of class analysis. In 1998 David Cannadine claimed that 'class as hierarchy' was – and is – the most accurate description of the English social structure (1998: 22). Similarly, the major paradigm of cultural studies is a view of the social formation where dominant and subordinate groups contest the meaning of culture in its widest possible sense. Both these omit any reference to how the class which owns the means of production is in a position to exploit those who own nothing but their labour power. Both fail to realise how the concept of 'domination', whether expressed in hierarchical terms or understood as a struggle for hegemony – the right to determine cultural meaning – does not in and of itself imply any specific economic interests by those who dominate. As Olin Wright observes, 'parents dominate small children but this does not imply that they have intrinsically opposed interests to their children' (1989: 5). Exploitation, by contrast, does imply a set of opposing material interests; it implies that 'the rich are rich because the poor are poor; and that the welfare of the rich depends upon the effort of the poor' (ibid.: 8). It entails 'both economic oppression and appropriation of at least part of the social surplus by the oppressor' (ibid.).

It is possible to give a history of class in terms of exploitation and this is what Marx had in mind when he wrote that '[t]he history of all hitherto existing societies is the history of class struggles' (Marx and Engels 1848 & 1968: 35). For example, although I have said that the *word* 'class' did not exist in ancient Greece, exploitation certainly did. As G. E. M. De. Ste. Croix notes, 'wealth consisted in the ownership of land and in the control of unfree labour which enabled the propertied class to exploit the rest of the population: that is to say, to appropriate a surplus out of their labour' (1981: 33). Similarly, the specific form of exploitation under feudalism was the lord's power to extract 'surplus value' from the peasant by making him work on the lord's land without pay. The class struggle in feudalism was therefore over the individual liberty of the peasant. However, as we have already noted, the fact that peasants did not encounter each other on a large scale meant they did not develop a consciousness of themselves as a class. There are, in other words, other factors to be taken into account when discussing class apart from exploitation, though that is its defining feature. The link between exploitation and exchange is that each is market-based: both labour power and the commodity are sold for money. However, our focus will be the mechanism of exchange and its relation to literature.

EXCHANGE AND 'LITERATURE'

Both the exchange relation and literature are forms of representation: money represents commodities, literature 'reality'. Although exchange and literature are forms of representation, they do not represent their respective objects in the same way. Money, it will be remembered, pays no attention to the unique qualities of the commodity, only to what it has in common with other commodities. By contrast, F. R. Leavis (1895–1978), an important twentieth-century critic, stated that literature dealt with the concrete, not the abstract, the particular not the general. However, this distinction is not an absolute one for, in the eighteenth century, Samuel Johnson (1709–84) observed that the 'business of the poet ... is to examine not the individual but the species' (1759 & 1996: 875). Such differences over the nature of 'literature' draw attention to the historicity of the term. Very schematically, 'literature' derives from the Latin *littera* meaning a

letter. *Litterature* was the common early English form and signified being able to read; it was therefore close to our modern word
literacy (Williams 1977: 46). By the late eighteenth century, the
term had come to mean the ability to discern qualities of artistic
excellence, while in the nineteenth and twentieth centuries it
denoted creative or imaginative works, the 'best' of which constituted a tradition embodying the various aspects of 'British' identity (ibid.: 46–54). There are many reasons why the idea of
'literature' has changed over the centuries but the one which concerns us is its relationship to exchange. This links it to the rise of
the bourgeoisie though it does not follow that literature is an
expression of bourgeois values. The point is rather that both literature and exchange are forms of representation, ways of structur-
ing and imagining the world, whose relationship is sometimes
complementary and sometimes contradictory.

This relationship will be a major focus from the late medieval
period to the end of the eighteenth century. We start with the
late fourteenth century because that is the moment when English
replaces Latin or French as the preferred medium of writing. At
the same time, money takes on an increasingly important role in
the feudal economy: the development of 'literature' keeps pace
with the development of the capitalist economy. In general, these
early chapters will describe the social divisions of the period
before considering a specific work or works and its or their relationship to exchange. There will be two lines of argument. The
first will be that 'literature' enacts aspects of the exchange relation and, in doing so, reveals how its logic is contradictory. The
second will be that, in the absence of a theory of economics, 'literature' itself becomes a means of imagining, negotiating and
even institutionalising the mechanism of exchange. 'Literature'
will be shown to be both the ally and the enemy of exchange. In
addition to analysing the transactions between 'literature' and economics at the level of exchange, these chapters also make occasional
reference to the fact that 'literature' in all its various meanings,

was a mark of social division in its own right. As one anonymous commentator of the fourteenth century remarked, '[t]he comyn people ... without lyterrature and good informacyon ben lyke to brute beestes' (cited *Oxford English Dictionary* 1963). A variation of this view was still current in the twentieth century with F. R. Leavis claiming that only an elite minority were capable of judging true literary worth. To view 'literature' in this way is to see it in terms of status rather than class, whereas to view it in relation to exchange is to see it in terms of class rather than status.

We shift the focus in the nineteenth and twentieth centuries from the relationship between 'literature' and exchange to the rise of the working class. The reason for this change of focus is that the Industrial Revolution has precipitated into existence a group whose interests are clearly opposed to those for whom they are forced to work in order to survive. We will look at the formation of the working class, its organs of expression, its internal divisions and its relations with the middle class. We will also look at how the working class was represented in some of the 'literature' of the period and how its own culture begins to be eroded by the development of mass culture. Indeed, the term 'culture' becomes increasingly important during the course of the book. Up to the end of the eighteenth century what concerns us is the relationship between 'literature', 'class' (in the form of exchange) and status; thereafter it is the relationship between 'literature', 'class' and 'culture'. The chief issues here are the relationship of 'culture' to the economic base; the question of the existence of an 'authentic' working-class culture, the relations between 'high' and 'popular' culture, and whether the current conception of culture in cultural studies as a form of 'resistance' to the dominant order is either accurate or adequate. In addition we shall also be considering the problem the idea of the individual poses for class. This issue arises in the medieval period but it becomes particularly pronounced in the twentieth century where it is the alibi of consumerism. The mention of consumerism brings us back to

exchange since it too is based on the idea that commodities represent human qualities, such as desirability and happiness, which
can be bought. The question of exchange, in other words, is not
forgotten but continues to be a point of reference in our discussion of the working class. Indeed, by the twentieth century we
shall see how the abstract system of representation, which characterises exchange, has come to condition nearly all other perceptions of the social order. The exchange relation begins with the
rise of the bourgeoisie but it eventually transcends them to
become the mode of apprehension common to all classes. We conclude by reiterating the view that it would be false to assert that
the particularity of 'literature' always opposes the generality of
exchange for, throughout the period covered in this book, 'literature' has also supported it. This is the case now where some of the
ideas of critical theory in respect of 'literature' have analogies to
market philosophy.

Inevitably the concentration, first on the relationship between
'literature' and exchange, and then on the representations of the
working class, means that other issues related to class do not
receive the attention they should. The most obvious and regret-
table omissions are feminism, race, region and sexuality.
However, the extensive coverage these have received elsewhere
goes some way to mitigating their exclusion here. But there is
another problem, namely that feminism, race, region and sexuality
are somehow seen as separate from the issue of class. Andrew
Milner goes further by suggesting that the politics of class have
become 'progressively "decentred" by an increasing pre-occupation
with ... gender, race, ethnicity, [and] sexuality' (1999: 7). Similarly,
Stefan Collini asserts that '[i]n the frequently incanted quartet of
race, class, gender and sexual orientation, there is no doubt that
class has been the least fashionable ... despite the fact that all the
evidence suggests that class remains the single, most powerful
determinant of life chances' (1994: 3). We need to address why,
say, feminism and class appear to be mutually exclusive before we

can analyse the class relations of gender, and that is too large an undertaking for a book of this size.

To try to deal with gender, race, region and sexuality without considering this problem would be to give a highly misleading account of their relationship to class. Not to deal with them, however, implies either that they have no relationship to class or that class is a more urgent topic of attention. There is some justification for this latter view in as much as class has been ignored in literary studies for the last twenty years. But it is not just a question of refocusing attention, it is also a question of asserting the primacy of class analysis over the various types of identity politics manifest in gender, race, region and sexuality. There is no doubt that women, ethnic groups, gays and lesbians have all suffered discrimination, hence it is reasonable to view society as characterised by a plurality of oppressions, each rooted in a different form of domination. But we need to explain why a system of domination should arise at all and it is here that Marx's claim, that the class which owns the means of production can determine the character of a society, is relevant. In short, class provides an account of the origin of inequality from which other forms of oppression arise. 'Literature' is one of those forms of oppression, but it also has the potential to transcend the mechanism of exchange with which it is otherwise so unwittingly complicit.

1

MEDIEVAL

This chapter describes the structure of late medieval society (roughly 1200–1500) and considers how far we can view it as a class society. To that end, it looks at the relationship between landlords and peasants and the 'rise of the bourgeoisie' as measured by the growth of the exchange relation of capitalism compared to the decay of the personal obligations characteristic of feudalism.

THE ESTATES MODEL OF SOCIETY

The standard view of the society of the Middle Ages is that it was divided into three estates: the clergy, whose business was with prayer and spiritual well-being; the warriors, who defended the land and the people with their arms; and the labourers who supported the other two. As one contemporary succinctly put it: 'the cleric prays, the knight fights and the peasant tills the soil' (cited in Medcalf 1981: 58). It was believed that these divisions were divinely ordained and that birth determined destiny. William Langland, in *Piers the Ploughman* (1379) says that God placed each person in their respective estates:

> He gave to some men Intelligence ... by which to earn their living as preachers and priests. ... He taught some men to ride out on horseback and recover unlawful gains by speed and strength of arm, and some he taught to till the soil, to ditch and to thatch.
>
> (1379 & 1966: 237–8)

Hence a person's Christian duty lay in 'working joyfully in the role assigned to them' (Medcalf 1981: 58).

The relationship between the three estates was strictly hierarchical. The priest came first, then the knight and then the labourer. 'To the knight it sufficeth not that he be given the best arms and the best beast but also that he be given seignory', that is, lordship over other men (cited in Keen 1990: 3). This lordship, however, entailed certain obligations. As Janet Coleman points out, 'each man of each estate should be recognised to have his due, and that the rich and powerful should support the poor and virtuous' (1981: 99). The relationship was, however, unequal. The lord's main responsibility towards his tenant farmers was to protect them in return for which he received money, food and livestock and labour on his land (Bloch 1962: 250). The lord's relation to his tenant was a class relation to the extent that he was able to exploit him by extracting his surplus labour. But the lord also had to pay homage to his liege lord, that is the person of a higher rank than himself who, in turn, would pay homage to his feudal superior and so on all the way up to the king. Known as vassalage, this homage consisted, in the first place, of military service, but it also involved attendance at the lord's court where, in return for his aid, the vassal received land, gifts and a share in the exercise of authority (ibid.: 219–30). The technical term for land granted to a lord was 'fief'. The lord did not own this land but held it on condition that he was loyal to his liege lord, a conception of property which differs profoundly from the idea of absolute ownership which characterises capitalism (Reynolds

1994: 53–4). 'Fiefdom' complicates the question of class since it implies a distinction between the lord's possession of the land and his exploitation of those who worked on it. Marx, however, believed that ownership and exploitation could not be separated since the former was the basis of the latter (Marx and Engels 1848 & 1968: 47).

Just as there were distinctions within the nobility so were there within the peasantry. The main dividing line, inherited from the Classical world, was between the free and the unfree. The former were able to move from one place to another, and dispose of their goods as they saw fit; the latter, serfs or villeins, were 'restricted as to freedom of movement, freedom of alienation of land and goods, and freedom of access to public jurisdiction' (Hilton 1985 & 1990: 68). With the revival of serfdom in the late middle ages, many peasant families were forced into dependence on aristocratic and church landowners and this rather blurred the distinction between the free and the unfree. However, there were other divisions within the peasantry, the main one being between those who had sufficient land to pay their rents and taxes and those whose holdings yielded a mere subsistence level. The very poor depended on what they could earn, in money or kind, to supplement the little they grew.

The variations within each estate suggest that, as a description of society, the model of the three estates was not entirely adequate. Indeed, within the third estate, no distinction was made between rich and poor, or between town and country. Hence, as Maurice Keen has noted, 'the conception of the three estates and their relations to one another was an ideal vision: it never did and never could have corresponded to reality' (1990: 3). John of Salisbury (1112–70) gives us another version of this model when he describes society in terms of the body: the priesthood as the soul, the warriors as the armed hands and the labourers as the feet. Like the three estates model, the emphasis was on harmony and cooperation. Each person, like each organ in the body, had their part to play in the smooth functioning of society. The estates model and the metaphor of society as a body are both status-based conceptions of the social order. As was noted in the introduction, status denotes an essentially static view of the social formation, with each group having a clearly defined function in relation to the whole. It will also be remembered that status was originally a legal term stipulating those marks of distinction which defined a person's place in society in relation to another: thus a knight could bear arms but a peasant could not. Similarly, a person's status determined what obligations, duties and responsibilities were owed to those above and below him or her. Within the Church, for instance, 'the bishop demanded homage from the abbots of his diocese; the canons required it from their less well provided colleagues and the parish priests had to do homage to the head of the religious community on which their parishes were dependent' (Bloch 1962: 348).

A status-based conception of the social order assumes that stability not change is the governing principle of society. However, the late medieval world, like all periods in history, was characterised by a number of developments that prefaced profound upheaval. One of the most important was the growing power of the mercantile bourgeoisie manifest in the growth of urban industries such as iron, paper and textiles. The growth of commodity production, together with the increase in the use of money, began to undermine the system of personal obligations that characterised feudalism (Anderson 1974 & 1996: 22). Put simply, coinage began to replace homage as the key social relation, though the full effects of this would not be felt until the nineteenth century. One sign of this change was a new conception of property. In feudalism, as we have seen, the possession or holding of land was conditional on the discharge of certain obligations but, as Anderson notes, 'the recovery and introduction of Roman law [in the late medieval world] with its concept of absolute and unconditional private property was fundamentally propitious to the growth of free capital in town and country' (ibid.: 24–5). In short, land began to be seen as a commodity rather than as the literal ground of a complex hierarchy of relationships. These changes led to a conflict of interest between the urban bourgeoisie and the landed nobility. The former had the economic initiative but the latter had the political power. We will look at how the rise of money affected the estates model of society when we discuss *Piers the Ploughman* (1379) and *Sir Gawain and the Green Knight* (1380). In the meantime we need to consider a much more obvious conflict of the late medieval period, that between landowners and peasants.

CLASS AND THE PEASANTS

The relation between landowners and peasants can be seen as a class relation to the extent that the former owned the land upon which the latter worked. As we have seen, the landlord was able to exploit the peasants, extracting from them surplus value in the form of rents, labour services or agricultural produce. Rodney Hilton (1985 & 1990) argues that the struggle between peasants and landlords over these matters was the main feature of late medieval society. This conflict was particularly sharp in the second half of the fourteenth century, culminating in the Peasants' Revolt of 1381.

The various tensions leading up to this were aggravated by the dramatic decline in population following the Black Death of 1348–9. This affected both rents and wages. The shortage of tenants meant that landlords were forced to rent at a lower rate, while the depleted population led peasants to demand not only a reduction of labour services but also higher wages. The landlords reacted by asserting their rights over their tenants with renewed vigour and by passing the Statute of Labourers in 1351, which sought to lay down maximum wage rates and to control the movement of labour. Peasant resistance to this took a number of forms, from legal challenges whose basis was that since they were the king's subjects, and therefore free men not villeins, landlords could not arbitrarily increase their services, to non-performance of these same services by refusing to plough the lord's land or thresh his wheat or carry his goods. There were also organised attacks in Middlesex (1351), Lincolnshire (1352) and Northamptonshire (1359), on the sessions of the Justices of the Labourers whose specific task was to enforce the statute of 1351. The revolt of 1381 was sparked by the introduction of another poll tax. Not only was this the third since 1377, it was also three times the rate of the previous two. The reason for the tax was mainly the cost of the Hundred Years War (1337–1453), which the Crown sought to pass on to the peasantry, but it was also to satisfy 'the expanding need of the ruling class for luxury goods' (Aers 1988: 15).

The rebels' main demand in 1381 was for the abolition of serfdom. In practical terms this would mean 'low fixed money rents; freedom of movement; freedom to buy and sell livestock; freedom to buy and sell land; freedom from arbitrary exactions such as tallage, marriage fines, death duties and entry fines' (Hilton 1985 & 1990: 148). Other demands included the end of all lordship except for that of the king; the abolition of the whole Church hierarchy except for one bishop; the division of Church property among the commons; and the payment of tithes only if the priest were poorer and more worthy than the parishioners (ibid.: 149). Together, these demands amounted to a wholesale rejection of the estates view of society. The peasants wanted to abolish private property and replace hierarchy with equality. In the words of John Ball:

> things cannot go right in England, and never will, until goods are held in common and there are no more villeins and gentlefolk, but we are all one and the same. In what way are those whom we call lords and masters greater than ourselves? Why do they hold us in bondage? If we all spring from a single

father and mother, Adam and Eve, how can they claim or prove
that they are lords more than us?

(cited in Froissart 1388 & 1978: 212)

The mouthpiece of political and social criticism was the ploughman, who emerged as a radical and disturbing figure in this
period (Hilton 1985 & 1990: 176–7). The anonymous poet of
Pierce the Plowman's Crede (1396) challenged the clergy by claiming that the ploughman could teach the creed better than friars or
monks. 'Ploughing', wrote Iolo Goch, a Welsh contemporary of
Langland, 'is "wisdom's way"' (cited in Hilton 1985 & 1990:
176). The prologue to *The Ploughman's Tale* (1400) complains that
while the ploughman provides for the clergy, he gets nothing in
return: 'They have the corn and we have the dust' (ibid.: 177); a
sentiment echoed by the speaker in *Gode Spede the Plow* (1409),
angry that those who 'mayntayne this worlde' (ibid.) should
receive so little reward for their labour. Ploughmen are thus represented as supporting the world with their labour and questioning how the fruits of their labour are distributed. This
'working-class' critique of social organisation will echo, in different forms, down the centuries, as will the contrast, in many of
these poems, between the industrious many and the idle few.

Marx claimed that there was no class consciousness among the
peasantry because they lived in scattered communities which
rarely came into contact with one another (1859 & 1968: 171).
Although the existence of poetry which placed the ploughman in
opposition to the nobility and the clergy would suggest otherwise, it is the case that we cannot really describe the peasant's
sense of grievance in terms of class consciousness. Compared to
the nineteenth-century industrial working class, peasants lacked
the means to organise themselves and to promote their cause. Of
more immediate relevance, however, is the fact that the hierarchical nature of feudal society prevented that polarisation of the
'classes' which Marx regarded as an important constituent of class

consciousness, others being an awareness of oppression and an awareness of the role of class in the revolutionary transformation of society (1844 & 1961: 178–87). It was not just the diffusion of power through the various ranks of society which inhibited the development of class consciousness but also the divisions within the peasantry itself. Those at the top end of the scale, the yeomen, identified more with the nobility than with their own group while their chivalric ballads, celebrating the exploits of 'gentle-man outlaws', were rejected by 'ploughman poets' on the grounds that their romantic idealism was 'inapplicable to the problems of everyday life' (Morgan 1993: 17): a criticism that reveals an early preference for the 'realism' which will characterise much 'work-ing-class' writing. The value attached to chivalry in yeoman ballads also reminds us that, broadly speaking, what mattered to contemporaries were social relationships based on status rather than economic relationships based on class. In the end, it was not the class consciousness of peasants that was crucial to the devel-opment of capitalism but changes in their condition of labour. Briefly, the custom-based relation to the lord was slowly com-muted to a cash-based relation with a guild master or merchant. The latter represented the new productive forces, the technical and commercial advances, that would slowly erode the political order of feudalism.

Capitalism requires that individuals be free to pursue their own economic interests irrespective of the condition into which they are born. The expansion of capitalism in the late medieval period, therefore, undermined the idea that people should remain in the station to which God had appointed them. Similarly, the demands of the market diversified social life beyond the capacity of the estates model to represent it. Inventors, merchants, manu-facturers, artisans and journeymen did not really fit into a scheme devised for clerics, knights and peasants. Chaucer, in *The Canterbury Tales* (1387 & 1992), tried to extend the estates model to include new social types such as the man of law, the Franklin, the Merchant, the Shipman and the Wife of Bath. There were also legal attempts to defend the traditional hierarchy by making people dress according to their rank, not their inclination. The sumptuary laws of 1363 and 1463, for example, aimed to regulate 'the outrageous and excessive apparel of divers people, against their estate and degree' (Edward III cited in Bolton 1980: 321). However, neither literature nor legislation, nor even dire warnings that any violation of the social order would lead to natural disaster, could save the estates conception of society. Contemporaries were aware of the growth of commodity production and of the power of money to usurp traditional values. 'Wynne whoso may', declares the Wife of Bath, 'for al is to selle' (1387 & 1992: 169), while Langland observes that 'the cross on the back of a gold coin is worshipped above the cross of Christ' (1379 & 1966: 194). What happens in the late medieval period is that money begins to usurp the estates model as a representation of the social order in a process which is still continuing today. It is not simply that a society is judged by its wealth, or that money becomes the measure of a person, it is rather the way in which the exchange mechanism, an essential part of the bourgeois rise to power (Marx 1849 & 1968: 80), moulds all social experience.

THE 'INDIVIDUAL'

The development of the idea of the individual is closely related to the rise of the bourgeoisie; however, the term obscures its relation to class because it emphasises how people are different rather than what they have in common. I put the term 'individual' in inverted commas because, strictly speaking, the late medieval period did not have a concept of the 'individual', at least not in our sense of the term. The word 'individual' was generally found in theological argument and meant 'indivisible' particularly in disputes about the Trinity. It could also mean 'a vain or eccentric departure from the common ground of human nature' (Williams

1988: 162). It was not until the late eighteenth and nineteenth centuries that the modern meaning of the word – unique, singular – came into being. We have already seen that the medieval conception of society saw people in terms of their functions rather than their being, and their duties rather than their qualities. To this we must add that the dominant mode of medieval thought was allegory, which saw things not as they were but as the signs of some other reality. Hence the value of the phenomenal world lay in what it revealed about the spiritual world: red and white roses blooming amid their thorns were not merely flowers but 'virgins and martyrs shining with glory in the midst of their persecutors' (Huizinga 1924 & 1968: 196). The personal was subsumed under the universal: 'all individual suffering is but the shadow of divine suffering, and all virtue is a partial realization of absolute goodness' (ibid.: 199). A similar pattern is discernible in the poetry of courtly love where 'individual' feelings are made to fit conventional expressions. 'Even when an actual love affair is described', writes Huizinga, in his classic *The Waning of the Middle Ages* (1924), authors 'cannot free [themselves] from the accepted style and technical conceptions' (ibid.: 118). By subordinating the earthly to the spiritual, the particular to the general, medieval allegory mirrored the hierarchic conception of society.

However, a number of developments combined to undermine these mutually reinforcing views of the world, the most important of which, for our purposes, was the growth of the market. Its encouragement of 'individuals' to take charge of their own economic destiny was complemented by two related developments: the beginnings of national self-consciousness and the first stirrings of humanism (Bloch 1962: 106 & 433). Very generally, the spread of trade nurtured a nascent sense of nationhood already apparent in such things as the increased use of English rather than French as the language of the court from about 1250 (Anderson 1974 & 1996: 22). Similarly, the rediscovery of antiquity led to the 'growth of a new self-consciousness' (Bloch 1962: 434) which took many forms, including the spiritual autobiography of the wife of a King's Lynn burgess, *The Book of Margery Kempe* (circa 1427). Such cultural expressions of 'individualism' served to underpin the entrepreneurial activity of capitalism. The idea of the 'individual' entailed mobility rather than stability and personal responsibility rather than social obligation hence, as we have seen, it posed a threat to the estates model of society (Aers 1988: 16). We can see how the experience of social mobility affected the estates model of society by looking at Thomas Malory's tale in *Le Morte Darthur* (1470), 'Sir Gareth of Orkney'.

'SIR GARETH OF ORKNEY' AND SOCIAL MOBILITY

'Sir Gareth of Orkney' relates how the hero, initially known as Beaumains, hides his true identity in order to prove himself a knight by his actions alone. Working in the kitchen earns him the scorn of Sir Kay, who dismisses him as 'a villein born' (Malory 1470 & 1998: 121). More vitriolic is the abuse he receives from the 'damosel Lyonet' who says that he 'stinkest all of the kitchen' and that his clothes are 'bawdy of the grease and tallow' (ibid.: 125). This alerts us to how those lower down the social scale are often represented in terms of the body. The poet Gower, for example, sees peasants as 'defying reason' and 'obeying no law but natural urges' (cited in Coleman 1981: 134). Beaumains' forbearance towards Lyonet, however, and his prowess in combat with other knights, convince her that he comes 'of gentle blood', which he soon afterwards confirms by informing her that he is the son of King Lot and Arthur's sister, Dame Morgause (Malory 1470 & 1998: 135, 139). The story of 'Sir Gareth of Orkney' therefore negotiates fears of social mobility, fears of someone from a servile class being the equal of someone from a superior one, but it reassures by showing that action is a direct expression of station. The story may raise the possibility that birth does not determine identity, but it allays that anxiety by confirming Beaumains as Gareth, a true knight of the round table. The shape of the table is important because it symbolises the perfect fit between the individual and his estate; the former an individual, the latter a collective expression of chivalric values, each mirroring the other in a mutually reinforcing relationship.

This affirmation of the relationship between the individual and his estate is, however, more a function of the romance form than a reflection of its reality in late medieval England. As Coleman observes, the chivalric elements of romance were ways of avoiding contemporary life (1981: 92). Indeed, the emergence of the romance was marked by 'a simultaneous decline of the knight' (ibid.: 91). We can see this in the contradiction between the meaning of reward in romance and in reality. In 'Sir Gareth of Orkney' Beaumains declares 'I will no reward have but God reward me' (Malory 1470 & 1998: 126). This contrasts with the way in which, as Gower complains, 'the knight now neglects his honour for gold' (in Stockton 1962: 35). The round table tournament organised by Edward III in 1344 to promote Arthurian values offers an image of knighthood at variance with the reality, which was that war 'was fought for booty rather than for moral ends' (Coleman 1981: 147).

The gap between the romance and reality does not mean that the former is mere escapism. We have already seen how 'Sir Gareth of Orkney' addresses the problem of the relationship between the individual and his estate but, even as it affirms that relation, it also calls it into question. For example, the very fact that knights are expected to embody only the values of their estate can be seen as a potential denial of their individuality. Moreover, the estate itself is defined in the narrowest terms – the court – whose social exclusiveness takes no cognisance of the wider world, except in so far as it provides opportunities for the exercise of chivalry. The concentration on the court also means that the relations between the different orders of society are transposed to the relations between the sexes. Thus instead of serving and protecting the clergy and the commons, the knight carries out these functions for his lady. The displacement of a relation between different levels of society to a relation between the sexes is a recurrent strategy in 'literature' for negotiating social tension and it also points to the profound connection between gender and class. This diminution of social relations reaches its conclusion in the knight's essential isolation. Sir Gareth is depicted as alone and embattled, a representation which suggests that the relation between the individual and his estate has broken down. In attempting to affirm that relation, 'Sir Gareth of Orkney' only succeeds in demonstrating its impossibility.

PIERS THE PLOUGHMAN

If 'Sir Gareth of Orkney' deals with the problem of social mobility, *Piers the Ploughman* is concerned with the disruptive effects of money on the estates model of society. The increasing use of money, affecting everyone from 'kings' down to 'workmen' (Langland 1379 & 1966: 50), was a sign of the growing power of the bourgeoisie. Langland is highly critical of money because it 'smiles on falsehood and tramples on the truth' (ibid.: 49). He also claims that money inverts the social order by, for example, turning knights into drapers and vice versa (ibid.: 68). It therefore ignores status distinctions in favour of a single division between rich and poor. Finally, he asserts that the love of money prevents clerics and nobles from discharging the duties of their station. Instead of 'guiding' and 'leading [the people] along the highway, going before them as a good standard bearer', the Church 'gobbles up wealth' and indulges in 'merry making and gluttony' (ibid.: 114–15, 191). Langland's complaint, in short, is that money disrupts the social hierarchy and inhibits its proper functions.

Long Will, the narrator of *Piers the Ploughman*, quotes Solomon's remark that 'There is not a more wicked thing to love than money' to make his point that riches are a bar to truth and goodness (1379 & 1966: 122, see also 32–7). The values of religion and the market appear to conflict but, as the poem progresses, it becomes clear that capitalism and Christianity begin to converge. Langland, in fact, deploys the language of money to explicate the doctrines of Christianity.

> [A] merchant may lose money again and again, yet if at last he makes some wonderful bargain which sets him up for the rest of his life, what does he care about his previous losses? – Through the grace of God he has acquired a fortune ... And I too am banking on a treasure – a sudden windfall of God's grace, to begin a new epoch in my life and turn all my past to profit.
>
> (ibid.: 259)

The reason why the idiom of the market lends itself to matters of the spirit is because, at the heart of them both, lies the act of exchange. Money, because it is 'the universal equivalent [by] which commodities can be equated as values and have the magnitude of their values compared' (Marx 1867 & 1995: 52), enables goods to be exchanged in the market. In the Christian scheme of *Piers the Ploughman* the human race is expected to obey God in exchange for his having sacrificed his only son to free them from their sins (Langland 1379 & 1966: 37, 143). 'Pay back what thou owest' (ibid.: 236) is the poem's chief refrain.

Piers the Ploughman is preoccupied with the nature of exchange and is so because the expansion of the market was beginning to have a corrosive effect on the feudal idea of duty and obligation as, for instance, in the commutation of labour services into cash payments. Langland tries to reconcile the new commerce with the traditional hierarchy by casting the problem of exchange in Christian terms. Thus the credit and debit transactions of trade are displaced on to the soul's indebtedness to God. The focus of the poem is how the soul can repay God for his gift of eternal life by, for example, recognising the meaning of the crucifixion, giving to the poor or 'forgiving those who have sinned against you' (1379 & 1966: 83, 93, 143). Seen in these terms, the exchange relation appears to be quite compatible with the feudal order: repaying God by giving to the poor is at once an act of exchange and the discharge of an obligation. However, the very fact that the soul's relation with God is expressed in a monetary idiom – '[p]ay back what thou owest' – suggests that we can turn the argument round so that instead of seeing exchange in terms of Christianity, we should really see Christianity in terms of exchange. From this point of view, God is seen as a 'capitalist' who expects a good return on his investment. 'Wherefore then gavest thou not my money into the bank, that at my coming I might have required mine own with usury?' (Luke cited in ibid.: 94). It is on this basis that Truth tells merchants to 'buy up boldly all the best goods [and] then sell again at a profit ... to assist religious orders and to give them a better endowment' (ibid.: 92). This monetary idiom not only conditions our perception of Christianity in the poem but also the social relations of feudalism. Piers views the labourer purely in economic terms, as someone who should be 'worthy of his hire', 'content with his wages' and, if he does not work, then he 'can starve to death' (ibid.: 41, 86, 171).

Piers the Ploughman negotiates the tensions between a declining feudalism and an emerging capitalism in the form of the exchange relation which prioritises monetary transactions over social obligations. We cannot say that Langland's poem represents the interests of the new bourgeoisie over the old nobility but it does enact the clash of their respective 'world-views'. More importantly, it is a mark of how the mechanism of exchange was becoming the mould of social representation. Despite its strong critique of the corrupting effects of money, *Piers the Ploughman* is dominated by monetary idioms and metaphors of trade, with the result that medieval allegory undergoes a curious reversal. Instead of earthly existence being understood in terms of spiritual essence, the true meaning of religion reveals itself in commercial activity. What is lost, as exchange insinuates itself as the general form of representation, is a sense of transcendence which will henceforth make it more and more difficult to conceive of an alternative to the market. What is gained is a fusion of business and Christianity that will serve the bourgeoisie very well as capitalism continues to expand in the coming centuries.

SIR GAWAIN AND THE GREEN KNIGHT: IDENTITY AND EXCHANGE

Sir Gawain and the Green Knight (1380 & 1998) is concerned with the effects of exchange on identity. The tale begins with a Green Knight appearing at the court of King Arthur and challenging any member of the round table to cut off his head providing he is allowed to return the blow a year hence. This is a dramatic expression of the intrinsic violence of the exchange relation which, in order to function, must strip 'individuals' of their existing 'identity' and impose on them the only one that matters for the market: their ability to buy or sell (Marx 1867 & 1995: 52). The Green Knight's violence is most evident in his vicious ripping of animals killed in a hunt (1380 & 1998: 48–9, 58).

The hunt, too, is part of the pattern of exchange in the poem. The Green Knight, who is Gawain's host, although the latter does not recognise him because his name and appearance have changed, proposes a bargain whereby 'Whatever I win at hunting will henceforth be yours; / And you, in turn, will yield whatever you earn' (1380 & 1998: 40). This, the first of three such bargains (ibid.: 51, 60), extends and alters the original one, though their relation to it is withheld from Gawain. He is also unaware of the terms of this agreement, which refer to how the Green Knight's wife will attempt to seduce him while her husband is out hunting, and Gawain is to 'yield' to him whatever he 'earns' from her. Although Gawain does not succumb to her temptations he does accept a magic girdle whose power means he 'cannot be cut down by any man nor slain / By any cleverness or cunning under the whole Heavens' (ibid.: 66). By not surrendering this to the Green Knight, Gawain reneges on his bargain to 'yield' everything he has earned. When the time comes for him to fulfil his part of the original bargain, he receives two mock blows and one which slightly nicks his neck because, by accepting the girdle, he 'failed the test' (ibid.: 84). It follows from this that the act of exchange cannot be understood as an isolated event. The original agreement of 'one stroke for another' (ibid.: 12) is mediated through three others. The result of this is that the act of exchange has to be seen as a system whose total operation transcends Gawain's experience of it.

Sir Gawain and the Green Knight also shows that exchange cannot be considered apart from its effect on identity. The identity of the Green Knight, for example, is uncertain. He appears as a mythic, nameless figure at Arthur's court and as the mortal Sir Bertilak at his castle. He takes one shape when he proposes the first bargain and another for the second. The act of exchange creates identity. The Green Knight implies as much when he tells Gawain that 'I have tested you twice and I have found you true / But "third time, winner takes all" ... recall my words / Tomorrow' (1380 & 1998: 60). Gawain loses his identity because he accepts the girdle: 'Craven fear of your blow', he cries, made 'me / ... go against myself / And the noble and generous code of knightly men' (ibid.: 84). The consequences of the various patterns of exchange in the poem mean that Gawain can no longer be defined in terms of the court and the code of chivalry (see also Aers 1988: 153–78). He cannot, in other words, be defined in terms of his community, which suggests that one of the effects of exchange is to introduce a rift between the individual and his or her society. It might be too much to say that, from this point on, the individual is seen in terms of a lack or, as Gawain puts it, 'false, faulty' and 'haunt[ed] by failings' (1380 & 1998: 85), but there can be no doubt that such an individual is both a condition of, and a necessary stimulus to, the growth of the market.

CONCLUSION

'Sir Gareth of Orkney' and *Sir Gawain and the Green Knight* are examples of how aristocratic romances tried to accommodate the experience of the market and its effects on traditional hierarchy. *Piers the Ploughman* and *Sir Gawain and the Green Knight* focus on the exchange relation, registering a shift from a *social* to an *economic* basis of identity: a move from the pyramid of estates to the mechanism of exchange. Consequently, all three works point to the beginnings of a momentous change in the social formation, the growing power of the bourgeoisie. They all resist that process while simultaneously testifying to its inevitability because of the way a system of representation, based on exchange, installs itself at their centre. A bourgeois system of representation is in place long before the 'bourgeois' revolution of 1642 and long before the institutions of bourgeois political power have been established. Although we can define the bourgeoisie in terms of their relation to production, their relation to exchange renders them a more nebulous group. This is because the mechanism of exchange requires, in contrast to feudalism, not a fixed but a flexible notion of identity, since this better serves the capitalist dynamic of constant change. We have seen how, in *Sir Gawain and the Green Knight*, identity varies according to different transactions and it is precisely because the market negates the idea of a stable, durable identity that we have difficulty in defining not only the 'middle' but also the 'working' class. The bourgeois system of economics generates, as it were, problems of identity to which 'literature' responds, reproducing as much as resolving them because, as we have seen in this chapter, its own 'economy' of representation is steeped in that of exchange.

2

THE RENAISSANCE

This chapter begins by questioning to what extent criticism can be seen as part of the 'class struggle' before moving on to consider how applicable the term 'class' is to Renaissance England. The remainder of the chapter is concerned with the growing importance of the exchange, particularly in relation to the 'bourgeois self'.

CRITICISM AND CULTURAL PRODUCTION: WARRING SIGNIFICATIONS

Marx declared that 'the history of all hitherto existing society is the history of class struggle' (Marx and Engels 1848 & 1968) and it is sometimes possible to interpret rival critical accounts of a work or an era as part of that struggle. One example of this may be the way that cultural materialists take issue with traditional or humanist critics in their approach to the Renaissance, a period which stretched roughly from the end of the War of the Roses in 1485 to the outbreak of Civil War in 1642. In order to determine whether we can examine this disagreement in terms of class, we first need to describe the two forms of criticism and the differences between them.

The conventional view of Shakespeare's England can be found in E. M. W. Tillyard's *The Elizabethan World Picture* (1943 & 1976). He argued that Shakespeare subscribed to the hierarchical model of Elizabethan society whereby human beings occupied the mid-point in the 'great chain of being' between God and the angels and the animal and plant kingdoms. This order was reflected in a finely tuned social structure stretching from the monarch to the beggar. Its various gradations were expressed through the sumptuary laws governing not only what kind of clothes people could wear, but also the material of which they were made. Gentlemen with lands or fees of a £100 a year were allowed velvet in their doublets but only satin or damask in their gowns and coats. Since the social order was believed to mirror the cosmic one, any attempt to interfere with it was deemed unnatural and likely to provoke the wrath of God. To discourage potential rebellion the Homily of Obedience was read out in church, attendance at which was compulsory every Sunday. The Homily stated that '[e]very degree of people, in their vocation, calling and office, hath appointed to them their duty and order ... [without which] there must needs follow all mischief and utter destruction both of souls, bodies, goods and commonwealths'. Tillyard (ibid.) believed that Shakespeare endorsed this view and cites Ulysses' speech from *Troilus and Cressida* in support of his claim. This equates the order of society with that of the cosmos and warns of the dreadful consequences should it be violated. 'Take but degree away, untune that string / And hark, what discord follows' (1603 & 1988: 721).

What is missing from Tillyard's account of Elizabethan society 'is any clear theoretical sense of how power functions' (Drakakis 1985: 15), which is a particular concern of cultural materialists like Jonathan Dollimore, Graham Holderness and Alan Sinfield, to mention but a few. Where Tillyard sees the ordered conception of society merely as 'a mode of thought', a 'basic assumption about the world' (1943 & 1976: 12), they see it as an attempt by the Tudor monarchy to legitimise itself and prevent criticism of its rule. The Elizabethan emphasis on order was not a spontaneous perception, but 'an official orthodox and conservative world-view imposed and preached through church and state through executive government, legislation and the voices of an organic establishment intelligentsia' (Holderness 1992: 4). In short it was an ideology, 'a collection of beliefs, practices and institutions which work to legitimate the social order especially by the process of representing sectional or class interests as universal ones' (Dollimore and Sinfield 1992: 182). Ideology justifies the economic divisions on which class interests are based by presenting them as decreed by God and/or as part of nature; either way they appear immutable and unalterable. Tillyard's failure to grasp the ideological nature of the 'chain of being' is matched by his tendency to conflate the England of the sixteenth century with the England of the twentieth century. 'We still have', he argues, 'that Elizabethan habit of mind in our own bosoms' (1943 & 1976: 117). Such assertions lend support to the idea that literature transcends the time in which it was written because it deals with subjects that are 'the commonplace of every age' (ibid.: 83). In general, this is the view taken by humanist critics whereas cultural materialists adopt a more historical approach. Hence they would claim that *King Lear* (1605–6) is not so much about the universal nature of suffering as about a determinate situation arising from particular relations concerning 'power, property and inheritance' (Dollimore 1989: 196). And if they wanted to highlight the class aspect of the play, they might draw attention to how Lear's downfall 'represents' the 'crisis of the aristocracy' (Stone 1967) while Edmund 'represents' the rise of the bourgeoisie by his determination to make his fortune at the expense of feudal obligation.

In addressing problems specific to his period, Shakespeare promotes certain solutions as more desirable than others. For example, he appears to believe that people had neither the right to rebel against tyrants nor to establish a representative form of government in their place. Instead, as in *Richard II* (1595), the eponymous monarch is deposed by Bolingbroke, a decision eventually vindicated in *Henry V* (1599) where we see order restored to the state (Holderness 1992: 1). The fact that Shakespeare upheld certain conceptions of the social order in preference to others is a reminder of the volatility of early modern culture, divided as it was between monarchists and republicans, and Catholics, Protestants and puritans. It is not clear whether we can interpret these divisions in terms of class since they turned on political and religious differences rather than economic ones. However, we should note that approximately fifty years after the production of the history plays, Britain was plunged into Civil War. Shakespeare's plays are animated by these and other conflicts and the resultant clash of meanings opens his work to different and even contradictory readings. Catherine Belsey (1992), for example, argues that the history plays are more concerned to interrogate kingship than to idealise it, because they show that the exercise of power depends less on divine right than on the skilful manipulation of its signs, 'the balm, the sceptre, and the ball / the sword, the mace, the crown imperial' (*Henry V* 1599 & 1988: 586). As Henry V himself acknowledges, there is nothing that divides him from his subjects 'save ceremony, save general ceremony' (ibid.). This perception of the equality of human beings is very much at odds with the play's endorsement of kingship and hierarchy.

In contrast to the humanist critic, the cultural materialist aims to politicise and de-mythologise Shakespeare, to dislodge that view of him as 'an all-wise, all-knowing genius, possessed of astounding capacities of insight into the human psyche' (Hawkes 1996: 9) by understanding how he is used to make sense of the world in which we live, how he is used to 'commend and promote' the conservative values of 'tradition, individualism, patriotism and permanence' (ibid.: 58). His place at the heart of the English curriculum in schools and universities is intended to promote class and racial harmony by encouraging people to identify with and take pride in the 'national' language (Newbolt 1921; Scarman 1981). Shakespeare also serves to inspire 'men' to pursue spiritual not material realities (Newbolt 1921: 255). Hence in 1926, the year of the General Strike, workers were encouraged to see productions of Shakespeare as these would 'induce them to look beyond the paltry advantage of the moment ... to something more substantial' (Hawkes 1996: 58). In that same year, *Coriolanus* (1608) was chosen to celebrate Shakespeare's birthday because it upheld the value of the individual against the politics of class (ibid.: 51–3). This conservative use of Shakespeare was also apparent in the 1980s when Nigel Lawson, the Chancellor of the Exchequer in the British Conservative government, cited Ulysses' speech, to which we have already referred, in support of his view that equality was 'not only unworkable but "wholly destructive"' (cited in Dollimore 1989: l–li). Belsey, like other cultural materialists, aims to counter this conservative use of Shakespeare. Her book, *Shakespeare and the Loss of Eden* (1999), challenges those who appeal to 'the Bard' to strengthen their advocacy of family values by arguing that they ignore how the emergence of the concept of 'the nuclear family' in Elizabethan England was characterised by 'unresolved ambiguities' (ibid.: 22). Hence we cannot invoke Shakespeare simply in support of 'family values' since his work also reveals alternative and possibly more liberating relations between men, women and children (ibid.: 17–25). The question is, who has the power to get their version of Shakespeare accepted?

THE INTELLIGENTSIA AND CLASS

To what extent, then, can we consider the differences between humanist critics and cultural materialists in class terms? It all depends on how we define class. If we look at it in strictly Marxist terms, then humanist critics and cultural materialists belong to the proletariat because they do not own the means of production. But if we look at it in terms of occupation, then they belong to the middle class in as much as they work in a white-collar profession. In either case, humanists and cultural material-ists belong to the same class and so any differences between them cannot be the result of diametrically opposed economic interests. As university lecturers, critics belong to the intelligentsia, itself part of the 'new middle class' (Giddens 1981: 177–97) that appeared in Britain – and indeed Western Europe – after the Second World War. The novel feature of this class was that its members, unlike the middle class of the first half of the century, did not occupy clear positions of either authority or high status in relation to manual labour. The French sociologist Pierre Bourdieu (1979 & 1984) argues that the intelligentsia are the dominated fraction of the dominant class because of their ownership of 'cul-tural' rather than economic capital. Simply, 'cultural capital' refers to forms of knowledge and understanding in the arts and sciences used to differentiate the 'educated' from the 'non-educated' and it therefore reinforces social and economic inequality. The position of the intelligentsia within the dominant class is ambiguous because, while their possession of 'cultural capital' moves them closer to the centre of power, its subordinate nature in relation to economic capital distances them from it. Although there may be inter-class disagreement over the relative value and importance of cultural capital as opposed to economic value, both groups have a common interest in maintaining their privileges *vis-à-vis* the dominated classes.

John Frow takes issue with Bourdieu's claim that the intelli-gentsia are part of the bourgeoisie, arguing that it is a separate, albeit weakly formed class, because it is constituted around claims to knowledge rather than property (1995: 121, 125). Frow goes on to suggest that this relative autonomy from the bour-geoisie allows it to take a more critical stance towards the values of capitalism and his analysis is therefore more applicable to understanding the cultural materialist project of 're-working the authoritative text so that it is forced to yield, against the grain, explicitly oppositional kinds of understanding' (Sinfield 1992: 22). However, the loose structure of this class, together with the sort of internal, intellectual divisions we have described, militates against any strong sense of class identity. Furthermore, the concept of class has been undermined by the rise of postmodernism and its questioning of 'grand narratives' such as Marxism. Hence, as Sinfield acknowledges, the concept of class 'has sunk from view' in recent years (ibid.: 39), thus providing only the weakest of contexts for the work of cultural materialists even though they may, as Sinfield does, locate their work in the Marxist tradition.

In any case, the oppositional stance of a part or the whole of the intelligentsia needs to be set against the changes in higher education where market pressures are transforming a traditional academic culture into a management-led, business-orientated one. The university's traditional function of social discrimination on the basis of educational qualification always undermined the claims of radical critics whose audience was largely the white middle class but, lately, the very principles of knowledge and critique have given way to an emphasis on skills which serves the needs of corporate capitalism more completely. And what Isobel Armstrong argued in 1989, that attacks on the concept of 'literature' and particularly Shakespeare, 'play[ed] into conservative hands' (1989: 5), is still true today. Such attacks on the literary, while perfectly valid and well intentioned, inadvertently reinforce the government view that, since the humanities have little to offer the self-help society, their subsidy can be drastically cut. Here, perhaps, is a modern instance of the cultural materialist's insight that 'subversion may be appropriated by authority for its own purpose' but whether it can then 'be used against authority' (Dollimore and Sinfield 1985: 12) remains to be seen.

The dispute between humanists and cultural materialists, then, is not a class one because they are or were members of the same class, because their class structure is too weak to generate a strong sense of class consciousness, and because the concept of class itself has fallen into abeyance eliding, in the process, the class position of the cultural materialists themselves. Moreover, although cultural materialists talk in terms of opposition to the established order, that opposition cannot be understood in class terms because it is not related to a theory of exploitation based on the ownership or non-ownership of the means of production. While cultural materialists are right to emphasise the autonomy of cultural production, too great an emphasis on this autonomy obscures its relation to the function of the university in the 'free' market. The fact that the market can direct the use of 'knowledge' and, in more subtle ways, harness radical meanings to reactionary ends, is a salutary reminder that there is a definite relation between base and superstructure and that the dominant class still has a great deal of power in determining the kind of society in which we live. Criticism, as well as Shakespeare, needs to be set in context. Cultural materialists have pointed out that the chaos and carnage of the Second World War (1939–45) was an important factor in Tillyard's concern with order (Hawkes 1996: 6) but their reaction to him still needs to be located within the transformations of British society within the late 1970s and 1980s.

RENAISSANCE ENGLAND

Most of the work of cultural materialists has been concerned with the operations of power, with how Renaissance literature – in its widest sense – both reproduced and resisted the dominant ideologies of the period. However, as Dollimore notes, it is difficult to reconcile this approach with traditional class analysis, for while the former stresses the plurality of opposing voices to state power, the latter assumes a unified class consciousness based on a common experience of economic exploitation (Dollimore and Sinfield

1985: 14). This then raises the question of whether Renaissance England was a class society. Peter Laslett thinks that 'status society' would be a more appropriate description, though he notes that the two terms are ultimately interdependent and any distinctions between them are a matter of convenience rather than fact (1965 & 1971). As we noted in the introduction, status is mainly a system of fine gradations between groups, class a sharp division of economic interests. Since the social structure of late fifteenth- and early sixteenth-century Britain was defined more 'by custom and law' than by 'the ebb and flow of economic movements' (Tawney 1926 & 1990: 75), it would be reasonable to assume that it was a status rather than a class society.

Certainly that is how it was viewed by a number of contemporaries. Sir Thomas Elyot, in his *Boke named the Governour* (1531), drew on status categories when he distinguished between the gentlefolk and 'the multitude wherein be contained the base and vulgar inhabitants not advanced to any honour or dignity' (cited in Briggs 1983 & 1997: 17). Another contemporary, Sir Thomas Smith, divided the country into four groups, also on the basis of status. The first was the *Nobilitas Major*, that is the aristocracy, then there was the *Nobilitas Minor*, that is the gentry which was subdivided into knights, esquires and gentlemen. This group was followed by one composed of citizens, burgesses and yeomen and, finally, there was the fourth group whom Smith curtly describes as 'men which do not rule' (cited in Laslett 1965 & 1971: 31). As already mentioned, the nobility were clearly demarcated from the rest of society by their clothes. They were also distinguished by their right to bear arms, and to play bowls and tennis while the 'lower orders' were restricted to archery. Lawrence Stone briskly summarises these and other marks of status by saying that the difference between the nobility and the rest of society could be symbolised by the hat and the whip. The former 'was forever being doffed and donned to emphasise the complex hierarchy of ranks and authorities' while the latter was 'used by the Crown upon its lesser subjects, and by the nobleman upon his servants' (1967: 20).

THE NOBILITY AND THE GENTRY

Stone's concern is with the economic, moral and social 'crisis of the aristocracy' in this period as manifest in the growth of the gentry and the bourgeoisie relative to the decline of the nobility. There were many reasons for this decline, including the failure of the nobility to provide male heirs, borrowing to finance the conspicuous consumption which was the 'prime test of rank' (1967: 26) and the ravages of inflation which had a ruinous effect on those landowners whose incomes came from fixed rents. 'How many noble families have there been whose memory is utterly abolished!' wrote an Englishman in 1603 (cited in Kamen 1971: 181). The growing power of the Crown over the nobility was also an important factor in their demise: the sale of honours, the forced reductions of armaments and retainers, legislation against duelling and 'the development of the monarchy as the one overriding focus of allegiance and loyalty' (Stone 1967: 97) made them dependent on the throne for wealth and position. They lost their traditional warrior status and gravitated towards the court where they became 'generals in the royal army, functionaries in the royal administration or attendants upon the monarch in the performance of the elaborate rituals of the Court' (ibid.: 183). But it was not just the promise of lucrative rewards which made members of the nobility desert their estates; there was also the attraction of London whose excitements contrasted favourably with the boredom and loneliness of the country. From this time forward, the figure of the noble is less likely to be a Hotspur, 'the king of honour' who seeks glory in single combat: 'O, would the quarrel lay upon our heads, / And that no man might draw short breath today / But I and Harry Monmouth!' (I Henry IV 1598 & 1988: 473, 478) than the scheming courtier, wit or fop. This

dwindling of aristocratic ideals was part of a general decay of deference, whose more violent manifestations included two draymen
overturning the Earl of Exeter's coach and a beggar assaulting the
Earl of Westmoreland with a truncheon (Stone 1967: 350). The
nobility, it seemed, no longer had the whip hand.

We have already mentioned some of the ways in which the
gentleman was distinguished from the rest of society; another was
that he could 'live idly and without manual labour' (cited in
Stone 1967: 27). The life of the nobleman was one of comfort and
leisure but that of the gentry and the bourgeoisie was one of
enterprise and hard work. The gentry, along with a small part of
the nobility, sought to exploit their estates thereby underlining
that change in the conception of land which we noted in the previous chapter; namely that property was increasingly seen more
in terms of the profit it could yield than the obligations it
entailed. The most dramatic example of this was the enclosure
movement, that is the mass eviction of peasants from their holdings and the commons by landlords eager to take advantage of
the rise in agricultural prices either by improving cultivation or
raising sheep. Since enclosure could lead to unrest and even riots,
some landowners preferred to turn instead to the extraction and
refinement of mineral ores such as iron and coal; but the greatest
undertaking was the drainage of the Fens, a project organised by
the fourth Earl of Bedford. This business-like approach to nature
is quite different to the idea of it in Shakespeare's plays where, as
we have seen, nature is a model for the social order itself. The rise
of commerce, however, required a different attitude to nature, one
which saw it not as the image of an integrated cosmos, but as a
resource to be exploited. In a similar vein, the conception of
human nature begins to shrink from an ideal to be attained, to an
appetite to be fed (Danby 1948: 15–53) thereby stimulating that
acquisitive spirit characteristic of the bourgeoisie and necessary to
the development of capitalism. Iago's view of human nature as
'blood and baseness' means he casts aside the feudal ideal of 'love

and duty', declaring that 'In following [Othello], I follow but myself' (1604 & 1988: 821, 826).

THE BOURGEOISIE

The bourgeoisie of the sixteenth and early seventeenth centuries differed from their medieval counterparts by being more international in outlook and by dispensing with the artificial protection of the guild to carve their own independent careers (Tawney 1926 & 1990: 84). Protestantism, but especially puritanism, played a key role in this development by giving a theological justification to the economic conception of the individual which was – and indeed still is – central to bourgeois ideology. Briefly, what separated Protestants and puritans from, in their contemporary parlance, 'Papists', was the belief that a person's relation with God was a private matter which did not require the mediation of the priest. This trust in the individual's own experience rather in the authority of the Church was a further factor in the decline of deference to which we have already referred. The independence of individuals in the religious sphere matched – and even sanctioned – those qualities of ambition and self-improvement which drove economic developments such as the expansion of trade, the growth of industry and the rise of commercial companies. However, a shared philosophy of self-reliance and a commitment to self-scrutiny are not by themselves sufficient to convert individuals into a class. Nevertheless, we can tentatively say that they *did* form a class to the extent that they were at the forefront of economic change and that they shared a cluster of attitudes, such as thrift, hard work and competition, in strong contrast to those of the nobility, which revolved around duelling and leisure. Louis B. Wright maintains that what he terms the 'middle class' was a distinct group with its own way of life, code of ethics and set of ideals (1935 & 1958: 3). Tawney agrees, arguing that these merchants, lawyers and prosperous craftsmen:

were conscious of themselves as something like a separate order, with an outlook on religion and politics peculiarly their own, distinguished, not merely by their birth and breeding, but by their social habits, their business discipline, the whole bracing atmosphere of their moral life, from a Court which they believed to be godless and an aristocracy which thèy knew to be spendthrift.

(1926 & 1990: 207–8)

Despite this we should not forget that the term 'bourgeoisie' primarily refers to a relationship to production and it therefore has only a limited applicability to a group whose main characteristic was diversity. The true bourgeois elements were small masters and wealthy merchants, but the term also includes shopkeepers, doctors and government administrators. These masters and merchants were united not against a property-less proletariat but against a state whose monopolies and price-fixing and whose statutes against usury were seen as interfering with free trade. 'It is against the natural right and liberty', declared a House of Commons Committee in 1604, 'to restrain [free trade] into the hands of some few' (cited in Tawney 1926 & 1990: 183). This was one of the tensions which contributed to the outbreak of the Civil War discussed in the next chapter. In contrast to those who wished to expand their trading and financial concerns were a substantial number who, after amassing wealth, sought to become members of the nobility by buying estates and adopting an aristocratic lifestyle, living in a substantial, well-furnished house, wearing rich clothes, keeping plenty of servants and, above all, maintaining a lavish table. Such mobility prompted a contemporary to complain '[w]ho ever saw so many discontented persons, so many irked with their own degrees, so few contented with their own calling, and such numbers desirous and greedy of change and novelties?' (cited in Kamen 1971: 181).

The *nouveaux riches* could find themselves ridiculed on stage.

Lord and Lady Frugal, in Philip Massinger's *The City Madam*, are both chastised for imagining that, having become rich through trade, they can pass for aristocrats; the former is rebuked for his 'harshness of table' the latter for her 'pride above rank' (1632 & 1964: 52). Both characters must learn that it is not money alone which guarantees esteem but style of life, a reminder that status considerations were more important than class ones – though not in the case of one Sir Baptist Hickes, later Viscount Camden, who defied the aristocratic disdain for trade by keeping a shop even after being knighted. Although these different examples testify to the existence of social mobility, we should not assume that the social structure was becoming any less rigid; dividing lines were crossed over, not crossed out. The aristocratic Lacy may marry the 'middle-class' Rose in *The Shoemaker's Holiday* to the chagrin of Oatley, his father, but when the king knights Lacy she is made a lady and social distinctions are thus reaffirmed at the very moment they appear to be questioned. 'Tell me now', says the king, 'tell me in earnest, Oatley, canst thou chide, / Seeing thy Rose a lady and a bride' (Dekker 1599 & 1997: 99). If the titular peerage was a status group with marked internal gradations it was also a class based on the ownership of land and it ruled through the court, the Lords and government. It is true that many established noble families disappeared in this period, but their place was taken by new ones, and so, while the landed class may have changed its personnel, its grip on power was largely the same.

MASTERLESS MEN

Smith's description of society does not include 'large groups of lowly persons' (Laslett 1965 & 1971: 32) who, because they were part of 'the base and vulgar multitude' and therefore lacking in any honour or dignity, did not even merit surnames. We can see this in a quite literal way if we look at Henry V's relief after the battle of Agincourt that the only dead are 'Edward the Duke of York, the Earl of Suffolk, / Sir Richard Ketly, Davy Gam, esquire; / None else of name' (1988). While the dead are dismissed, the living are either silenced or their attempts at speech ridiculed. In *1 Henry IV*, Prince Hal diverts himself not only by preventing the 'lower-class' Francis from speaking but also by claiming that he is incapable of speech: he has, says Hal, 'fewer words than a parrot' (ibid.: 464). Francis is only one example of many Shakespearian 'clowns' whose misuse of language is a source of humour for their 'betters'. Shakespeare's contrast between the titled and eloquent nobility and the nameless and tongue-tied 'lower orders' derives from the division between owners and non-owners of land. Formerly peasants had enjoyed some security on their lords' estates but the enclosure movement meant that they swelled the ranks of those other 'masterless men', rogues, vagabonds, beggars, the London poor, and cottagers and squatters on commons, who formed the 'ready-made material for what began in the later seventeenth century to be called the mob' (Hill 1972: 39–43, 41). Poets of the period complained of landlords, 'Whose vast designs engross the boundless land / By fraud or force; like spiders stand / Squeezing small flies' (1626, cited in Saintsbury 1905: 11). The enclosure of common land – an example of how the interests of property triumphed over customary liberties – deprived many of their traditional rights to collect fuel, pasture cattle or glean after the harvest. As a result, those who were cast off the land had to depend solely on what they earned. We can thus regard them as the forerunners of Marx's proletariat since they owned nothing but their labour power.

The appearance of this 'class' state signalled a change in the conception of poverty. Previously it could be seen as holy because Christ himself was poor, but where those without means were once told 'not to be ashamed to beg and be needy for He who created the world chose to be so' (Langland 1379 & 1966: 246) they were now regarded as idle vagabonds who should be forced to work. The Statute of Artificers (1563) not only required all able-bodied people to seek work, but also to accept whatever employment was offered to them. Those who were forced into wage labour had no rights. They could not leave their jobs without the consent of their employers nor could they combine to raise wages as this was a treasonable offence (Hill 1996: 46). In the words of Sir Thomas Smith, 'labourers have no voice nor authority in our commonwealth and no account is made of them but only to be ruled' (cited in ibid.: 67). Deprived of their traditional rights, and denied any new ones to reflect their changed circumstances, this group had no protection against either the widespread unemployment or the rise in prices in the early seventeenth century. Where once they might have looked to their lords to mitigate the effects of an economic crisis, they were now left to shift for themselves. One option was to seek work in another parish but this was tantamount to advertising themselves as 'vagabonds' thus incurring penalties of whipping or branding. Moreover, local communities were reluctant to embrace those in search of employment partly because they believed they would depress wages even further and partly because they viewed them as 'the scum and dregs of many counties from whence they had been driven' (cited in ibid.: 66).

CLASS OR STATUS?

The enclosure movement, the commercial exploitation of land, the growth of manufacture and the mobility of a large group of 'masterless men' were changes in the means of production which inevitably affected the social relations of production, that is, the rules governing how people work together. There is an accentuation of the shift from the notion of reciprocal obligation to the idea of individual responsibility. In the previous chapter we noted that 'individual' had a pejorative ring because it signified a departure from common human nature. Now it has a more positive sense with writers recommending that 'a man should be something that men are not, and individual in somewhat beside his proper nature' (cited in Williams 1988: 162). However, the clear implication that men could be individuals but not women links the term 'individual' with that of class since they both involve relations of domination and subordination. Generally speaking, though, the notion of the individual in the late sixteenth and early seventeenth centuries indicates a weakening of the hierarchical principle rather than the existence of class society.

Social mobility and the crisis of the aristocracy meant that outward markers of status, such as clothing, were no longer adequate to identify a person as a member of the nobility. The higher ranks therefore insisted on the idea of a blood elite and either traced or concocted genealogies to establish their superiority over newcomers to their lists. Nobility now resides more in lineage than in the traditional signs of status. 'I am Duchess of Malfi still' asserts Webster's eponymous heroine from her prison cell (1623 & 1987: 255), showing that inner substance need not be compromised by external events. At the opposite end of the social scale, 'masterless men', shaken out of their place in the social hierarchy, also faced the task of redefining themselves, which was made more difficult by them being labelled as outcasts (Hill 1996: 50). As we saw in the last chapter, the bourgeoisie, too, had difficulty in being accommodated within the existing social framework, hence 'their object was to find a new master in themselves, a rigid self-control shaping a new personality' (Hill 1972: 48). They therefore looked inwards with a view to altering their behaviour; the puritans, for example, were driven by an internal sense of being damned to work hard. The connection between inner self and outward expression was thus transformed. Instead of being an external display of a fixed social position, identity, at least in sections of the bourgeoisie, was now a complex dialectic between an inner relation to God and economic performance. However, the fact that identity was located more on the inside than the outside meant that it was more elusive, and could therefore seem 'empty' or non-existent in comparison to the embodied identities of status and society. We will pick up this point again towards the end of the chapter where it will be tied in with the mechanism of exchange. The meaning of the term 'individual', which has very little relevance to 'masterless men', thus varies according to whether it applies to the nobility or the bourgeoisie. For the nobility, it designates an internal quality based on a bloodline. For the puritan bourgeoisie, it designates a work ethic derived from a relation to God. We can therefore say that in so far as the term 'individual' refers to economic behaviour rather than social status it is a class notion; one, moreover, which belongs more to the bourgeoisie than the nobility. As Simon Eyre notes in *The Shoemaker's Holiday*, courtiers lack the inner substance of the bourgeoisie, being nothing more than 'painted images – outsides, outsides' (Dekker 1599 & 1997: 56).

We have suggested that economic developments undermined signifiers of status thereby giving a further boost to the evolution of the idea of the 'individual', a process whose origins can be traced back at least to the late medieval period (Aers 1988). The destabilisation of status categories meant that it was harder to describe the social order by recourse to the conventional metaphors of the body or the 'great chain of being'. The fact that Menenius quells the rioting citizens in *Coriolanus* by comparing the role of the belly with that of the Roman senators – 'No public benefit which you receive / But it proceeds or comes from them to you' (1608 & 1988: 1068) – is significant only because the metaphor has already failed to keep the citizens in their place. The Britain of the late sixteenth and early seventeenth centuries saw a number of uprisings, such as the Oxfordshire one in 1596, causing one pamphleteer to remark that the 'poorer sort of people are apt to assist rebellion and to murder many wealthy persons for their wealth' (cited in Hill 1996: 58). The use of the word 'sort' is important here for, as Keith Wrightson has argued, it belonged to 'a terminology of social simplification, sweeping aside the fine grained distinctions of the hierarchy of degrees and regrouping the English into two broad camps … the haves and the have nots' (1991: 45–6). Thomas More certainly saw England divided between 'a few rich men' and the people (1516 & 1965: 48). A polarised conception of the social order is also found in some peasant ballads: 'There be many rich men / That for their own private gain / Hurt a whole country' (cited in Hill 1996: 37). More ominous for the authorities was the question of an Essex labourer: 'What can rich men do against poor men if poor men rise and hold together?' (cited in Kamen 1971: 384).

To see society divided between rich and poor does not, by itself, constitute class consciousness. 'Separate individuals', Marx wrote, 'form a class only in so far as they have to carry on a common battle against another class' (Marx and Engels 1846 & 1996: 82). This does not apply to those 'masterless men' of our period because, while some fought against the gentry and enclosure, others fought against the bourgeoisie and their new discipline of wage labour. Indeed, the sheer variety of protest in this period from poaching to the sexual licence preached by the Ranters during the Civil War makes it difficult to talk of 'masterless men' forming a single class on the basis of a common experience of exploitation. Crime rather than organised resistance was the response to a rapidly changing and repressive social order. The second murderer in *Macbeth* probably speaks for many when he says: 'I am one … / Whom the vile blows and buffets of the world / Hath so incensed that I am reckless what / I do to spite the world' (1606 & 1988: 986). Between 1559 and 1624, 24,147 men and women were hanged, a further 516 were pressed to death while 11,440 died in jail; mostly for stealing in order to eat (Barker 1993). Given the fact that people were 'either cheated or bullied into giving up their property' (More 1516 & 1965: 47) and therefore forced to steal, it is surprising that there were not more rebellions. Those that did occur such as the Pilgrimage of

Grace (1536), and the Western rebellion (1547–9) were often conservative, demanding a return to the feudal order. As such they illustrate the tension between new economic developments and an old social structure or, in Marxist terms, between the forces of production and the relations of production.

Was Renaissance England a class society? In one sense yes, because the nobility mostly owned the means of production and were conscious of themselves as a distinct group. In another sense no, because many people continued to think of society in terms of status and hierarchy rather than as a conflict of economic interests. The situation was, however, more complicated. The development of trade and industry was creating a new class, the bourgeoisie, who had economic but not political power. Some of them viewed the nobility with hostility while others sought to join their ranks. Peasants who had lost their land through enclosure formed another group, but one which seemed to have no place in the social order. The protests of this group had the power to unite the other two against it, or to exacerbate the difference between them by appealing to the nobility for a restoration of feudal relations. It was from tensions such as these that the Civil War arose.

MONEY, EXCHANGE AND SELF

We saw in the last chapter that money, in the form of the exchange relation, was beginning to impact on the social hierarchy, conceptions of identity and even the mechanism of representation itself. This process intensified in the sixteenth century, particularly with the flow of bullion from the silver mines in America which was one of the factors behind the unprecedented rise in the cost of living. 'Sixpence a day', complained Sir Thomas Smith, 'will not now go as far as fourpence would aforetime' (cited in Kamen 1971: 58–9). For Henry Kamen, 'the continued commutation of feudal dues to cash, the expansion of industry, trade and markets [and] the collapse of the ban on usury meant that money was assuming a more important part in the affairs of the community' (ibid.: 103). The sixteenth century 'may not have had the reality of a money or a cash economy', but says Kamen, 'it certainly had the *form* of one' (ibid.: 102) and we should understand that 'form' as I shall argue shortly, as exchange.

Raymond Southall argues that, during the course of the sixteenth century, love poetry moved from a feudal to a monetary idiom. In the first half of the century, 'the heart's affections were felt to be as natural and unchanging as feudal bondage' but, as it progresses, 'the lover weighs up his profits and losses like a businessman preparing a balance sheet' (1973: 28, 61). According to Southall, there was a direct correspondence between the growth of trade and the imagery of Elizabethan poetry where 'the lover is a merchant, the beloved a desirable commodity and love itself a commercial transaction' (ibid.: 68). John Donne, for example, eulogises his mistress as 'my America ... / My mine of precious stones' (1633 & 1971: 125) while Edmund Spenser asks what need 'tradefull Merchants' have to 'seeke most pretious things' and 'both the Indias of their treasures spoile' when his 'loue doth in her self containe / all this worlds riches that may far be found' (1593 & 1975: 286).

The pursuit of money is an increasingly important element in the drama of the period. The action of Thomas Middleton's *A Trick to Catch the Old One* (1606) revolves around Witgood fooling his uncle into giving him money so he can discharge his creditors and win back the property out of which his uncle had cheated him. The major theme of the play is the corrupting effect of money. When the Host asks Witgood how one of the minor characters, Dampit, 'came by [his wealth]?', Witgood replies 'How the devil came he not by it?' (1606 & 1973: 17). Dampit, in other words, is prepared to do anything for money, as indeed are the other characters in the play. The same applies to the characters in *Arden of Faversham* (1592) whose desire for money overrides all other considerations. As a landlord, Arden has no regard for his tenants; being 'greedy gaping still for gain' he 'wrings from [them] the little [they] have' (in White 1982: 22) while his killers, Black Will and Shakebag, more examples of those 'masterless' men discussed earlier, 'will murder ... for gold' (ibid.: 21). The point to stress is that, although these characters differ from one another in terms of status, they are the same in their desire for wealth: greed makes them equal. The principle of equivalence, as it were, undermines the principle of hierarchy, thus advancing the interests of the bourgeoisie. This is similar to the way that money, in the form of the exchange relation, cancels out the difference between commodities by submitting them to a common measure.

The development of a money economy also has a material effect on the evolution of theatre. Originally a space for the expression of communal energies, it became, in the late sixteenth century, an essentially commercial arena. One consequence of this was that plays began to be geared more towards entertainment than instruction (McLuskie 1996). Thomas Dekker complained that playwrights now had to 'barter away' their 'muse' to 'merchants' who demanded that they please 'that great beast', the audience (cited in Kastan 1987: 335). In very general terms, this meant a shift of focus from the tragic destinies and comic intrigues of the nobility to the solid virtues and sober activities of the bourgeoisie which were, accordingly, presented in a 'realistic' rather than in a 'stylised' or 'exaggerated' manner (Holbrook 1994: 90). *The Merchant of Venice* shows the nobility dependent on the business acumen of merchants. Hence Antonio secures a loan to fund Bassanio's courtship of Portia since he, along with many nobles of the period, has 'disabled [his] estate, / By something showing a more swelling port / Than [his] faint means would allow' (1598 & 1988: 428). Simon Eyre in *The Shoemaker's Holiday* displays good business sense when he accepts 'a bargain in commodities' from a ship-owner: 'He shall', says his foreman Hodge, 'have a reasonable day of payment' by which time 'he may sell the wares and be an huge gainer himself' (Dekker 1599 & 1997: 35). Eyre's rise from shoemaker to Lord Mayor underlines this gener- ally positive portrayal of the bourgeoisie in Dekker's play. By con- trast, Francis Beaumont's *The Knight of the Burning Pestle* derides 'citizens' for presuming to act the part of their betters and partic- ularly for their ignorance of dramatic conventions. The attempts of George, the grocer, to dictate the action are 'contrary to the plot' (1613 & 1970: 30) and this, together with his wife's failure to distinguish between what is real and what is represented on stage – 'Away George, away! Raise the watch at Ludgate and bring a mittimus from the justice for this desperate villain' (ibid.: 40) – marks them down as unsophisticated in their approach to theatre. The differing portrayals of the nobility and the bour- geoisie and the relations between them show that the stage was an important site for the cultural expression of 'class' conflict. Indeed, we can read George's interventions and his apprentice Ralph's impersonation of a knight errant in precisely this way, for they are attempts both to be included in a dominant form of rep- resentation, the romance, and to manipulate that form to their own ends. Their actions draw attention to the fact that the bour- geoisie had yet to find their own idiom and form of expression. That will come with the novel.

The changes in poetry and drama testify to the growth of a bourgeois system of values in which money predominates. Only an inhabitant of Utopia is puzzled over 'why a totally useless sub- stance like gold should now ... be considered far more important than human beings' (More 1516 & 1965: 89). The minor poet Richard Barnfield asserts that 'Friends may prove false and leave thee in thy need; / But still thy Purse will bee thy friend indeed' (1598 & 1995: 320). Ben Jonson's Volpone sums up the prevail- ing outlook when he declares that 'gold' is 'the world's soul and mine' (1607 & 1966: 51). His practice of deceiving others into giving him money, his desire to 'coin ... profit' (ibid.: 53) at their expense can be seen as an early example of the extraction of surplus value. True, Volpone does not employ the people he cheats, but the fact that he makes money out of them points the way to the exploitation of the proletariat by the bourgeoisie: in both cases one party benefits by using the other in a wholly instrumental fashion. This objectification of others lies at the heart of the capitalist enterprise. It involves defining them in purely economic terms: when the masterless men did begin to acquire surnames, they were based on their occupations; Peter the smith became Peter Smith. Even the family relation, as Marx noted, 'reduced it to a mere money relation' (Marx and Engels 1848 & 1968: 38) as we can see from Shylock's notorious cry in *The Merchant of Venice*: 'My daughter! O my ducats! O my daughter!' (1596 & 1988: 436).

But the capitalist system involves more than an objectification of others, it also, through the operation of exchange, restructures 'the self'. The main feature of exchange is that it separates the actual commodity from its value as money. Money measures what commodities have in common, their labour power, and so it ignores what is unique about them, their different uses. This split between the bodily form of the commodity and its 'purely ideal or mental form', that is its value (Marx 1867 & 1995: 59), is implicated in the decline of status and the rise of the 'inner self'. The difference between the two types of identity is that whereas status is directly expressed in bodily form, for example clothing or jewellery, the 'inner self' has a much more indirect relation to its 'outer appearance'. This 'dual' nature of 'the self', split between mind and body, seems to correspond to the 'dual' character of the commodity, split between 'value' and 'use' and is, accordingly, an appropriate form of identity for a society based on exchange. The 'split self' also inaugurates the great 'bourgeois' project of self-knowledge whose many forms include the puritan conscience, Freudian psychoanalysis and the stream of consciousness novel. Just as exchange structures the conception of the self, so too it has an impact on the conception of 'reality', for, broadly speaking, whereas in the medieval period the things of the world were luminous with meaning, in the Renaissance and onwards there is a divorce between 'appearance' and 'reality', a lesson that Portia's suitors have to learn in the three caskets episode in *The Merchant of Venice*.

The exchange relation, then, helps generate a form of self that applies most directly to the bourgeoisie, since this is the class most actively engaged in the sort of economic activity, investment, trade and manufacture, that is based on exchange. 'The self', in short, is class-based and, because of that, we can view the contrast between different conceptions of 'the self' as a form of class conflict. We can find examples of such conflicts in those Shakespearian meditations on the nature of 'man' where the 'empty self' of capitalism clashes with the 'full self' of feudalism. Hamlet's 'quintessence of dust' (1604 & 1988: 667) could not be more different from Coriolanus' absolute nobility. The tension between the two types of 'self' characterises the portrait of Shylock in *The Merchant of Venice* where there is a constant play between his Jewishness and his humanity. His Jewishness is an essence which sets him apart, but at the same time it is the ground of his common humanity. 'I am a Jew. Hath not a Jew eyes? hath not a Jew hands, organs, dimensions, senses, affections, passions?' (1596 & 1988: 438). Although this ambiguity is never finally resolved, Shylock's identity seems to reside more in his likeness to others than his difference from them. And, if this is the case, then his role as a moneylender is important because it highlights the connection between a particular kind of identity, similarity not separateness, and a particular kind of economic organisation, exchange, which functions according to the common denominators of objects, not their unique qualities. Shylock's contract with Antonio, repayment of 3,000 ducats or lose a pound of flesh, is also a reminder of the violence of exchange that we saw in *Sir Gawain and the Green Knight*. Furthermore, the fact that the contract stipulates the potential destruction of Antonio's body, partially evokes Marx's claim that exchange dispenses with the body of the commodity.

CONCLUSION

We have, at the end of this period, a fairly complex picture of Britain shortly before the outbreak of the Civil War. There are economic and social tensions between the declining nobility, the rising bourgeoisie and the rootless 'masterless men', but we cannot refer to these three groups as 'classes' – partly because the continuing transition from feudalism to capitalism complicates the relation of the nobility and the bourgeoisie to the means of production, and partly because people still thought of the social order in terms of status which, by internally differentiating the nobility and the bourgeoisie, made it still harder to see them as 'classes'. The idea of hierarchy was, however, being undermined by the extension of exchange, which functions according to the principle of similarity rather than difference. In terms of social relations this means a shift from the 'full self' of status to the 'empty self' of exchange. Lear thinks he's found essential 'man' in Poor Tom: 'thou art the thing itself' (1605–6 & 1988: 961) but he doesn't know that 'Poor Tom' is Edgar acting a part. There is no 'real self', 'all men and women are merely players' as Jacques notes in *As You Like It* (1600 & 1988: 638). The 'empty self' of the bourgeoisie is best represented by the metaphor of acting. 'Man in business is but a Theatricall person', opined John Hall in his *The Advancement of Learning* (1649 & 1953: 57). Bourgeois art and philosophy is preoccupied with this 'empty self' at the expense of class, which brings us to the paradox of exchange: on the one hand it is associated with the rise of the bourgeoisie and is therefore 'class'-based, but on the other hand it transcends class by assuming the essential equality of all in the market place. It is important to understand the nature of exchange, not just because it is a bourgeois form of economic organisation, but also because of the way it insinuates itself into structures of representation. This reminds us that there is a link between base and superstructure, and that criticism perhaps needs to take more account of it than has sometimes been the case over the past few years.

3

THE CIVIL WAR AND AFTER

This chapter considers to what extent 'class' was a factor in the English Civil War. It then examines how economic changes impacted on representations of self and society, and how these related to the bourgeoisie, before concluding with a discussion of how John Milton's *Paradise Lost* negotiates problems of money and exchange, and the bearing that has on the 'class' character of the poem.

THE ENGLISH REVOLUTION: A CLASS WAR?

Oliver Cromwell (1599–1658) said, at the start of the Civil War (1642–8), that he did not believe its causes were religious, but that he did by the end. Certainly the Catholic leanings of Charles I (1600–49) were a cause for concern, as were the reforms of his Archbishop of Canterbury, William Laud (1573–1645), because of the way in which they 'shifted the emphasis of religion from the sermon to the sacrament' (Manning 1996: 14). Laud's 'popish innovations', such as the conversion of communion tables into altars, did provoke attacks on churches in Essex and Hertfordshire, but religion was only one factor in the conflict. One Huntingdonshire puritan declared 'I am not to obey a wicked King's Lawes upon

Earth ... but I am to obey the King of Heaven' (cited in Greaves 1992: 15). Although this was a religious declaration, it also pointed to the tension between the king and Parliament over the treatment of his subjects. Of particular concern was Charles's failure to consult MPs over the extension of the ship money tax; that, together with the imposition of tariffs and the granting of monopolies, aggravated the worries already raised by religion.

These worries deepened when Charles' attempt to impose the Book of Common Prayer on the Scots led to the latter invading the north of England (1640), and were further exacerbated by the Catholic rising in Ireland (1641) which seemed to confirm the king's connection with 'popish plots'. Charles' relations with MPs continued to deteriorate and John Pym, one of the most formidable figures in the Commons, presented the Grand Remonstrance, which set out in detail the wrongs of Charles' reign. The Remonstrance divided Parliament into Royalists and Parliamentarians and Charles' continued refusal to meet Parliament's demands for curbs on royal power, as set out in the Nineteen Propositions, made Civil War inevitable. Royalists fought for the traditions of religion and monarchy and their fundamental principle was loyalty – 'an instinct etched deeply in the patriarchal nature of their society' (Kishlansky 1997: 151). The Parliamentarians fought for true religion and liberty, and their fundamental principle was consent – 'an ingrained belief in the co-operation of subject and sovereign that maintained the delicate balance between prerogatives and liberties' (ibid.). However, these simple divisions take no account either of the variety of issues that were raised during the course of the conflict or of the internal tensions within the two groups.

Some aristocrats sided with the Parliamentarians and some with the king. In Nottinghamshire, the Grey family declared for the former while the Hastings family declared for the latter. Their differences, as with so many cases of this kind, were not caused by a clash of principles but by local power struggles. The aristocracy, in other words, cannot be seen as a unified class, and neither can the bourgeoisie. A number of merchants fought on the king's side because they benefited from royal charters of monopoly. The Merchant Adventurers, for example, excluded retailers and craftsmen from overseas trade. This not only maximised the profits of merchants, it also upheld the concept of hierarchy since it 'elevated the status and function of merchants above those of shopkeepers and craftsmen' (Manning 1996: 67). The challenge to the king opened the way for a number of radical ideas about the social order which also split the Parliamentarians. Cromwell may have stripped all peers of their military command in his New Model Army but he nevertheless intended to 'keep up the nobility and the gentry', for it was in such distinctions 'that the best interests of the nation lay' (cited in Manning 1996: 118).

This was in stark contrast to the various demands of the Levellers, the Diggers and the Ranters. The Levellers, led by John Lilburne (1614–57), Richard Overton (1612–62?) and William Walwyn (1603–56?), were a diverse group of apprentices, tradesmen, preachers and 'the odd not so distinguished gentleman' (Sharp 1998: xv) who, in 1647 and then again in 1648–9, proposed sweeping reforms of the constitution and the Church. They wanted to abolish the monarchy and the House of Lords and make the Commons a truly representative body by giving the vote to all adult males (not women). They believed that the authority to govern came from the people and not from custom or tradition and it was this, together with their belief that all men were by nature equal, that earned them the name of 'levellers'. There is some confusion between the Diggers and the Levellers because the former, under the inspiration of Gerard Winstanley (1609–76), called themselves the 'true levellers' but whereas the Levellers believed in political equality, the Diggers believed in economic equality. They held that the earth was 'a common treasury' and claimed that '[t]he poorest man hath as true a title and just right to the land as the richest man' (Winstanley cited in

Hill 1972: 133). The Diggers tried to put this principle into practice by establishing communes whose produce would be evenly distributed among those who worked on them, but they were ruthlessly suppressed.

Although the Levellers and the Diggers had scant regard for the institution of the Church, they did use the Bible to justify their radical vision. Overton, for example, declared that Parliament had no 'power at all to conclude the people in matters that concern the worship of God' (1640 cited in Sharp 1998: 43) while Winstanley believed that the 'Great Creator' was 'mightily dishonoured' by a situation where a few 'delighted in comfort' while many lived in 'miserable poverty' (cited in Hill 1972: 132). The Ranters, by contrast, interpreted the Bible for personal rather than social ends. They believed in individuals not groups and taught that, to the pure, all things were pure, demonstrating this by practising free love and swearing blasphemous oaths, hence their name.

The divisions within the nobility and what Manning calls the 'middling sort' (1996: 13) make it difficult to view the English Civil War as a class war (MacLachlan 1996). It may be true that 'an aristocratic ethos dominated the Royalist party' while the ethos of a 'middle sort' held sway in the Parliamentarian party (ibid.: 71) but this eclipses internal differences within the warring factions. It also assumes that the main reason for the conflict was economic, but we have seen that religious, constitutional and even status issues played a part in the hostilities. I do not mean to imply by this that these issues are separate from those of class, only that they weighed as much if not more heavily with contemporaries than economic matters, whereas in traditional Marxist analysis it is the latter which are crucial. Moreover, the view of the Civil War as a class conflict between Royalists and Parliamentarians overlooks the greater part of the population and their response to the conflict. Manning argues that assaults on the property of wealthy landlords were 'indicative of underlying class hatred' (ibid.: 50), but many refused to get involved in the fighting, demanding a cessation of hostilities because it interfered with their daily struggle of putting bread on the table. Hence the risings of the 'clubmen' against conscription and their petitioning of the king and Parliament for peace. There were even some in the country who did not know that Civil War had broken out. At the time of the battle of Marston Moor (1644), a patrol found a farm labourer on the field of battle and told him to clear out as king and Parliament were at war. 'Whaat!' he exclaimed, 'has them two fallen out then?' (cited in Ashley 1968: 81).

The question of whether the Civil War was a class war is, then, debatable. The abolition of feudal tenure in 1646 seemed to suggest that the bourgeois conception of property had replaced the feudal one: land was no longer the basis of social relations but a resource to be exploited. However, this was the culmination of a process that had been going on since the late medieval period. Moreover, the legislation of 1646 related more to the gentry than to the bourgeoisie, whose main concern was the abolition of the restrictive practices of the guilds and Crown monopolies, that is the sale to a particular individual of exclusive rights of production and/or sale of a particular commodity. The different economic reforms benefiting different groups again complicate the question of class. But its contours become much clearer when we consider not the relations between the nobility and the bourgeoisie but between these two as owners of land, capital and 'industry' and the mass of the population who owned nothing and who continued to suffer from the effects of enclosure, exploitation and the uncertainty of employment.

CLASS SOCIETY VERSUS STATUS SOCIETY

The government of Oliver Cromwell abolished the episcopacy – Church government by bishops (1646) – the monarchy and the House of Lords (1649). But they were all restored in 1660 when

Charles II returned from exile. Although, in the last analysis, the House of Commons was supreme, the return of these institutions and the survival of the aristocracy and gentry ensured the preservation of many traditional values (Hill 1980 & 1997: 30). The basic social division was still between those who were 'gentle' and those who were 'common' (Kishlansky 1997: 25) but, as capitalism continued to develop, economic divisions came increasingly to the fore. It is the predominance of the economic as opposed to other relations that characterises class society which, in contrast to the apparent unity of a status-based one, is marked by division. In the words of R. H. Tawney:

> a hierarchy of values, embracing all human interests and activities in a system of which the apex is religion, is replaced by the conception of separate and parallel compartments between which a due balance should be maintained, but which have no vital connection with each other.
>
> (Tawney 1926 & 1990: 22)

The decline of the small family farm or business is one example of how an integrated life, the household as unit of production, little church and little school, disintegrates due to the effects of enclosure and the rise of the factory. The move into the slavery of wage labour or the poverty of unemployment represented a divorce between economy and society, a dissolution of traditional social relationships and responsibilities. Such developments augmented the power of the bourgeoisie. The most important point for our purposes, however, is that changes in the economy meant that commercial considerations not only penetrated ever deeper into 'social' life but also that they altered habits of perception and valuation in subtle ways. The ascendancy of the bourgeoisie was matched by the elevation of market imperatives over moral claims, and the establishment of a structure of representation that rested ultimately on the operation of exchange.

Even before the Civil War, economic perceptions were beginning to displace social ones; the sumptuary laws for example, were repealed during the early part of the century. Thereafter laws were directed more to the protection and promotion of English manufacture than to the reinforcement of status distinctions. Thus a resolution of 1678 required '*all persons whatsoever* to wear no garments, stockings or other sort of apparel, but what is made of sheep's wool only, from the Feast of All Saints to the Feast of Our Lady inclusive' (italics added, Lipson 1964: 46). A person's 'price', what they were worth on the labour market, began to matter more than any other quality they may have possessed. Thomas Hobbes put the point bluntly when he declared that '[t]he Value or WORTH of a man, is as of all other things, his Price; that is to say, so much as would be given for the use of his Power' (1651 & 1985: 42). This perception of a person was institutionalised at the end of the century in Gregory King's *Naturall and Political Observations* (1696) which differentiated people according to their income. A husbandman earned only a quarter of the wages of a seaman, reflecting the fact that the latter made a greater contribution to England's trade (Wilson 1965 & 1996: 228). King's tables confirm that people were now valued more for their productive capacity than for their powers of consumption, as had been the case in the medieval period.

Christopher Hill argues that 'the main ideological driving force of the Revolution was religious' but that 'its long-term significance was economic' (1980 & 1997: 34). Of course it is hard to separate the two, since demands for freedom of conscience seemed to lead directly to freedom of trade. The puritans had always believed that work itself was a means of glorifying God, and that success in business was a sign of salvation. However, the language of religion moved ever closer to that of commerce so that spiritual matters were routinely discussed using the metaphors of trade. 'Here are no monopolies', wrote Bartholomew Ashwood writing of the distribution of God's grace, 'or hard impositions upon this trade: no restraint from setting up, or sell-ing out ... in any part of the world' (cited in Greaves 1992: 27). Starting out with the intention to spiritualise commerce, the puritans ended up by commercialising the spirit. And, as the century progresses, we find Robert Boyle, a principal founder of the Royal Society (1662), arguing that, with the restoration of the episcopacy, '[r]eligion must be made to serve commerce and industry as well as the clergy and the gentry' (Jacob 1980: 245).

Yet another example of how commerce was coming to dominate social life was in the emergence of 'economic man' who was described in terms of his 'interest' rather than his 'passion' (Hirschman 1977 & 1997). Simplifying greatly, the passions were held to be responsible for the 'brutish fury' (Marvell 1655 & 1976: 131) of the Civil War, whereas care for one's own economic 'interest' was seen as the basis of an ordered society. The pursuit of profit, in other words, introduced an element of predictability into social activity. Thomas Mun, Sir Josiah Child and Nicholas Barbon were among a number of writers on economic affairs who held that commerce promoted reason in 'men' and pattern in society. In the words of one contemporary: 'If you can apprehend wherein a man's interest doth consist you may surely know how to judge of his design' (cited in Gunn 1969: 557). The market was not only the basis of social stability, it also promoted peace and prosperity. The by-product of individuals acting predictably in accordance with their economic interests was the expansion of trade and increased cooperation and interdependent relationships between different groups and nations. The people who proclaimed such views were the very ones who had most to gain from the new economic arrangements. Others were less sanguine in their opinion. 'What does the merchant care, so that he be rich, how poor the public is? Let the commonwealth sink, so that he gets his profits' (cited in Lipson 1964: 5). If, as the late seventeenth-century proverb stated, 'Interest Governs the World', then it did so for the benefit of the few rather than the many, which is the quintessential class relation of capitalism.

THE BODY AND THE BOURGEOISIE

The expansion of an economic mode of thought into ever new spheres both altered the meanings of the traditional representations of society and instituted new ones. The perception of people in terms of their productive capacities promoted a mechanistic view of the body. 'For what', asks Hobbes, 'is the *Heart* but a *Spring*; and the *Nerves* but so many *Strings*; and the *Joynts*, but so many *Wheeles*, giving motion to the whole Body?' (1651 & 1985: 81). This description of the body signifies a further step in its separation from the mind, a process whose beginning we noted in the previous chapter. The idea of the mechanistic body could not be more different from the earlier view of it as an organic unity whose parts cooperated with one another and which served as a model for the working of hierarchical society.

T. S. Eliot described the divorce between mind and body as a 'dissociation of sensibility' seeing it as a crucial moment in the history of literature where 'language' is sundered from 'feeling', the former becoming ever 'more refined', the latter ever 'more crude' (1932 & 1976: 288). Eliot's account was enormously influential in traditional literary criticism but it did not explain how this 'dissociation' took place. There is, of course, no one answer, but we cannot properly understand the division between mind and body without taking into account the division of labour. This was not widespread in the period but the new factories and the 'wholesome rule of commerce' that the manufacture of a commodity should 'pass through as many hands as it can' (Thirsk 1978: 83) were early indications that the division of labour was set to become an important part of the capitalist economy. The separation of mind and body, in other words, is not a spontaneous event but a specific effect of economic changes that were benefiting the bourgeoisie. As such it has a determinate class character. The trope of the divided 'self' underwrites the division of labour and the new inequalities based on ownership of production.

However, it also speaks of the alienation at the heart of capitalism. The mind has been dispossessed of the body which, in taking on a mechanical character, is identified with the productive process from which the mind is quite separate. '[T]he alienation of man from himself and from nature', writes Marx, consists, in the fact that he is 'forced' to work for another, that his labour is therefore 'external' to him and that he is only ever involved in producing a part of the finished product (cited in Bottomore and Rubel 1956 & 1961: 169–70). *Paradise Lost* presents one example of alienation that arises from the division of labour. Eve's proposal that she and Adam 'divide [their] labours in Eden' (Milton 1667 & 1977: 376) results in her being alone when Satan approaches to tempt her to eat the forbidden fruit of the tree of the Knowledge of Good and Evil. Quite literally, the division of labour leads to the expulsion from Paradise; an event we might also read in terms of the enclosure movement.

The mechanistic view of the body is an example of that objectifying vision which characterises the labour relations of capitalism: a worker is not seen as a person but as a unit of production. Ultimately, this means that there is not only a division between body and mind, but that the body itself can be subdivided into smaller and smaller units. A good example of this is the way factory operatives in Victorian fiction are referred to as 'hands', but the process is already at work in Andrew Marvell's 'To His Coy Mistress' where the poet breaks down the woman's body into its various components:

> An hundred years should go to praise
> Thine eyes, and on thy forehead gaze;
> Two hundred to adore each breast
> (But thirty thousand to the rest);
> An age (at least) to every part,
> And the last age should show your heart.
>
> (1681 & 1976: 50–1)

This fetishisation of the different parts of the mistress' body also points to the beginnings of a commodity culture. Indeed, we can detect, in this period, the first stirrings of consumerism with the growth of shops in English provincial towns and 'the speed with which new-style consumer goods penetrated the length and breadth of the kingdom' (Thirsk 1978: 74).

We noted in the last chapter that to view 'man' in terms of bodily appetites rather than spiritual aspirations was seen as a travesty of Nature, but, in the latter part of the seventeenth century, it was an economic orthodoxy. Sir Dudley North was one of many who argued that the desire for gain was natural and that it was therefore a perfectly acceptable motive for economic activity. By the end of the century, the economy comes to be seen as 'a projection of endless human appetite on to the world at large' (McKeon 1988: 202). The problem was that appetite could never be satisfied:

> ... men like Ants
> Toyle to prevent imaginaire wants;
> Yet all in vain, increasing with their store,
> Their vast desires, but make their wants the more
> (Denham 1688 & 1974: 102)

The view of the body as solely appetite informs the sexual intrigues of Restoration comedy and the poetry of John Wilmot, Earl of Rochester (1647–80), who notes, of the countess of the Cockpit, 'when all her old Lovers forsake her I Trow / She'll then be contented with Signior Dildo' (1680 & 1996: 472). The body, as mechanism and appetite, serves the interest of the bourgeoisie by promoting production and stimulating consumer demand. Expenditure, however, existed in some tension with the puritan injunction to curb appetite in order to accumulate wealth, which was a sign of God's election (Weber 1930 & 1967: 155–83). However, writers, particularly Restoration dramatists, who drew on the aristocratic tradition of conspicuous consumption to endorse the pleasures of 'plays, visits, fine coaches, fine clothes, fiddles, balls, [and other] treats of town life' (Wycherley 1675 & 1976: 97), unwittingly demonstrated that two apparently opposed ideologies, arising from different economic interests, could complement one another. The use of the aristocratic custom of display vindicated the existence of commodities that the bourgeoisie produced but were constrained from enjoying by the rigours of their work ethic.

CLASSIFICATION AND CAPITALIST ECONOMICS

The division between the body and the mind and the subdivisions of the body were part of a new way of representing the social order that relied more on classification than on status distinctions. We have already mentioned one example of this, King's *Naturall and Political Observations*, but there was also William Petty's *Verbum Sapienti* (1668) which was the first serious attempt at calculating the national income. E. Victor Morgan argues that there is a close relationship between economic thought and scientific development. 'The essence of the scientific method', he writes, 'is accurate measurement, systematic classification, and logical deduction and these are just the processes which accounting brings to bear on economic life' (1965: 56). We can see an example of the link between economics and classification in the puritan Richard Baxter's divisions of the poor into separate categories. First there were the 'impotent poor', those who could not work, such as the physically or mentally incapacitated, and then there were the 'idle poor', those who could work but would not. These could be further divided into 'vagrants', who populated the underworld of vice and crime, and 'sturdy beggars' who were believed to be fleeing from employment instead of actively seeking it (Kishlansky 1997: 28–9).

The principle of classification is associated with the operation of exchange. Both work by emphasising what objects have in common, not how they differ. We have seen how this works with exchange, money does not compare commodities as unique entities but as embodiments of human labour. Similarly, classification organises phenomena not by their individual traits but by their shared features: spiders may all have eight legs but this does not make them the same. Although there is a parallel between exchange and classification, problems arise if we push it too far: classification, unlike exchange is also a means of differentiation, spiders are not insects. Nevertheless, to the extent that classification, to a greater or lesser extent, concentrates on likeness rather than difference it reinforces the operation of exchange and therefore the dominant mode of bourgeois representation. But this raises a problem, namely isn't there a contradiction between the sameness imposed by exchange and the ideology of the individual? How can they both be bourgeois? There is no easy answer to this question but although these characteristic representations of the bourgeoisie seem to conflict, they both hide the reality of class. The mechanism of exchange equalises all human labour in the medium of money (Marx 1867 & 1995: 43) while the idea of the hard-working individual diverts attention from questions of ownership and exploitation.

To return, however, to classification. It not only serves the bourgeois interest by its association with exchange, it also seems to give an objective account of social divisions. Sociology and national income studies 'were born in the seventeenth century' (Wilson 1965 & 1996: 17), partly as a reaction to the upheavals of the Civil War. In contrast to the partisan language of politics and religion, they promised an impartial description of the social structure. However, as Mary Poovey contends, classificatory thinking 'reproduces as inequalities' the social differentiations it purports to describe (1994: 19). For example, Petty's *Verbum Sapienti* may have been the first serious attempt at a calculation of the national income, but its real aim was to show that property could be taxed less and the people more (Wilson 1965 & 1996: 227–8). In short, classification serves the bourgeoisie by describing economic divisions in scientific terms thereby making them seem a law of nature which must be accepted since it cannot be changed.

Classification was part of a scientific approach to the world. The chemist Robert Boyle (1627–91), the physiologist William Harvey (1578–1657) and of course the astronomer and mathematician Sir Isaac Newton (1642–1727) were among many who believed that it was possible to explain the world methodically in one coherent system. Science was the ally of the bourgeoisie, not only because the Royal Society was actively involved in trade and agricultural improvements, but also because certain findings seemed to endorse the dynamic nature of capitalism. William Harvey's discovery of the circulation of the blood (1628, published 1653) quickly began to inform descriptions of trade. Petty, for example, described merchants as 'veines and arteries, to distribute back and forth the blood and nutritive juyces of the Body Politic, namely the Product of Husbandry & Manufactures' (cited in Wilson 1965 & 1996: 50) while Newton's discovery of the law of perpetual motion (1686) provided an alibi for what Marx called the 'constantly revolutionary' nature of capitalism (Marx and Engels 1848 & 1968: 38).

THE PLAIN STYLE AND THE BOURGEOISIE

The growth of science had an enormous effect on the English language. Thomas Sprat (1635–1713), in *The History of the Royal Society*, claims that 'until the beginning of the late Civil Wars' the language 'sound[ed] tolerably well' (1667 & 1963: 113). However, during the conflict, it 'received many fantastical terms [and] outlandish phrases' which it was now time to remove as the 'ill effects of this superfluity of talking have overwhelmed most other Arts and Professions' (ibid.: 113, 116). Sprat blames the inflation of the language on 'the *dissention* of Princes and Religious sects' (ibid.: 117), saying it must be purged of 'amplifications, digressions, and swellings of style' and be 'returned to the primitive purity and shortness, when men deliver'd so many *things* almost in an equal number of *words*' (ibid.: 118). He describes this sense of proportion as 'Mathematical plainness' and links it directly to the speech of 'Artizans and Merchants' which is to be preferred to that of 'Wits and Scholars' (ibid.). In short, Sprat makes clear the relationship between language and class: the court and nobility speak in 'tropes and figures', the city traders and businessmen with 'unaffected sincerity and sound simplicity' (ibid.: 117–18). Moreover, the desired bourgeois idiom was one that mimicked an aspect of exchange in its ideal equivalence of words for things. Sprat's purpose in promoting this particular conception of language was to create consensus and prevent a return to the polemics of the Civil War. This was a language for all classes, but it was designed by and for the bourgeoisie.

A number of writers advocated that the plain style be adopted in 'literature'. Roger Pooley suggests that 'literature', in the sense of fine writing, was applicable only from the second half of the eighteenth century and that rhetoric would therefore be a more suitable term (1992: 1–2). There was certainly much discussion about the nature of poetry and drama following the upheaval of the Civil War. The abolition of censorship in 1640 precipitated an avalanche of newspapers, pamphlets, ballads and almanacs which not only ended the state Church's monopoly of opinion-forming, but also swept away the traditional relation between genre and social position. In the tumult of the period, the idea that poetry and drama were the preserve of the aristocratic court while prose was the province of the 'middle sort of people' (Parfitt 1985 & 1992: 17) simply did not survive: old genres disappeared and new ones emerged (Smith 1994). The essay, for example, makes its appearance in this century, its provisional character well suited to the turmoil of the age where institutions like the monarchy, previously thought to be permanent, proved quite transitory.

There was some attempt to reassert old hierarchies when Charles II returned from France in 1660 and the theatres were re-opened. The hero of Restoration comedy was the antithesis of the puritan. His was a life of leisure not work, of elegant dress not plain garb, of sophistication not sincerity, and of sexual licence not restraint. Although characters like Horner in *The Country Wife* do not strictly belong to the nobility, they nevertheless personify the pursuit of pleasure that characterised the court of Charles II and, to that extent, they uphold an aristocratic over a 'bourgeois' culture. Horner is able to cuckold the banker Sir Jasper because of the latter's attachment to his work: 'business must be preferred always before love' (Wycherley 1675 & 1976: 86). The poet and playwright Sir William Davenant (1606–68) believed that poetry was a mark of refinement, exclusively a court activity which 'should not be levell'd to the reach of Common men' (1650 & 1963: 14). Sir Richard Blackmore (1654–1729), poet and physician to Queen Anne, agreed, advocating that poetry should concentrate, in a style 'Rich in Fancy [and] abound[ing] in Beautiful and Noble Expression', on 'Characters of the first Rank and Dignity, Illustrious for the Birth' (1695 & 1963: 229). Others, however, took a different view. Wentworth Dillon (1633–85), who had the distinction of being the first critic publicly to praise *Paradise Lost*, declared in 'An Essay on Translated Verse' that poets should write of 'useful subjects' and avoid 'affected, *meretricious* Arts' (1684 & 1963: 301). John Sheffield (1648–1721), a patron of the poet and critic John Dryden (1631–1700), dismissed 'Figures of Speech which Poets think so fine [as] Art's needless Varnish to make Nature shine' (1682 & 1963: 291) while Joseph Glanvill (1636–80), a rector at Bath, believed that 'plainness' represents things better than '*Affected Rhetoric* and *Phantastical Phrases*' (1678 & 1963: 273).

Although many of those who wrote on poetry were 'sirs' or 'lords', they promoted values that more properly belonged to the bourgeoisie. Poetry did not require inspiration but 'time and labour' (Davenant 1650 & 1963: 25). The ideal, however, was to balance contrary qualities: poems should have 'invention and liveliness of wit' but they must also, argued the diplomat and poet William Temple (1628–99) have 'good sense and soundness of judgement' (1690 & 1963: 81). 'Without the forces of Wit', he continued, 'all poetry is flat and languishing; without the succours of Judgement 'tis wild and extravagant' (ibid.). It was not just mental attributes that needed to complement each other in poetic composition, so too did the relations between the part and whole in the work of art. Dryden maintains that the superiority of English to French drama resides in its structure, which reconciles a number of different elements: 'the parts are managed so regularly that the beauty of the whole be kept intire', the parts themselves being a 'variety' and the whole 'a pleasing labyrinth of design' (1668 & 1997: 56).

The concern to establish equilibrium between conflicting elements is a political as well as an aesthetic consideration. The attention to symmetry in the work of art, in other words, cannot be separated from the anxiety about the balance of power between the Crown and Parliament where the scales needed to be fairly even to avoid the repetition of civil strife. At another level, the desire to connect part and whole is a reaction to the dissolution of an integrated hierarchy of values 'embracing all human interests and activities', resulting in a society divided into 'separate compartments ... between which a due balance should be maintained' (Tawney 1926 & 1990: 22). John Guillory argues that it is at this moment that the work of art becomes important for its 'order, proportion, [and] harmony' could be used analogously to represent the social totality (1993: 305). The allegory of medieval literature, which expressed the fundamental unity of creation, has given way to an art which must piece together the broken world.

The plain style is charged with this enormous task, but its concern for equivalence between words and things, its association with exchange, its being modelled on the language of merchants, its concern with balance and its preoccupation with the relation of part and whole, identify it as the class idiom of the bourgeoisie. It therefore does not so much restore a lost world as create a new one in its own image; and it disguises the ideological nature of this enterprise by casting the relations between, for example, part and whole in a poem or a drama in entirely naturalistic terms. Well, not quite: Dryden's *Of Dramatic Poesie: An Essay*, announces its bourgeois sympathies when it describes the plots of English drama as being 'weav'd in English looms', but it suppresses that allusion to production almost immediately by describing the relation between main plots and subplots as like the 'motions of the planets' (1668 & 1997: 50, 52).

MONEY, SELF AND CLASS

One way of describing some of the changes discussed in this chapter is to say that there is a shift from a domestic to a political economy. In the feudal era, broadly speaking, the term 'economy' referred to personal management or husbandry 'without any financial or monetary suggestion' (Thompson 1996: 42). However, with the financial revolution of the 1690s, which saw the establishment of credit, the foundation of the Bank of England and the recoinage of the currency, the word 'economy' comes to be associated with money and exchange. In the words of James Thompson:

> political economy consists of a language or discourse of and about money, about making money, accumulating money, improving money, but it is also about the form of money and its nature, how to direct or control money, how to make money work smoothly, efficiently and profitably.
>
> (ibid.: 43)

These developments not only represent a further extension of exchange, thereby consolidating bourgeois power, they are also implicated in responses to art. As Guillory observes, 'the problem of aesthetic judgement was as essential to the formation of political economy as the problem of political economy was to the formation of aesthetics' (1993: 303). In the late seventeenth century, and throughout the eighteenth, this relationship centred on the question of representation. How accurately does a banknote represent monetary worth and how well do words represent the reality they purport to describe? It was partly this problem of the non-coincidence of 'appearance' and 'reality' that the creation of a transparent language was expected to resolve.

The origin of the problem lay in the anxieties surrounding the debased state of the currency in the late seventeenth century. Not merely was it old and worn, but coins were deliberately clipped to produce small parings that were then melted down and exported as bullion. The resulting shortage of silver raised prices while 'golden guineas (with milled edges less vulnerable to clipping) rose in value and a complex, accelerating distortion of England's trade balance, exchange rates and domestic economy followed' (Roseveare 1991: 38). The solution was to recoin and there were two approaches to this. James Hodges declared that the 'whole value that is put upon Money by Mankind, is extrinsick to the Money' (cited in Buchan 1997: 104). It was such considerations that made William Lowndes, the Treasury Secretary, propose that the name of the coin remain the same but its weight be reduced. This was unacceptable to John Locke (1632–1704), the philosopher and member of the Council of Trade, who countered that it was a coin's weight in precious metal that determined its value: 'the intrinsic Value of Silver and Gold ... is nothing but their quantity' (cited in Thompson 1996: 57). It was Locke's view, summarised in his phrase 'silver is silver', which held sway, and, by the terms of the Recoinage Act of 1696, the currency was restored to the old high standard.

Despite this, contemporaries continued to worry about the question of whether gold and silver were inherently valuable or whether their value was conventional and arbitrary. The sense that there was a gap between value and representation was aggravated by the growing use of credit and paper money, and was to be the subject of much debate in the late seventeenth and eighteenth centuries. In the late seventeenth century, the distinction between intrinsic and extrinsic value appears, in 'literature', as the tension between 'appearance' and 'reality'. These terms can also apply to money. James Buchan notes that what the numerous seventeenth-century tracts on money had 'in common [was] their claim to distinguish between appearance and reality' (1997: 103). This distinction applies particularly to Restoration comedy, especially that written in the 1670s, a decade of intense debate about Britain's financial institutions and practices (Roseveare 1991: 27). Harriet, in *The Man of Mode*, talks of 'the dear pleasure of dissembling' while at the same time complaining that '[v]arnished over with good breeding, many a blockhead makes a tolerable show' (Etherege 1676 & 1967: 54, 51). Manly, in William Wycherley's *The Plain Dealer*, scorns Freeman as one 'who esteems men only by the marks value and fortune has set upon them, and never considers intrinsic worth', while he himself 'weighs the man, not his title' (1676 & 1967: 19). Such remarks recall the problems of how to value, and how value should be expressed, which were key features of the recoinage debate.

More particularly, it is the metaphor of money that provides the means of conceptualising the difference between 'appearance' and 'reality' in Restoration comedy. In *The Man of Mode*, love is seen as a form of 'counterfeit coin' that 'gilds us over ... but soon the gold wears off and then again the native brass appears' (1676 & 1976: 45). The whole process of love is cast in a financial idiom. For instance Olivia, in *The Plain Dealer*, speaks of lovers as 'creditors' and love as a form of 'debt' (1676 & 1967: 59). Furthermore, despite Freeman's protestations to the contrary: 'I value you only, not your jointure' (ibid.: 73), it is money which determines the value of the 'loved' one. 'I would marry her', the same character declares earlier, 'to the comfort of my creditors' (ibid.: 67). Although there is, as we have seen, a distinction to be drawn between a person and their wealth in these plays, this is largely rhetorical. A great deal of their imagery is drawn from theatre and acting, suggesting that the idea of a substantial self which transcends its social roles is a mere chimera. This is in contrast to our earlier point that there is a 'true' self of the mind if not the body. These different 'selves' represent different relations to the capitalist economy and so they are both versions of the 'bourgeois self'. The division between mind and body is related to the division of labour, whereas the 'empty self' is related to money and exchange. Very briefly, as we noted in the last chapter, the 'split self' mirrored the split in the commodity between its actual form and its value form. This division could be maintained only if the concept of money was itself secure. Once a rift occurred between the form of money and its actual value, the distinction between mind and body, between a real and an ephemeral self, started to crumble. The establishment of the institutions of a money economy seems to drain the self of substance. That this is evident from Restoration theatre shows that the 'truth' of the bourgeois economy can register itself in a non-bourgeois art form.

PARADISE LOST (1667): BEDDING DOWN THE BOURGEOIS ECONOMY

It is a commonplace that John Milton's *Paradise Lost* is an attempt to come to terms with the failure of the republican experiment in England, but what is less noticed is the way that it negotiates the experience of exchange in literary terms. The fact that this is not carried on at a conscious level already implies that there is a deep connection between the form of money and structures of representation.

Derrida notes that economy 'implies the idea of exchange, of circulation, of return' (1994: 6) and God, 'from whom / All things proceed, and up to him return' (1667 & 1977: 309) is the perfect example of this. The metaphor of exchange characterises God's relationship to Satan and Adam and Eve: in return for creating them he expects 'adoration pure' (ibid.: 292). Exchange seems to have two meanings which contradict one another. The first is that when one thing is exchanged for another it should be of an equal value to it. The second is that there is always an imbalance in the act of exchange. Since God adjudicates each matter by weighing it in 'his golden scales' (ibid.: 298), it would seem he has a quantitative view of exchange. This takes the form of a mirror in which God's image is reflected back to him from his creation without loss of value. The rebellion of Satan and the disobedience of Adam and Eve are seen in terms of the corruption of this image, its 'disfigurement', or 'debasement' (ibid.: 435–6). These actions disrupt the return of God's image to himself and so constitute an excess in an economy of which God should be the origin and the end. God then contributes to that excess by declaring that Adam's crime 'makes guilty all his sons' (ibid.: 263). The structured imbalance of this new economy is different in heaven to what it is on earth. The single action of Christ's sacrifice redeems 'Death's due' and discharges the human race's 'debt' while, for humans, the opposite is the case: it needs 'many deeds well done' to 'cover one bad act' (ibid.: 262, 249).

The above account suggests that a restricted economy gives place to a more general one. This is certainly what happens as society moves from the closed order of feudalism to the open-ended one of capitalism. However, it is not easy to separate the two kinds of economy because, as MacLachlan notes, 'pre-capitalist communal arrangements co-existed and perpetuated themselves alongside the individualist imperatives of trade and commerce' (1996: 17), a fact reflected in Milton's conflation of the idioms of feudalism and capitalism throughout *Paradise Lost*. More specifically, as Adam points out, God's bounty to himself and Eve is far in excess of anything they can do for him (1667 & 1977: 285) showing that excess is already a feature of an economy apparently based on equal exchange. The basis of this excess is a trope; the comparison of heavenly beings to humans. This lies at the heart of Raphael's account of Satan's rebellion, which God had instructed him to relate to Adam in order to warn the latter of the dangers of transgression.

Raphael's problem is how to make Adam understand God's message: 'how shall I relate / To human sense th' invisible exploits / Of warring Spirits?' (1667 & 1977: 311). His solution is to use similes: 'what surmounts the reach / Of human sense I shall delineate so, / By lik'ning spiritual to corporal forms' (ibid.: 312). By doing so, however, he brings about the opposite effect to the one he intended. Instead of reminding Adam of the virtue of obedience, he unwittingly incites him to disobedience. His similes stimulate Adam with a 'desire to know' more than he should (ibid.: 341–3) and, in that respect, he achieves Satan's aim of 'excit[ing] their minds / With more desire to know' (ibid.: 287). Raphael's analogies produce this excess because they appeal more to the body and the fancy than to reason and the mind. Adam relishes their sensuous quality; 'sweeter thy discourse is to my ear / Than fruits of palm tree' but it is a 'sweetness' which 'bring[s] no satiety' (ibid.: 360). It excites the fancy to search for more delight but, like the now awakened desire, so here too, 'of her roving is no end' (ibid.).

The trope of similitude not only generates an excess that upsets the idea of economic balance, it is also an analogue for the exchange relation itself. In establishing likeness between different things it eliminates what is unique about them. This likeness then becomes the basis of value. What gives Adam and Eve their worth is their resemblance to the divine, the source of value (1667 & 1977: 283). In this respect, God behaves like money. That is to say, just as it is not goods which are important in exchange, but what they represent in terms of money, so what matters to God is not the particularity of the characters but how much they reflect his glory. At the same time, similitude resists the uniformity demanded by exchange because it is based on a relation of difference. The very idea that one thing is like another implicitly acknowledges that they can be distinguished, that they are not identical and this links similitude with the perceived disparity between nominal and real value in money terms.

According to Marc Shell, the paper money debate 'was concerned with symbolisation in general, with the relationship between the substantial thing and its sign' and so referred to aesthetic as well as financial matters (1982: 6). One means of overcoming the gap between value and representation in money was the king's stamp, and this perhaps has some bearing on Milton's concern with the debasement of God's image in *Paradise Lost*. The importance of this stamp grew as it was gradually accepted, during the course of the eighteenth century, that money was not simply the measure of wealth but a commodity – silver and gold – that also fluctuated in price (Thompson 1996: 71). As such it had no intrinsic value and this is, in part, suggested by the nature of God's image in *Paradise Lost*. God is 'invisible', it is only through Christ, the 'Divine Similitude', that he becomes visible, a process described in terms which evoke the minting of money: 'on thee / Impressed the effulgence of his glory abides' (1667 & 1977: 265–6). The point I want to stress is that God *himself* is never seen, only his reflection. His essence can never equate with his appearance. Extending this to money, we can say that there is no correlation between value and its representation. Paradoxically, it is only because value cannot be seen, that it can be represented. Its visible form is necessarily displaced from its source.

It should be clear from the above that there is no direct correlation between the economy and cultural expression. Indeed, it is questionable whether that distinction is itself reliable given that *Paradise Lost* shows that we cannot imagine exchange without similitude, nor similitude without exchange. The idea of the economic relies on literary tropes just as these tropes are themselves modified by economic activity. The circulation of the blood conceptualises a certain view of how the economy functions, while the development of trade fosters a new interest in the physical properties of objects which stimulates the growth of realism and hence the novel. The relevance of this for class is that it complicates the view that literature can be determined by the economic base or express the interests of the dominant group. The close association between literary tropes and economic concepts suggests that Milton's epic prepares the mind to accept a life lived according to exchange. Consequently, the poem represents not the defeat of the English Revolution but its triumph, the triumph of a bourgeois economic logic implacably opposed to the freedom Adam and Eve enjoyed in the feudal splendour of Paradise.

4

THE EIGHTEENTH CENTURY

This chapter considers the extent to which eighteenth-century society can be considered as a class society. Its main focus is the rise of the middle class and how the nature of the bourgeois economy affected literary forms and representations of reason and the self. I will use the terms 'bourgeois' or 'bourgeoisie' instead of 'middle class' when I wish to emphasise the economic character of cultural forms in capitalism.

PATRICIANS, PLEBS AND THE PERSISTENCE OF HIERARCHY

We noted in the last chapter that the basic social division was still between those who were 'gentle' and those who were 'common'. This bipartite view of the social structure persists into the eighteenth century with the novelist and Justice of the Peace, Henry Fielding (1707–54), aligning 'Mankind under two great divisions, those that use their hands and those that employ the hands of others' (1743 & 1947: 12). Fielding's distinction, however, contains a shift of emphasis that reflects a growing awareness of 'class' rather than status categories in conceptions of society. He distinguishes between employers and employees whereas commentators in previous eras were more concerned with birth, manners and learning. By contrast, many of Fielding's contemporaries continued to think in terms of the old tripartite model of society, based on the medieval estates, but instead of knights, priests and labourers the division was between the upper orders, the middle ranks and the rest (Cannadine 1998: 29).

This model, however, suffered from a number of limitations. In the first place it took no account of the internal diversity of the different groups and, in the second, it was ill adapted to represent the many changes that resulted from the intense commercial activity of the period. Roy Porter notes how the term 'gentry' ranged from baronets to squires, while the 'middling sort' included, among others, businessmen, merchants, professionals, shopkeepers and tradesmen. The lower orders, too, were far from uniform, moving 'from weavers to watermen, from ostlers to shepherds, from ploughman to pieman, from crossing sweepers to coal miners' (Porter 1990: 49). The diversity within these groups, Porter continues, led to a constant struggle over status differentiation: 'the distinctions between being a servant in or out of livery ... mattered no less at their own levels than the pecking-order between baronets and earls, marquises and dukes' (ibid.). The conventional view of the social hierarchy, as 'providentially ordained, hierarchically ordered and organically interconnected' (Cannadine 1998: 28), was based on the idea that society did not change, that its order, in the words of the critic Samuel Johnson (1709–84), was 'fixed and invariable' (cited in ibid.: 26). The increase in population, the growth of trade and industry and greater social mobility all contradicted this view and led to attempts to update and expand the traditional model. In 1709, Daniel Defoe (1660–1731) produced a seven-tier classification, from 'the great' who 'lived profusely' to 'the miserable' that 'really pinch and suffer want', while an anonymous author of 1770 postulated a fourfold division consisting of 'the Nobs', 'the

Citizens and their Ladies', the 'Mechanics and Middling Degrees' and 'the Refuse' (cited in ibid.: 28). What is noticeable about these and other attempts is that they try to accommodate a town-based and commercial vocabulary within a land-based social structure. The resulting picture is less a clear image of a society than a testament to the tensions within it.

Although it was true that the 'middling class' owned most of the industrial capital, and that they were responsible for the viability and growth of the national economy, there was little evidence that 'the basic structure of property ownership was changing dramatically' (Langford 1997: 388). It is this observation that has made a number of commentators on the eighteenth century reluctant to use the word 'class' to describe the social formation. In addition, the traditional Marxist identification of class with economics tends to play down other factors that were important to contemporaries such as region, local loyalty, family and religion. Moreover, as Porter asserts, eighteenth-century people 'did not think of their society in a way anticipating Marx as turning upon struggle between two distinct classes, defined essentially in relation to ownership and deployment of capital' (Porter 1990: 53). And he goes on to point out that when there was social or political disturbance it was less likely for classes to be confronting one another than rival trades or interest groups. In any case, Porter concludes, '[t]he Marxist schema could hardly apply to a nation in which smallholders, yeomen, self-employing tradesmen and craftsmen still comprised much of the workforce' (ibid.: 53).

Be that as it may, a Marxist could still make the case that society began to polarise as the century wore on (Hay and Rogers 1997: 201–7); it should not be forgotten that the age of reason ended in the upheaval of revolution. E.P. Thompson claims that the primary relationship of the eighteenth century was that between what he calls the patricians and plebeians, by which he means the gentry and 'the labouring poor' (1993: 16). The gentry were seen as the oppressors because this was the period in which 'the commoners finally lost their land, in which the number of offences carrying the capital penalty multiplied, in which thousands of felons were transported and in which thousands of lives were lost in imperial wars' (ibid.: 18). The labouring poor responded with riots against food prices, road tolls and, in the 1760s and 1770s, with protests against the monarchy. These latter demonstrations were countered with repressive legislation against the press and trade unions, and there was also a concerted effort to suppress the plebeian culture which had flourished in the early part of the century thanks, in part, to the decline of puritanism. When this aspect of the eighteenth century is emphasised, Marx's observations about class seem to have some relevance. However, there is an ambiguity in Marx which needs to be borne in mind. According to Michael McKeon, Marx employs:

> 'class' as an abstract term to describe a kind of socio-economic relation and conflict that is generally characteristic of all human societies. On the other hand, the category describes a very particular historical reality, that of modern industrial capitalism, whose particularity is registered by the fact that it directly experiences itself in the terms of class – by the fact, that is, of class consciousness.
>
> (1988: 164)

This would seem to bear out Thompson's observation that, in the eighteenth century, there was class conflict but not class consciousness. The relationship between the patricians and the plebeians was not based on a conflict of economic interests because the economic connection between them had been severed. The eighteenth century saw 'the final extinction of labour services and the advance of free, mobile wage labour' which resulted in 'independence from the gentry' (Thompson 1993: 36). It was this independence which had to be policed, especially when it was linked with a potentially unruly plebeian culture of 'baitings, wrestling, dancing and drinking' (ibid.: 54). Even though the 'plebs' were aware of common economic problems, evident in the desire of some to transcend the guild mentality and establish a trade union movement, their culture could not be described in class terms; partly because it lacked consistency of self-definition, partly because it had no clear objectives and partly because it gave priority to moral over economic imperatives (ibid.: 11, 57, 72). It was a culture of resistance rather than revolution, invoking the name of custom in its struggle against technological innovation, work discipline and the free market in grain. Despite the many riots of the period, most opposition to the gentry concerned the importance of local customs rather than the need for economic reorganisation or political reform: dancing round the maypole was a more urgent matter than the extension of the franchise. It was not until the American Revolution (1775–83) and later the French Revolution (1789–99) that the 'mob' began to challenge the principles of the social order; but though the threat of revolution was then in the air, it was not directly related to 'class', a concept which comes into its own in the nineteenth century.

In the eighteenth century, the main metaphors of the social structure were still predominantly feudal. We have already mentioned the durability of the estates model and the 'great chain of being' was 'still the most widely recognised and accepted view of society' (Cannadine 1998: 26). An example is Alexander Pope's (1688–1744) 'An Essay on Man' where he writes:

> ... Parts relate to whole;
> One all extending all preserving Soul
> Connects each being, greatest with the least;
> Made beast in aid of Man, and Man of Beast;
> All serv'd, all serving! Nothing stands alone
> The chain holds on, and where it ends, unknown.
>
> (1744 & 1978: 259)

The chain of being shows the cosmos as a living organism of interdependent parts such that 'From Nature's chain whatever link you strike, / Tenth or ten thousandth, breaks the chain alike' (ibid.: 248). This echoes Ulysses' remark in *Troilus and Cressida* 'Take but degree away, untune that string, / and hark, what discord follows' (Shakespeare 1603 & 1988: 721). The chain is less a description of the existing order than an attempt to justify it in the face of a number of challenges to its essential principles. 'Masters', for example, were 'complain[ing] at the breach of the "great law of subordination" and the diminution of deference among the labouring poor' (Thompson 1993: 37). Defoe looked into this issue in his 'Great Law of Subordination Consider'd; or the Insolence and Unsufferable Behaviour of Servants in England duly enquired into' (1724).

THE MEANINGS OF 'CLASS' AND THE RISE OF THE MIDDLE CLASS

An idiosyncratic use of the term 'class' appears in *The Spectator* in 1712. The author of the article, one 'Hotspur', allocates women into 'three distinct and proper classes, the ape, the coquette and the devotee' (cited in Cannadine 1998: 29). More generally, the term was used interchangeably with 'estate' or 'degree', hence Johnson's definition in his *Dictionary of the English Language* (1755) of class as 'rank or order of persons' (cited in Cannadine 1998: 31). Another meaning, also found in Johnson's *Dictionary*, is class as classification, 'a set of beings or things, a number arranged in distribution under some common denomination' (ibid.). Jonas Hanway (1712–86) uses the term 'class' in the preface to his *Letters on the importance of the rising generation of the Labouring part of our fellow subjects* (1767) but incorporates it into the title of his next work, *Observations on the Causes of the Dissoluteness which reigns among the Lower Classes of People* (1772). This represents yet another use of the word since it associates it with both the rise of labour and its discontent. The idea of class and conflict are very close here. However, it was more usual to apply the term 'class' to the middle section of society as the novelist Samuel Richardson (1689–1761) does in *Clarissa* as early as 1748.

Raymond Williams has suggested that the appearance of the word 'class' coincides with the rise of the 'middle sort' since it 'relates to the increasing consciousness that social position is made rather than merely inherited; [a]ll the other words, with their essential metaphors of standing, stepping and arranging in rows, belong to a society in which position was determined by birth' (1988: 61–2). The period saw a proliferation of descriptions for the middle class: 'the Middling People of England', 'the middling sort', 'the middle station of life' or, in the words of the poet William Cowper, 'Tenants of Life's middle state, / Securely placed between the small and great' (cited in Seed 1992: 115). It is to this group that Robinson Crusoe belongs. His father tells him that:

> [his] was the middle State ... which he had found by long Experience was the best State in the World, the most suited to human Happiness, not exposed to the Miseries and Hardships, the Labour and Sufferings of the Mechanick Part of Mankind, and not embarass'd with the Pride, Luxury, Ambition and Envy of the Upper Part of Mankind. [Rather] Temperance, Moderation, Quietness, Health, Society, all agreeable Diversions and all Desirable Pleasures, were the Blessings attending the Middle Station of Life.
>
> (Defoe 1719 & 1972: 6)

John Seed gives a minimal definition of the middle class in this period when he says they were distinguished from the aristocracy and gentry 'by their need to generate income from some kind of active occupation' and from the labouring majority 'by their possession of property' (1992: 115). This class was made up of a number of different elements: merchants, traders, businessmen, shopkeepers and professional groups such as lawyers, doctors and teachers.

Despite this diversity, it did have a number of common features. From rich bankers to modest tradesmen it provided the commercial backbone of the nation, while the poet and playwright, Oliver Goldsmith (1730–74), claimed that 'in this middle order of mankind are generally to be found all the arts, wisdom and virtues of society' (cited in Cannadine 1998: 32). The middle class saw itself as moderately placed between the two extremes of high and low, thereby holding society together. There is a certain irony in this since it was the belief in economic individualism that dissolved social ties, something that the middle class tried to address in the eighteenth century by the cultivation of sensibility. As Terry Eagleton notes, 'the ultimate binding force of the bourgeois social order [were] habits, pieties, sentiments and affections' (1990: 22). These found their highest expression in the work of art, or the aesthetic, whose essential concern with the relation between parts and whole runs counter to the fragmentation of the capitalist economy. Although we can identify a middle class in terms of its relation to production, this does not cover all who may qualify for membership, such as journalists or civil servants. These may belong to the middle class by virtue of their sensibility, but this characteristic, because it is associated with social cooperation, exists in some tension with economic competition. Such internal rifts inhibited the formation of the 'middling sort' as a coherent class. It is therefore not surprising that some of their number sought assimilation into the aristocracy, and their fidelity to the fashions and habits of their social superiors helped to sustain 'the impression of a dominant and patronising elite' (Langford 1997: 395). At the same time, however, the middle class were creating their own 'shadowy civil society or public sphere' (Thompson 1993: 32) thus freeing themselves from the patronage of the nobility upon which they had previously relied for access to power.

The increasing wealth, influence and power of the middle class raised anxieties about who was and who was not a gentleman. Was he, in Defoe's phrase, 'a born gentleman or a bred gentleman'? (cited in Cannadine 1998: 33). The traditional idea of the gentleman was a landowner, with a coat of arms denoting his pedigree of lineage, who possessed the qualities of courage, chivalry, generosity, hospitality and a sense of duty. However, this ideal had been eroded throughout the seventeenth century by the sale of titles and offices. It was further weakened in the eighteenth century by the ability of the more wealthy part of the middle class to buy large estates and, with them, the appearance of gentility. This was particularly pronounced with the 'nabobs', the name given to men who, having made their fortune on the slave plantations of the West Indies, were able to buy their way into Parliament. Consequently, property was no longer deemed to be a reliable guide to gentlemanly status and instead the emphasis fell on qualities of character. 'The Gentleman', wrote Defoe, is 'a Person of Merit and Worth; a Man of Honour, Virtue, Sense, Integrity, Honesty and Religion' (cited in McKeon 1988: 156).

A term that is missing from this list is 'taste' which is 'the utmost Perfection of an accomplished Man' (Addison 1712 in Steele and Addison 1988: 364). The concept of taste introduces an aesthetic element into the definition of a gentleman. Previously we noted that the aesthetic was the basis of sociability but, in being factored into the make-up of a gentleman, it also becomes a tool of discrimination. Taste was simultaneously a condition to which one was born and a state one achieved. 'It is', writes Addison, 'very difficult to lay down Rules for the Acquirement of Taste. ... The Faculty must in some degree be born with us ... but there are several Methods of cultivating and Improving it' (ibid.: 366). The dependence of the idea of the gentleman on the concept of taste creates the possibility that 'gentility' can be either inherited or acquired and, to that extent, the term 'gentleman' is less a source of anxiety than a compromise between the conflicting claims of class and status. It could not, however, maintain this poise because, as McKeon notes, 'the traditional, qualitative criteria of honorific status were being definitively infiltrated by the quantitative criteria of socio-economic class' (1988: 162). Concrete social distinctions, in other words, were gradually being replaced by an abstract idea of economic 'man' which underpinned the ideology of the free market.

THE FREE MARKET AND REPRESENTATION

The debate over gentlemanly qualities occurred in the 'century in which "money beareth all the stroke", in which liberties become properties, and use rights are reified' (Thompson 1993: 25). The financial reorganisation of Britain had begun in the final decade of the previous century with the foundation of the Bank of England (1694), the growth of paper money, the expansion of credit, the National Debt and the growth of the stock market (Roseveare 1991). These developments hastened the rejection of the moral economy and the acceptance of the market one. According to Thompson, the moral economy 'validated itself with reference to moral imperatives – what obligations the state or the landowners or the [corn] dealers ought to obey' (1993: 269). The market, however, implied a view of the economy as an objective mechanism that operated without regard to moral considerations and this receives its most famous expression in Adam Smith's *The Wealth of Nations* (1776). James Thompson makes the point that throughout the eighteenth century there was a 'drive toward an abstract and consistent and therefore predictable model of exchange, that is toward (new) scientific, quantitative, and mathematical modelling' (1996: 28). Such a model, rational and rule-bound, occludes questions of relations, duties and responsibilities. James Sambrook sums up this change by saying that cash relationships replaced those based on custom and tradition (1993: 100).

The essentially quantitative categories, derived from this con-

ception of the economy, permeated social experience. As Colin
Nicholson notes, they 'changed in decisive ways how people
thought and wrote about themselves and their world' (1996: 7).
Gregory King's audit of the income and expenses of families in the
1690s formalised the process of understanding society from a predominantly economic and therefore bourgeois perspective.
However, it failed to comprehend the social order as a dynamic system of mutual relations, power and purpose. We can see this to some
extent in the dominant verse form of the age, the heroic couplet, a
pair of rhymed lines in iambic pentameters, such as Pope's 'See
Mystery to Mathematics fly! / In vain! they gaze, turn giddy, rave
and die' (1728 & 1978: 584). The closed nature of the heroic couplet, its tightly structured format and epigrammatic quality, means
that it is complete in itself, that it has no vital connection with, but
is merely contiguous to those couplets that come before and after it.
Like the bourgeois capitalist, the heroic couplet accumulates, it
does not articulate. The Marxist critic Christopher Cauldwell,
(1907–37), who was killed in the Spanish Civil War, suggests that
the 'polished language and metre and curt antitheses [of the heroic
couplet] were a reflection of the bourgeois recognition' that, at this
stage of capitalist development, 'freedom can only be limited – man
must be prudent in his demands' (1937 & 1977: 99).

But if the heroic couplet is shaped by the exigencies of the
bourgeois economy and the bourgeois class, it is also a reaction to
the capacity of capitalism to expand beyond its means of representation. During the course of the eighteenth century, as John
Barrell has argued, the divisions of society on the basis of income
and occupation became too extensive to be contained in any one
scheme. Consequently, he claims, 'there is no comprehensive
view, society is no longer capable of being understood' (1983:
40). Class society exceeds the very classification systems it produced to understand itself. The closed form of the heroic couplet
was one response to this problem while the open nature of the
picaresque novel was another. However, even the latter's panoramic

vision could not encompass capitalism's endless expansion. As André Gorz notes, the '[q]uantitative measure inherently admits of no principle of self-limitation. The category of "the sufficient" and the category of "too much" are equally alien to the spirit of capitalism' (1989: 113). Defoe's fiction is an illustration of this point. Thompson observes that 'the chief desire throughout Defoe's writing is to accumulate money' but because money is regarded as unstable, 'subject to debasement, wear and theft, no amount can ever be enough' (1996: 96). This then creates problems of closure; how to conclude a novel whose motivating force is accumulation since no amount is ever going to be sufficient (ibid., see also Watt 1957: 118). The theme of accumulating money, in other words, also registers itself as a difficulty concerning artistic form.

It may be no accident that during the course of the eighteenth century the sublime, that sensation of terrified delight at being confronted by any object that 'is too big for [our] capacity', such as 'a vast uncultivated Desart ... or a wide Expanse of Water' (Addison 1712 in Steele and Addison 1988: 371), should become the dominant aesthetic. The impossibility of viewing society as a complex unity discovers an alibi in an aesthetic which valorises whatever is limitless and unbounded. In the nineteenth century, the concept of class functions both as a way of understanding the organisation of society and as a means of transcending it. It can thus be seen be as an idea that combines two contradictory elements: the principle of form – society as composed of classes – and the principle of the transcendence of form – the move beyond the present class-divided society to a 'classless' one. In short, the concept of class is both an answer to the eighteenth century problem of how society can be imagined as a whole and an endorsement of the sublime which exceeds any such whole.

REASON, THE PLAIN STYLE AND CLASS

The bourgeois economy is a determinate factor in the character of reason, traditionally regarded as one of the, if not *the*, most distinctive feature of the age. The philosopher Immanuel Kant promotes reason as 'man's release from his self-incurred tutelage' (1784 & 1995: 1). It represents freedom from the constraints of the old order and, to that extent, it is a quality associated more with the bourgeoisie than with the nobility. The movement of money also dissolved traditional ties to the extent that it could 'transform the master into a servant and the servant into the master' (Thompson 1996: 37). Thus reliance on one's own reason endorsed economic individualism. But the relations between reason and the economy go deeper than this.

Slavoj Žižek claims that it is the abstract nature of exchange, its discounting of morality, social relations and responsibilities that not only created the conditions for the development of abstract thought, but also determined its nature (1994: 17). The category of reason, like exchange, is a formal one; that is, it does not recognise the differences between individuals. Such thinking is also found in views of poetry in the period. 'The business of the poet' remarks Johnson's Imlac, 'is to examine, not the individual, but the species, to remark general properties ... not number the streaks of the tulip' (*Rasselas*, 1759 & 1996: 875). Paul Hazard refers to the eighteenth-century belief in 'the world wide uniformity of the reasoning faculty' (1965: 40), while Marx notes that 'the individuals, the subjects between whom this process [of exchange] goes on, are simply and only conceived of as exchangers' (1867 & 1973: 240). In the eighteenth century, reason and money ideally functioned as universal equivalents of exchange. Reason was the means by which ideas were compared and valued, as money was the means by which commodities were compared and valued. Money, argues Thompson, was 'the universal equivalent' whose value 'should be fixed, the unmoving centre around which all commodities and their relative values revolve' (1996: 73). Hazard makes a similar point about reason when he writes that 'it applies a common measure' against which all ideas and opinions can be judged (1965: 38). The close connection between reason and money is evident from the etymology of the term 'rational' which is derived from the Latin *ratio*, a reckoning.

In addition to its complicity with exchange, reason generated ideas of humanity that better served the ends of production, again underlining its association with the bourgeoisie. For example, John Locke's description of how the mind operates on sense data is analogous to the process of converting raw material into the finished product (1690 & 1995: 186) while Adam Ferguson's description of a workshop, 'the parts of which are men' (cited in Sambrook 1993: 106) identifies human capacity almost completely with the operations of production. Given the mutual interpenetration of reason and exchange, it is not hard to make a case for the eighteenth-century coffee house, scene of the free exchange of knowledge, as a reflection of the increasingly *laissez-faire* nature of the market, scene of the free exchange of commodities. The co-extension of reason and exchange compromises the former's status as an instrument of liberation. Reason is the mode of thought of an emergent capitalism and, as such, involves a certain acquiescence in the new order of things. Kant, who said that the motto of the Enlightenment was *sapere aude*, dare to know, also said that it was wrong to criticise the mechanisms by which government achieved 'public ends' (1784 & 1995: 3). In this he would have agreed with Pope, who wrote in 'An Essay on Man' that 'to reason right is to submit' (1734 & 1978: 245).

The language of the market, like the language of reason, favoured the plain style in contrast to the figurative language characteristic of aristocratic writing, particularly romance (Nicholson 1996: 17). As we noted in the previous chapter, the plain style was an attempt to make language as much like mathematics as possible. It was hoped that a language based on 'Number, Weight [and] Measure' would create a unified society in place of one divided by 'Opinions, Appetites and Passions' (Petty cited in Poovey 1994: 25). In suppressing these qualities the plain style may appear to contradict the bourgeois ideology of individualism but in fact it reinforces it because this 'individualism' refers only to the 'subject of exchange' and not a unique person. It is not, therefore, the plain style which suppresses 'individualism' but the bourgeois ideology of individualism itself, since it insists on defining people in terms of abstract economic categories and not concrete social and personal characteristics.

The preference for the plain style continued into the eighteenth century. Pope, in 'An Essay on Criticism', draws a familiar contrast.

> False Eloquence, like the Prismatic glass
> Its gaudy colours spreads on every place;
> The face of nature we no more survey,
> All glares alike without distinction gay:
> But true Expression, like th' unchanging Sun,
> Clears, and improves whate'er it shines upon,
> It gilds all objects, but it alters none.
>
> (1711 & 1978: 73)

Henry Fielding in *Joseph Andrews* exploits, for comic effect, the contrast between plain and figurative styles of writing.

> Now the rake Hesperus had called for his breeches, and, having well rubbed his drowsy eyes, prepared to dress himself for all night; by whose example his brother rakes on earth likewise leave those beds in which they had slept away the day. Now Thetis, the good housewife, began to put on the pot, in order to regale the good man Phoebus after his daily labours were over. In vulgar language, it was in the evening ...
>
> (1741 & 1960: 18)

In the first example, the plain style is identified with truth, the figurative style with error, while in the second example it is identified with economy and the figurative style with extravagance.

The period saw many attempts to consolidate the plain style, for example Johnson's *Dictionary* (1755) and *Rudiments of Grammar* (1761) by Joseph Priestley (1733–1804), the radical dissenter and discoverer of oxygen. These and other writers stressed the comparisons between law and language with the aim of showing that, just as the constitution had the power to unify those with different interests, so too, if it was properly standardised and reduced to rules, could language. In practice, this meant the 'subjugation of provincial English, and the modes of expression of different social classes, to the norms of the elite' (Barrell 1983: 112). Hence 'plebeian poets', to use Gustav Klaus' term (1985), were made to feel conscious of their shortcomings in respect of the canons of taste. One such poet, John Lucas, wrote:

> For me, I cannot boast the rules
> Which learned masters teach in schools;
> The useful rules of grammar clear,
> Alas! They never reach'd my ear,
> Yielding instruction how to write,
> Correctly, elegant, polite.
>   (cited in Klaus 1985: 27)

Two other plebeian poets, Stephen Duck (1705–56) and Anne Yearsley (1752–1806), had their work heavily edited to conform to established literary forms, namely ancient writers and the modes of expression suitable to a learned person. In addition, their respective patrons packaged them in such a way as to render them acceptable to polite readers. Their experience illustrates Klaus' remark that 'the pressure towards aesthetic integration was too strong for the poetic and intellectual capacity of the plebeian poets to be able to escape its effects' (1985: 19). To be heard, they had to adopt the conventions used by a Pope or a Johnson, but these conventions negated the very experiences they were trying to describe. The heroic couplet was not a suitable vehicle to express hunger pangs or the exhausting effects of labour.

The pressure on 'working-class' writers to use 'middle-class' forms not only defuses criticism of the existing order, it also inhibits imagining alternative ones. Yearsley advised 'unlettered poets' to ignore rules and regulations and to give free vent to inspiration which was greatest in 'untaught Minds' (cited in Klaus 1985: 19–20). But even this attempt at rebellion is neutralised by being couched in the language of the fashionable primitivism of the mid-eighteenth century. William Duff, for example, in his *Essay on Original Genius* (1767), declared that 'natural man' wrote better poetry because he was not tainted by the sophistications of civilisation (cited in Sambrook 1993: 146). There was, it seemed, no way out for plebeian writers except, perhaps, suicide; Duck drowned himself.

The treatment of Duck, Yearsley and others was consistent with wider suppression of plebeian culture during the latter part of the century. The ban on football and horse racing at Haworth in the 1760s, the suppression of the Midsummer fair at Pebmarch in 1778, and even the ban on the ceremony of the Dunmow Flitch – a competition to find the most happily married couple in the village – were driven by a desire to instil in the poor a proper respect for work. As one contemporary wrote, 'to promote and even advertise such ridiculous diversions as horse, foot or ass races … I consider as unlawful – How often do we see the whole inhabitants of a country village drawn from their harvest work to see cudgel playing, or a cricket match?' (cited in Porter 1990: 294). The outlawing of popular sports, church ales and fairs, traditional sports and festivities, amounted not just to a silencing of plebeian culture but a denial of any forms of subjectivity other than those modelled on the market. Servants, as Porter notes, 'might even lose their own names, being dubbed (like pets) "Betty" or "John Thomas"' (ibid.: 87). In this connection it is interesting to note Bruce Robbins' provocative claim that the early novel 'avoided representing in any sustained way the common people, occupying itself with servants rather than with proletarians' (1993: 67).

THE 'INDIVIDUAL', THE 'SUBJECT' AND MONEY

The identity of the 'middling sort' was inseparable from considerations of land and money. McKeon states that, traditionally, 'individualism' was based on the private ownership of land (1988: 145). Increasingly, in the eighteenth century, it comes to be based on money. As we have seen, 'individual' means different things in different periods, but in both feudalism and capitalism it is intimately related to class. This is not just a matter of the ownership of the means of production but of how the very idea of the 'individual' is shaped by the dominant forms of economic organisation. The term 'subject' better captures this sense of the 'self' being conditioned by outside forces than the term 'individual' which implies self-determination.

During the eighteenth century we see how much the idea of the self is conditioned by the structure of the exchange economy. Richard Steele observed that 'the greatest of all distinctions in civil life is that of a debtor and a creditor' (1711 in Steele and Addison 1988: 449) while Thompson claims that 'models of subjectivity' were embedded within descriptions of money, since money stipulates the existence of an 'exchanging subject' (1996: 44). A key feature of money in the period was that its value fluctuated: 'expanding and shrinking values of currency actively undermined once stable values associated with blood ties ... and a propertied stake in the country' (Nicholson 1996: 14). There was also the question of the relation between value and paper money. Prior to the introduction of notes, the value of a coin, it will be remembered, was equivalent to the amount of gold or silver it contained. The value of money was intrinsic. With the introduction of credit and promissory notes, however, its value became nominal. Unlike coins, paper did not contain precious metal, it only represented it. Money passed from being value itself to the representation of value. The economy, which was formerly the basis of fact, was now coming to be identified with fiction; its dominant force, wrote Defoe, was 'the Power of the Imagination' which gave birth to 'exotick Projects' (cited in McKeon 1988: 287). Since ideas of the 'self' were linked to money, any changes in the latter were reflected in the former. If the economy was a fiction, so too was the 'self'. This also had repercussions for the plain style which, because of its association with money, could now no longer be regarded as both the expression and guarantee of truth.

We have seen, in previous chapters, how the 'self' is rendered insubstantial by exchange. At first this takes the form of a split between mind and body and then is taken a step further in the eighteenth century by credit and financial speculation, both of which delay even the appearance of the subject. The operation of credit means that a subject defers fulfilment of that which *makes* him or her a subject in an increasingly contractual society, namely his or her word regarding future payment, while financial speculation means that the subject's identity is tied to the future value of stocks, shares and investments. The notion of the 'self-determining individual' is further undermined by the forms and operations of the economy itself. Adam Smith's idea of the invisible hand guiding the market undermines ideas of human agency, while Bernard Mandeville's diagnosis of human motivation, in 'The Fable of the Bees' (1714), reduces economic activity to the prompting of appetite. This emptying out of purpose and morality from the 'individual' is also reflected in contemporary descriptions of money as effecting 'its magic apart from any human hand or scene, a system of exchange happily working away out of the sight of human agency' (Thompson 1996: 82). One result of this is that the 'individual' is so completely 'subject' to the market that there is no position outside it that would allow a comprehensive view of its operations. This is in contrast to an identity based on land, where the gaze of ownership was analogous, Barrell suggests, to a complete view of the social whole (1983: 41). The loss of the transcendent position can be seen in the shift from poetry to the novel. Much of the poetry of the period assumes a speaker whose gaze is all-encompassing. Johnson begins 'The Vanity of Human Wishes' with the lines 'Let Observation with extensive view / Survey mankind from China to Peru' (1749 & 1996: 843) but, as the century progresses, this stance is progressively weakened.

THE NOVEL AND CLASS

The relatively open-ended nature of the novel makes it the most suitable form for a society that can no longer be comprehended in its entirety. Fredric Jameson (1988) suggests that the appearance of the novel is a function of the separation of the social and economic spheres, the move from the moral to the market economy. From that point onwards, he claims, political economy is the discourse that tells the general truth about 'society', while the novel is limited to individual, personal truths. They each complement one another as systems of exchange: whether it is vows or commodities, both are meant to be free. Thompson also sees the novel as the ally of the new political economy. In general terms, it reconfigures in the domestic realm those social relations that were being eroded by the increasing competitiveness of civil society. More specifically, both are concerned with the location of value; political economy asks whether it is in paper or coin, while the novel asks whether it is in appearance or character. The novel asserts the reality of intrinsic value – 'the heroine is loved for herself, not for extrinsic qualities such as family name and social status' – at the very moment that political economists were forced to acknowledge, *contra* Locke, that 'silver was not always silver' (Thompson 1996: 20, 22). The novel thus provides a fixed idea of value that acts as a basis for the fluctuations of exchange value. Eventually, this becomes the function of English itself which, in the words of Brian Doyle, promotes the idea of literary value 'not so much because it helps to sustain an inherent value for literature itself, but because in so doing it provides a self-sustaining transcendental ground for all use and exchange value' (1989: 14).

Nancy Armstrong (1987) argues that the novel is also important in the construction of class identity for it offered the nascent, dispersed middle class a unified image with which they could identify; on this basis the novel does not so much reflect the middle class as constitute it. There was a didactic element in this, for, as Clive Probyn notes, '[o]ne strand of the eighteenth century's novel's genesis can be traced to the Puritan conduct books of the seventeenth century' (1994: 11). In this sense, the novel can be regarded as a form of instruction. Samuel Richardson states in *Pamela* that the novel should not only teach 'religion, morality [and] the parental, the filial and the social duties' but also 'paint VICE in its proper colours ... set VIRTUE in its own amiable light [and] give practical examples, worthy to be followed' (1740 & 1962: 164). Fielding shows, in *Joseph Andrews*, that giving examples is not quite as straightforward as it may seem, principally because they are caught up in economic considerations which over-ride moral ones. Parson Adams is horrified when the bookseller refuses to take his sermons because 'they [w]on't sell' as well as a play (1741 & 1960: 54). 'But is there no difference' protests Adams, 'between conveying good or ill instructions to mankind?' to which the bookseller replies: 'the copy that sells best will always be the best copy' (ibid.). Moral issues are identified with and vindicated by economic success or failure. Quality is transformed into quantity.

The example that *Joseph Andrews* recommends its readers to emulate is chastity, but this too is inseparable from economics. Chastity is related to 'the gradual discrediting of the aristocratic honour, the resolution of its tacit unity into the problematic relation of rank and virtue, birth and worth' (McKeon 1988: 133). McKeon argues that the anxiety regarding honour is displaced on to the concern with female integrity, which must be respected if property, one of the meanings of honour, is to remain within the family. As a contemporary of Richardson wrote:

> in all societies there are families, inheritances, and distinctions of ranks and orders ... to keep these separate and distinct, to prevent them from falling into confusion ... the chastity and continence of women are absolutely and indispensably necessary.
>
> (cited in Stone 1977: 386)

In addition to being connected to land, chastity is also related to money. As an intrinsic virtue, chastity is the equivalent of the essentialist view of money characteristic of an economy based on property. Locke's central principle that 'an Ounce of Silver Coin'd or not Coin'd, is, and eternally will be, of equal value to any other Ounce of Silver' (cited in Thompson 1996: 58) assumes both conservation (nothing is ever lost) and continuity (the metal remains the same from moment to moment). And this, observes Thompson, is 'the most cherished principle of landed aristocracy – that the paternal estate is still bounded by the same hedgerows through the centuries' (ibid.: 60).

Chastity, then, through its association with property and a particular view of money, belongs to a society dominated by aristocratic assumptions. *Joseph Andrews* exemplifies this to the extent that the hero does not set out to acquire an identity but to preserve the one he has. This means that the theme of the novel, the importance of chastity, is at odds with its form, which implies development and change. This reflects another division in the novel which we mentioned earlier, namely that between plain and figurative language. The plain style, it will be remembered, is the expression of the exchange economy, which reduces subjectivity to a formal category, and it is also the language, in *Joseph Andrews*, in which improving examples are held up for imitation. The problem with the plain style is that it makes no appeal to the senses, with the result that the proffered example has little effect. As one of the characters comments, since 'the prospect of our good at a distance doth not so forcibly affect us, it might be of some service to mankind to be made thoroughly sensible' (Fielding 1741 & 1960: 198). But this would involve an appeal to the body which is ruled out by the novel's endorsement of chastity. The model of subjectivity which the novel offers is negated by the language in which it is presented. This fissure between substance and style is related to the gap between value and its representation in the economy, which itself stems from that split in the commodity between its body form and value form that we discussed earlier.

We have said that the plain style is the expression of the new economy and that is true to the extent that it is an exchange economy. But it is also the case that the plain style represents the aristocratic principle that expression should be equal to what is expressed. This is clearly not suited to an economy based on credit and paper money where there is an anxiety about value and its representation. This anxiety is registered in the numerous aesthetic tracts of the period where the emphasis is on the propriety, fitness or adequacy between the object and its means of representation. The sublime, by contrast, provides an aesthetic justification for the gap between value and its representation and thus is a means of coming to terms with this particular aspect of capitalism's development. Its idiom is the figurative language, formerly associated with aristocratic romance, but which now forms the basis of experiencing the characteristically open-ended nature of the bourgeois economy. The fact that the plain style is implicated in an aristocratic principle, while the figurative style of aristocratic writing serves as a means of apprehending the problems of a credit economy, shows that it is impossible to identify classes in terms of an exclusive idiom or outlook. This recalls what was said at the beginning of this chapter, that eighteenth-century society is a complex formation not least because the aristocratic class were as busy imitating the middle class as that class were busy imitating them.

CONCLUSION

The further extension of exchange in the eighteenth century represents the triumph of bourgeois thought. However, the idea that all subjects are rendered equal by exchange conceals real class divisions which are further obscured by the assumption that the market is merely the collection of individuals pursuing their own interests independently of one another. This leaves a dual legacy to the nineteenth century. First, what consequences follow as the evidence of economic inequality grows, and, second, how does the persistence of the category of the 'individual' affect the experience and the understanding of class?

5

THE NINETEENTH CENTURY

The chapter offers a wide survey of the problem of class in the nineteenth century. Its main focus is the nature of the nineteenth-century proletariat, its culture and its relations with the manufacturing class, but it also considers some of the issues which we have been looking at throughout this book, such as the problem of the 'individual' and class.

CLASS AND HIERARCHY

What distinguishes the early nineteenth century from previous periods is the prominence of the term 'class' in descriptions of society. Prior to this time, society had been described in terms of ranks, orders and degrees while the term 'class', was generally reserved for a number of people banded together for educational purposes or for subdivisions in schemes for classification (Briggs 1967 & 1983: 154). The development of the term 'class' was a consequence of the attempt to understand some of the major upheavals of the period 1780–1848. These included the radical ideas of the French Revolution, the rise in population, the intensification of the enclosure movement, the development of the factory system and the growth of towns. The effect of such changes was to undermine the idea of society as a harmonious hierarchy and to suggest, instead, that it was riven by conflict and division for which the term 'class' seemed more appropriate. Tom Paine, for example, saw society as polarised between a corrupt establishment and an oppressed minority. 'There are', he fulminated, 'two *classes* of men in the nation, those who pay taxes and those who receive and live upon taxes' (cited in Thompson 1963 & 1988: 97).

Geoffrey Crossick detects a clear change of emphasis from the eighteenth century, where class served as a synonym for rank, to the nineteenth century where class was 'determined by the relative position of groups within the productive system' (1991: 153). This made class more functional than hierarchical, and inter-class relations more antagonistic than cooperative (Himmelfarb 1984: 162). 'England', wrote William Cobbett, was 'daily advancing to the state in which there are but two classes of men, masters and abject dependants' (1830 & 1985: 106), or, as Marx termed them in *Manifesto of the Communist Party* (Marx and Engels 1848 & 1968), the bourgeoisie and the proletariat. Engels had used the term 'proletariat' in *The Condition of the Working Class in England* (1845, 1892 & 1958) to describe a new kind of poverty that had arisen as a result of the Industrial Revolution. The poverty of the proletariat was different from the poverty of the pre-industrial poor: this was 'a total unrelieved poverty that extended to every realm of life – cultural, moral, and intellectual as much as material – a poverty that created a class so different as to constitute a different "race" ' (Himmelfarb 1984: 285). But this very poverty, argued Engels, created a class whose size, unity and consciousness of itself meant that it would fight against the source of its oppression. In short, the term 'proletariat' designated a new kind of poverty which created a class determined to rebel against the economic system which had produced it.

The industrial labourer endured working conditions very different from his or her agricultural counterpart. Carlyle described the early part of the nineteenth century as 'the Mechanical Age' where 'nothing is done directly or by hand; all is by rule and calculated contrivance' (1829 & 1981: 47). It is not just that the 'living artisan is driven from his workshop to make room for a speedier, inanimate one' but also that 'men themselves are grown mechanical in head and in heart, [so that] their whole efforts, attachments, opinions, turn on mechanism and are of a mechanical character' (ibid.: 50). The language of class was both a reflection of and a contribution to this condition. It was, says Gertrude Himmelfarb, 'more mechanistic, less organic, connoting not a system of interrelations and interdependence but of separation and independence' (1984: 289). The change from agriculture to industry also saw priority given to economic issues over social and moral ones and this too was a major factor in the changed meaning and increased use of the term 'class' whose relations are 'based on interest and contract rather than tradition and status' (ibid.). The old feudal ideal of society, with its fine gradations, where each person had their allotted place and was related to every other by the duty appropriate to their rank, was replaced by a purely monetary connection. Robert Owen remarked that industrialism reduced the relations between employer and employee 'to the consideration of what immediate gain each could derive from the other' (1816 & 1972: 69). More forcefully, Carlyle declared that '[i]t is no longer the moral, religious, spiritual condition of the people that is our concern but their physical, practical, economical condition' (1829 & 1981: 54). The social relationships of feudalism had been stripped away leaving only 'Cash Payment as the sole nexus' between people; 'and there are so many things', Carlyle added, 'which cash will not buy' (ibid.: 50).

It should not be thought that a class-based view of society completely superseded the feudal view of it. As David Cannadine argues, 'it was hierarchy which remained for many people the natural, omnipresent and time-honoured and divinely sanctioned way of seeing British society and understanding their place within it' (1998: 85). William Otter's opinion, that the ideal social structure lay in the 'coherence and adaptation of its several parts, by which many ranks of men, rising in orderly gradation, and melting as it were into each other ... compose together one solid, well compacted and harmonious whole' (cited in ibid.: 62), can be regarded as representative. It is found, for example, in the view of Samuel Taylor Coleridge (1772–1834) that poetry was that 'species of composition' where 'the parts mutually support and explain each other; all in their proportion harmonizing with the ... whole' (1817 & 1986: 195). What was new about the traditional view of hierarchy in this period was that it was being vigorously defended against proponents of different visions of what society was, and how it should be. To the alarm of many, it seemed as if society was disintegrating into mutually exclusive groups. Hence Otter's concern that labourers in the manufacturing towns were 'an isolated class, without that due mixture of ranks and orders, which in all other cases tends by the infusion of benevolence, respect and intelligence, to temper and soften the whole mass' (cited in Cannadine 1998: 68). In addition, the food riots of 1810–13 and 1816–18, together with post-Waterloo 'monster' meetings and the Peterloo massacre of 1819, served to underline the social polarisation on which Cobbett and others had commented. It was believed that these various problems arose because the hierarchical principle was not being propagated strongly enough and so there was a determined effort to reassert its alleged cohesive properties. Thomas Estcourt argued that 'the imperceptible gradations of the different orders of society' meant that 'every person was at ease with the person immediately above or a little below him [or her]' while David Robinson extolled the intricate links of the social order which 'rendered the whole perfect in cohesion, strength and beauty' (cited in ibid.: 62).

These sentiments found expression in the Victorian interest in medieval society which seemed more ordered than the contemporary one. As Lord John Manners wrote in his poem, 'England's Trust' (1841):

> Each knew his place – king, peasant, peer or priest –
> The greatest owned connexion with the least;
> From rank to rank the generous feeling ran
> And linked society as man to man.
>
> (cited in Chandler 1971: 161)

This idealisation of the medieval world was present in a range of cultural phenomena from the Gothic architecture of Pugin to the attempt to stage a jousting tournament at Eglinton in 1839. The same tendency was observable in the literature of the period, for example in Sir Walter Scott's *Ivanhoe* (1819) or Tennyson's 'Idylls of the King' (1842). In all these instances, the medieval world was used 'as a weapon against the mechanism, calculation, selfishness and ugliness of the emerging industrial civilisation' (Gilmour 1993: 47).

The poetry of the Romantics had fulfilled a similar function. Writers such as William Blake (1757–1827), Percy Shelley (1792–1822) and William Wordsworth (1770–1850) used their art to uphold 'certain human values, capacities and energies which [they] felt industrial civilisation was threatening or even destroying' (Williams 1958 & 1975: 53). They emphasised the whole person against 'man as merely a specialized instrument of production', the importance of human relationships against competitive individualism and the 'eternal' truths of the imagination against the transience of political economy. Blake was especially outspoken against the new order, complaining that it changed 'the arts of life into the arts of death' and forced people into 'sorrowful drudgery to obtain a scanty piece of bread' (cited in Ackroyd 1996: 293). 'A Machine', he declared, 'is not a Man nor a Work of Art, it is destructive of Humanity and Art' (ibid.:

309). Wordsworth laments that 'Getting and spending we lay waste our powers / Little we see in Nature that is ours' (1803 & 1989: 120), while Shelley similarly observes that, though commerce may have 'enlarged the limits of the empire of man over the external world' it had 'proportionally circumscribed those of the internal world' (1821 & 1989: 213). The march of industrialism transformed Wordsworth's 'passions that build up our human soul ... with high objects, with enduring things / With life and nature' (1805 & 1989: 136) into Blake's 'mind-forg'd manacles' (1794 & 1975: 52) The same view about the distorting effects of industrial society resurfaced in the socialism at the end of the century. Tom Maguire, for example, was adamant about the need for socialism to cultivate 'the whole of man's desires and aspirations – physical, mental, social and moral' (cited in Waters 1990: 14).

Both the Romantics and the 'Medievalists' defined themselves, to a large extent, against the principles of *laissez-faire* capitalism. They were objecting not so much to the division of society into classes, since they accepted the principle of social differentiation, but to the reduction of all social life to, in Marx's phrase, 'egotistical calculation' (1848 & 1968: 38). Their antipathy to political economy precluded them from analysing it, they could see its general effect, the contraction of social life, but not its particular cause, the class-based nature of capitalism. The 'cash nexus' was to be repudiated, not incorporated into a comprehensive view of society. Accordingly, it was difficult for these thinkers to produce any general theory of the social order. Perry Anderson has argued that 'a deep, instinctive aversion to the very category of totality' is a characteristic feature of 'the British bourgeoisie' (1992: 57) as it is of postmodernism, famously defined by Lyotard as an 'incredulity towards metanarratives' (1984: xiii). This antipathy to totality is illustrated by Britain's failure, in the nineteenth century, to develop the discipline of sociology. Anderson argues that this failure was due to the manufacturing class of the nineteenth century, 'mindful of the French Revolution and fearful of the nascent working class' (1992: 56), adopting the ideology of the aristocracy as a means of ensuring social stability. It was able to do this because the agrarian economy had been capitalist since the seventeenth century. 'A common mode of production' united both classes, Anderson claims, and made 'their eventual fusion possible' (ibid.: 58). Since there was no real conflict between the bourgeoisie and the aristocracy, there was no need for the former to develop their own version of the social order. Similarly, argues Anderson, the insulation of the working class from continental Marxism meant that it revealed little intellectual stimulus to produce its own 'counter-totalising body of thought' (ibid.).

The absorption of at least a section of the bourgeoisie into the aristocracy shows that the development of class did not immediately threaten the principle of hierarchy. The Bishop of Norwich, in 1847, had no difficulty in using the two terms in the same sentence when he told the middle-class supporters of the Ipswich Museum that they were 'links in that great chain by which the higher classes of society and the lower are connected together' (*Suffolk Chronicle* 18 December 1847: 17). Nevertheless, by the time of the Bishop's remarks, the contours of class were being more sharply defined, making its continued accommodation with hierarchy increasingly less likely. This is evident in the Chartist Thomas Cooper's short story ' "Merrie England" – No More!' (1845). The very title announces the passing of the feudal era while the substance of the tale is an attack on the principle that providence allots people their place in society. As one of the characters says:

> I think all their talk about a Providence that disposes the lot of men, 'for His Own great mysterious purposes', as they phrase it, is mere mysterious humbug to keep us quiet. What purpose could a being have, who, they say, is as infinitely good as he is infinitely powerful, in placing me where I must undergo insult and starvation, while He places that man, – the oppressor and

> the grinder, who is riding past now, in his gig, – in plenty and
> abundance?
>
> (1845 & 1995: 54)

The characters are also aware that they form a class and must act
in their own interests for, as one of them declares, '[t]here is no
dependence on any of the middle class ... they are as bad as the
aristocrats' (ibid.: 56). This consciousness of themselves as a class
is based on their experience of economic exploitation where, in
Cooper's words, 'men compete with each other in machinery till
human hands are of little use, and rival each other in wicked zeal
to reduce man to the merest minimum of subsistence' (ibid.: 58).

COMPONENTS OF THE ENGLISH WORKING CLASS

The class consciousness of Cooper's characters is the result of radical traditions modified by the French Revolution and the experience of industrialism. E. P. Thompson, in his monumental study
The Making of the English Working Class (1963 & 1988), has
argued that the crucial period in its formation were the years
1790–1832. Thompson begins by noting that the character and
organisation of working people differed from one part of the
country to another. 'Radical London', for example, was 'more heterogeneous and fluid in its social and occupational definition than
the Midlands or Northern centres grouped around two or three
staple industries' (ibid.: 23). If the term 'working class' was used
at all in this early period – 'lower class' was the more usual appel-
lation – it was used in the plural; there was no sense of an homogeneous body united by a common purpose. The diversity of
working people was matched by a diverse radical tradition whose
main elements were a sense of the Norman yoke, dissent and
what Thompson calls 'tavern life' (ibid.: 63).

The Norman yoke was the powerful myth that, until the
arrival of William the Conqueror, the English, or more accurately

the Saxons, had a free Parliament based on manhood suffrage. The myth was used to argue for the recovery of ancient rights. The tradition of dissent was more complicated: its most important element was liberty of conscience but it also established the habit of self-government and local autonomy. This existed in some tension with Methodism, a major force in the tradition of dissent, since its founder, Charles Wesley, stressed the importance of centralised control over members and submission to authority. This, together with the requirement that the reformed sinner constantly monitor him- or herself, prepared the worker for the discipline of the factory with its strict rules and unremitting surveillance. Nevertheless, the central claim of Methodism, that everyone, not just the elect, was eligible for God's grace, promoted a more democratic ethos. The Duchess of Buckingham recognised this, complaining that Methodism was strongly 'tinctured with disrespect towards Superiors' and that '[i]t was monstrous to be told you have a heart as sinful as common wretches that crawl on earth' (cited in Whiteley 1938: 328).

The tradition of 'tavern life' affected the early working-class movement in a number of ways. Perhaps the most enduring was its mentality, described by Thompson as fatalistic, ironic and tenacious (1963 & 1988: 63). Some of these qualities are apparent in the dialect literature which flourished in the industrial north between 1860 and 1885. Fatalism, for example, is evident in dialect literature's assumption that the working class could do nothing about unemployment while its 'resilient, realistic comedy, that did not bow to snobbish literary or social assumptions' (Vicinus 1974: 187), echoes Thompson's view that 'tavern life' was ironic 'in the face of establishment homilies' (1963 & 1988: 63). The most immediate impact of 'tavern life' on the development of the working class was 'the phenomena of riot and the "mob", and the popular notions of an Englishman's birthright' (ibid.: 64). The latter is to be distinguished from the Norman yoke since it referred to the Settlement of 1688 which, embodied in the constitution of King, Lords and Commons, was believed to guarantee liberty and independence and equality before the law. Thompson makes the point that this aspect of 'tavern life' was 'not so much democratic as anti-absolutist' (ibid.: 87). The common Englishman, Thompson continues, 'felt himself to be an individualist, with few affirmative rights, but protected by the laws against the intrusion of arbitrary power' (ibid.). This emphasis on the individual ultimately militated against the development of *class* consciousness, encouraging instead the pursuit of respectability among the artisan section of the working class.

The 'mob' was basically a feature of the eighteenth century and, most commonly, riots were caused by bread shortages. These uprisings were legitimised by the assumption of the moral economy which stated that it was wrong to profit from the needs of the people. Hence they were not destructive, but an attempt to enforce standards of fairness, as in 1783 in Halifax when a crowd, led by Thomas Spencer, forced corn merchants to sell the grain that they had been hoarding at its regular, not their inflated price. The authorities also used crowds for their own ends. One example is the riots of 1780, led by Lord George Gordon against a bill for Catholic toleration. Charles Dickens (1812–70) describes these disturbances in *Barnaby Rudge*. The novel was published in 1841 when the language of class was already partly established as a means of conceptualising the social order and when Chartist agitation for universal male suffrage was well under way. Dickens confronts and contains the Victorian fear of working-class insurrection by depicting the rioters as filling the air 'with execrations, hoots and howlings. The mob', he continues, 'raged and roared, like the mad monster that it was, unceasingly, and each new outrage served to swell its fury' (1841 & 1964: 299). But he also contains these same fears to the extent that the events he describes are set at a safe distance in the past. After the excesses of crowd behaviour in the French Revolution, politicians were wary of trying to manipulate the 'mob', while reformers, for their part, 'worked to create an organised public opinion (Thompson 1963 & 1988: 78).

The French Revolution affected the development of the working class in two ways. First, it altered the language of political protest and, second, it made the authorities more repressive, thereby helping to create a sense of solidarity between disparate groups of workers. The rhetoric of the Englishman's 'birthright' and the Norman yoke endorsed the institutions of monarchy, Church and aristocracy, and upheld property rights not human ones. 'For a plebeian movement to arise', writes Thompson, 'it was essential to escape from these categories altogether and set forward far wider democratic claims' (1963 & 1988: 96).

Tom Paine was an important figure here and his *The Rights of Man* 'is a foundation-text of the English working-class movement' (Thompson 1963 & 1988: 99). He replaced a reverence for custom with a respect for reason and promoted a radical egalitarianism in place of hereditary distinctions. This equality, however, was based on an acceptance of free market capitalism where, as we saw in the last chapter, everyone was rendered equivalent by the principle of exchange. While Paine wanted every *man* to have equal rights as a citizen, he did not extend the same consideration to the economic sphere where differences of wealth were accepted as the result of enterprise or lack of it. Paine's considerable influence on the development of the British working class meant that the focus of its agitation was political rather than economic. Resigned to the economic system of capitalism, the working class sought to reform its political institutions. This separation of politics from economics meant that, like the middle class, the working class had no comprehensive vision of society.

The Rights of Man altered the language of political protest. It was no longer conducted in terms of the constitutional settlement of 1688 but in an entirely new idiom based on reason, equality and the principle of full representation. 'Considerable numbers', wrote one contemporary of disturbances in Durham in 1792, 'have manifested disaffection with the constitution, and the words "No King", "Liberty", and "Equality" have been written upon the Market Cross' (cited in Thompson 1963 & 1988: 112). Similar disturbances occurred all over the country and what was unusual about them was that, for the first time, working men were claiming general rights for themselves, a development 'which threw the propertied classes into panic' (ibid.: 114).

Their response was a policy of repression with the government using spies to infiltrate organisations such as the London Corresponding Society (1792–7) and troops to suppress demonstrations. The Combination Acts (1799–1800) prevented the growth of trade unions as well as working-class reading groups and debating clubs, while the Six Acts (1819) made it illegal for any periodical costing less than sixpence to appear more than once every twenty-six days, or for it to comment 'upon any Matter in Church or State' (cited in Murphy 1994: 46). Known collectively as the Seditious Publications Act, these measures effectively stifled working-class expression until 1836, by which time the combination of cheap paper and mechanical printing 'made a mockery of further prosecutions of publishers and sellers of unstamped periodicals' (James 1974: 19).

The result of this repression was to radicalise some sections of the working class, who now believed that revolution rather than reform was the way forward (Thompson 1963 & 1988: 146). Others, however, believed that it was only by an alliance with the middle class that working men could win the vote. The choice was between moral or physical force and the same dilemma was to run like a fault-line through the Chartist movement with the moderates of the London Working Men's Association on the one side and the East London Democratic Association on the other. This split was not just over tactics, it also reflected a growing social divide between a skilled artisan class and an unskilled 'mass'. This conventional characterisation, however, has recently been called into question (Walton 1999: 59), partly because 'moral' force always needed the threat of physical force to give it credibility, and partly because it diminishes the contribution of the Jacobins, or radicals, to the working-class movement.

Jacobinism left a legacy which stressed the importance of self-education, the rational criticism of institutions, republicanism and internationalism. Its chief characteristic, however, the emphasis on equality, was discredited by the excesses of the French Revolution. The massacres in Paris were also responsible for destroying 'the "natural" alliance between an impatient, radically-minded industrial bourgeoisie and a formative proletariat' (Thompson 1963 & 1988: 195). Frightened by the spectacle of violent anarchy across the Channel, the bourgeoisie united with the landowners to crush the cause of reform at home. In return, the manufacturers received important concessions in the form of repeal of paternalist legislation covering apprenticeship, wage regulations and the conditions of industry. Although the middle class and the working class were to make overtures towards each other during the course of the nineteenth century, the former when they wanted support for the repeal of the Corn Laws and the latter when they were trying to win support for the Charter, the new pattern was to be the middle class trying to mould the working class in its own image.

The factory owners, in particular, were keen to impose a new code of conduct on their employees, and this further widened the gap between the classes that the French Revolution had, if not opened, certainly highlighted. In their drive for greater economic efficiency, the manufacturers 'extended working hours, outlawed the traditional workshop pranks and diversions of the old craft culture and curtailed the number of local holidays' (Bailey 1978 & 1987: 30). Furthermore, workers were set production targets, subject to intensive surveillance and suffered a punitive system of fines, all for a wage that barely enabled them to survive (Thompson 1963 & 1988: 222–32). The aim, succinctly expressed by Richard Arkwright, inventor of the spinning jenny, was to train people 'to renounce their desultory habits of work and identify themselves with the unvarying regularity of the complex automaton' (cited in Inglis 1972: 107). This represented a new and more severe form of exploitation. As Thompson notes, '[t]he issues which provoked the most intensity were very often ones in which such values as traditional customs, "justice", "independence", security or family economy were at stake, rather than straightforward bread and butter issues' (1963 & 1988: 222).

THE ECONOMIC RELATIONS OF CLASS AND CLASS CONSCIOUSNESS

Marx, however, concentrated on precisely these 'bread and butter issues'. What interested him was the new economic relation between masters and men whose key feature was the production of surplus value which, Marx claimed, was the essence of capitalism (1867 & 1995: 163). Marx's highly technical argument rests on a distinction between 'the value of labour power and the value which that labour power creates in the labour process' (ibid.: 127). The value of labour power is 'the value of the means of subsistence necessary for the maintenance of the labourer' (ibid.: 111) while the value that the labour power creates in the form of the use value of the commodity 'is a source of more value than it has itself' (ibid.: 127). In other words, the capitalist sells his or her commodities at a price greater than it costs to produce them. If the cost of the labour power of the worker was £4 a day and the worker could embody £4 of value in the product after four hours then, if he or she worked eight hours, the last four hours would yield a surplus value of £4 – 100 per cent profit.

An embryonic version of this argument exists in *Manifesto of the Communist Party* (1848) where Marx claims that the essential condition for the existence of the bourgeois class is capital, and the condition for the existence of capital is wage labour (Marx and Engels 1848 & 1968: 45). The average price of wage labour,

Marx continues, is the minimum wage, that is, what is necessary 'to keep the labourer in bare existence as a labourer' (ibid.: 47). The poverty of the labourer, his reduction to being 'an appendage of the machine', the tendency of the machine to 'obliterate all distinctions of labour', and the labourer being crowded into a factory with other labourers where they are all 'daily and hourly enslaved by the machine, by the overlooker, but above all by the individual manufacturer himself' leads him to form combinations, or trade unions, first against the individual bourgeois, then against the class as a whole (ibid.: 41–3).

Class, in this context, is understood as the consciousness of a common experience of exploitation which unites those who experience it against those who perpetrate and perpetuate it. The class consciousness of the workers, or the proletariat, is different from that of the bourgeoisie. Put simply, the proletariat is distinguished from the bourgeoisie by its capacity to grasp society as a whole, to understand, that is, the connection between economic and social relations, thereby enabling it to realise its historic mission of overthrowing the bourgeoisie and establishing the classless society. The bourgeoisie, by contrast, in an effort to justify the existing order, conceives of society as a relation between individuals but, as Marx has pointed out, the relation between individuals is never a relation between one individual and another 'but between worker and capitalist, tenant and landlord, etc.' (cited in Lukács 1968 & 1990: 50). Consequently, the bourgeoisie never sees society as a whole but confronts it as a blind force beyond its control (ibid.: 50, 63). A good example of this is its conception of the free market with its laws of supply and demand.

The problem of class consciousness is an issue which has generated a great deal of debate (see Gorz 1982; Lukács 1968 & 1990; Lebowitz 1992). The apparently straightforward distinction between bourgeois and proletarian consciousness is complicated by the fact that the very forms of capitalism inhibit the development of a view of society as a whole. The division of labour, for example, 'leads to the destruction of every image of the whole' because it permits only a partial view of the labour process and, by extension, of society as a whole (Lukács 1968 & 1990: 103). Since the nature of capitalism is to fragment understanding, it is difficult to see how class consciousness, defined by Lukács as a class's consciousness of its relation to the whole (ibid.: 50), can ever arise. The distinction between bourgeois and proletarian consciousness is further complicated by Marx's claim that the proletariat is led by a section of the bourgeoisie who have 'raised themselves to the level of comprehending theoretically the historical movement as a whole' (Marx and Engels 1848 & 1968: 44) which suggests that it is they and not the proletariat who are the driving force of history. There is a further ambiguity in Marx concerning whether the proletariat is responsible for bringing about revolution or whether it is the inevitable outcome of the capitalist system of production. If the former, then we still have to explain how consciousness can arise in order for revolution to occur; if the latter, then 'history has a meaning independent of the consciousness of individuals and realises *itself*, whatever they may think, in their actions' (Gorz 1982: 18).

Perhaps the most problematic aspect of class consciousness concerns the relation between economic experience and social expression. To use Marx's terms, does the economic base wholly determine the superstructure, or does the superstructure have its own autonomy which then reflects back on the base? These questions correspond to the different positions taken by Thompson and Hobsbawm in relation to the problem of class in the nineteenth century. Thompson claims that a distinct working-class consciousness was established by 1832 while Hobsbawm argues that this was not the case until the latter decades of the century, when Britain had a mature industrial economy which alone could give rise to a true working-class consciousness (Hobsbawm 1964: 194–213). The disagreement between Thompson and Hobsbawm is more a matter of emphasis than a fundamental division. Thompson stresses how the working class makes itself whereas Hobsbawm stresses how it is made. Thompson stresses the role of culture in the working class coming to consciousness of itself; Hobsbawm stresses the role of economics. Neither category can be truly separated from the other but pinpointing their exact relation is an almost impossible task.

CHARTISM

One of the major working-class movements of the nineteenth century was Chartism. This had its roots in the dreadful conditions generated by the new factory system. The working class believed that these evils could be remedied if the working class were represented in Parliament. Consequently, they joined forces with the middle class, who were agitating for the extension of the franchise. However, the Reform Bill of 1832 did not give the working class the vote. Angry and frustrated, they withdrew their support from the middle class, whose true attitude to their former allies manifested itself in the passing of the punitive Poor Law Amendment Bill of 1834 and, in the same year, the transportation of a group of labourers from Dorset, known as the Tolpuddle martyrs, for trying to organise a trade union. It seemed that, if the working class were to be represented in Parliament, it would have to be by their own efforts. The Six Points of the Charter: universal manhood suffrage; annual elections; the payment of MPs; the abolition of the property qualification for MPs; the introduction of secret ballots; and the creation of equal electoral districts, were essentially political. The Chartists' aim was to reform Parliament, not to abolish the capitalist relations of production. Unlike the proletariat of Marx and Engels, the Chartists did not wish to overthrow the establishment, but to become an integral part of it. Their lack of revolutionary intent was evident in the fact that the demands of the Charter contained neither a challenge to the Crown nor any reference to abolishing the House of Lords. There was also no attempt to bring women within the pale of the constitution, though this issue was, at times, a source of animated discussion (Walton 1999: 7).

The Chartist desire for working-class representation in Parliament was paralleled by their desire for representation in literature. Indeed, for Cooper, the development of a specifically working-class literature would be instrumental in forging a distinct working-class consciousness. He wrote:

> It now becomes a matter of the highest necessity that you all join hands and heads to create a literature of your own. Your own prose, your own poetry ... would put you all more fully in possession of each other's thoughts and thus give you a higher respect for each other, and a clearer perception of what you can do when united.
>
> (cited in Vicinus 1974: 1)

Cooper's statement reflects a change in the working-class attitude to literature. In the early part of the century working-class journalists viewed imaginative writing with disdain. Richard Carlile summed up the general attitude when he urged that 'lovers of truth' should go to 'war with the fiction of the poet, the novelist and the romance writer' (cited in Murphy 1994: 68).

Carlile was also contemptuous of traditional lower-class forms such as the ballad, the broadsheet and the chapbook, because they 'catered to a demand for sensation and scandal' (Vicinus 1974: 10). More importantly, they interfered with the pursuit of 'useful knowledge' which would lead to a 'transformation in [one's] consciousness and in [one's] relationship with the external world' (Vincent 1981: 135). As this was deemed to be the goal of every self-respecting artisan, it marks a division within the industrial working class between the skilled and the unskilled man. The former occupied himself with serious learning in the hope of improving his situation while the latter remained ignorant of the world because distracted by the 'lies' of fiction (Murphy 1994: 68). The artisans' negative views about fiction correspond to those of middle-class Utilitarians and Evangelicals (Altick 1957). However, the artisan differed from his middle-class counterpart in respect of the ultimate end of useful knowledge. Where he saw it as a means of self-advancement, the middle class view was that it would 'make men more skilful, expert and useful in their particular kinds of work' (Brougham cited in Vincent 1981: 142). The real uses of knowledge were thus to increase production and ratify social divisions.

From approximately the mid-1830s, fiction, in particular, was regarded in a more favourable light. The work of Dickens showed that fiction could focus on the problems of the present rather than, as in Sir Walter Scott, be captivated by the pageantry of the past. There was also a recognition that 'political and social truths could be conveyed through imaginative as well as factual literature' (Murphy 1994: 63). Finally, the 1830s saw the development of cheap reprints of novels and serial publication as well as an explosion of magazines publishing fiction (Altick 1957). Since fiction was becoming an established part of working-class life, the debate was no longer over the respective merits of factual or imaginative literature but over how the latter could be used to promote working-class interests.

Chartist novelists wanted to win working-class novelists away from the 'cheap and nasty' products of serial fiction, which they believed were 'designed to drug political consciousness' (Vicinus 1974: 108). For, although they recognised the value of writers like Dickens, they believed that the majority of fiction aimed at the working class was 'replete with MYSTERY, HORROR, LOVE AND SEDUCTION' (cited in James 1974: 34) and that its general effect was to 'encourage a love of aristocratic romance' (Vicinus 1974: 113). Furthermore, the working class were portrayed in these tales, as they were in a number of middle-class novels, as a source of either humour or disorder (Keating 1971: 1). Accordingly, Chartist novelists sought to present a more positive image of their class. 'The virtues of the masses', declared William Thompson, 'should be extolled', and, added Ernest Jones, 'the dignity of the democratic character should be elevated' (cited in Vicinus 1974: 97, 113). At the same time, Chartist novelists were concerned to show that social problems were the result of human actions and could be remedied, even if that meant bloodshed. As one character notes: 'We are neither robbing nor murdering; killing we may be, for while the bad cause is supported by blood, the good has no alternative' (Somerville 1839 & 1995: 130). The Chartist concern with change was in contrast to the middle-class novel whose major preoccupation was the 'growth and consciousness of the individual' (Hemstedt 1978: 8). For George Eliot, individual development was inseparable from 'a consideration of another's need and trial' (1872 & 1965: 720). In contrast to Chartist writers, she did not believe that the 'growing good of the world' depended on the drama of political action, but on the 'unhistoric acts' of daily life (ibid.: 896).

How far the Chartist novelists were successful in their aims is debatable. For every story that suggested change was possible there was another, like Thomas Cooper's 'Seth Thompson, the Stockinger' which seemed to counsel despair. 'I see no hope for you, my friends', says Seth, as he prepares to emigrate (1845 & 1995: 51). Novels only became a significant feature of the Chartist movement when its political programme had begun to falter. To some extent imaginative fiction began to replace political action. Ian Haywood (1995), however, argues that Chartist literary aspirations were inseparable from their social and political ambitions, hence novels such as Thomas Martin Wheeler's *Sunshine and Shadows* (1849–50) and Ernest Jones's *De Brassier: A Democratic Romance* (1851–2), both written after the failure of the third Chartist petition (1848), are better understood not as a retreat into the realm of fiction but as a continuation of the struggle to win acceptance for the Charter by other means.

The portrayal of working-class characters is also problematic. On the one hand, there is a desire to move away from the negative stereotyping evident in popular fiction and promote, as one anonymous writer puts it, working-class 'intellectual attainments, their moral capabilities and kind feelings [so as] to enable those high in fortune's scale to form a true and proper estimate of their real worth' (Anonymous 1840 & 1995: 42). On the other hand, the need to emphasise the political aspects of a situation *still* involved stereotyping, even if it was of a positive kind such as in the character of Will Harper, 'an honest, hard working man [who], though frugal and care-taking, had at all times a hand ready to relieve the necessities of those upon whom Fortune had frowned' (Anonymous 1838 & 1995: 26). Chartist fiction, in other words, could not break with the essentially abstract paradigm that characterised the representation of the working class found in middle-class novels. Nor, despite freeing themselves from such standard middle-class plot conventions as inheritance and marriage, could Chartist novelists entirely dispense with 'the techniques of popular fiction, particularly sensationalism and melodrama' (Haywood 1995: 4). Moreover, there was a conflict between many of these 'techniques' which suggested that people could not control events – the heroine as passive victim, the villain brought to justice by fortuitous events – and the message of Chartist fiction, which said they could (Vicinus 1974: 122). The close association with popular fiction also meant that the villain in many Chartist works was not the middle-class factory owner but the aristocrat as in 'The Charter and the Land' where 'the baronet' orders his 'powdered lackey' to drive a starving woman from his doorstep with the result that she dies shortly after (Jones 1848 & 1995: 196). The English working class then, complicates Marx's analysis of capitalism to the extent that they were ranged against the aristocracy as much as, if not more than, against the bourgeoisie.

Chartist poetry follows much the same trajectory as Chartist fiction, professing faith in the time 'When thinking millions rise in power and might, / And peacefully assert an equal right / To eat their daily bread' (Hutton 1839 & 1995: 188). W. J. Linton and Gerald Massey were two poets who sought to portray the working class in a favourable light and to encourage readers to believe that they could transform existing conditions. Earlier versifiers such as 'the Corn Law rhymer', Ebenezer Elliot (1781–1849), had encouraged Chartist poets to abandon early attempts to reiterate the Romantic idea of Nature and to concentrate on their own personal experience. In addition, Ernest Jones urged poets to 'use plain words' and to avoid 'inflation of expression' (cited in Vicinus 1974: 109). The use of the plain style is not without its problems for, as we saw in the last chapter, it is implicated in the exchange mechanism which is at the heart of capitalism. Similarly, the protests of Chartist poets against poverty and oppression were blunted by their use of traditional verse forms such as the sonnet and the epic. The literature of Chartism, in short, failed to establish new categories of representation to comprehend the experience of industrialism. This mirrored their political programme which was to be represented within the existing institutions of democracy rather than create new, more accountable ones.

There can be little doubt that the rejection of the third Chartist petition signalled the end of Chartism as a mass movement. This, together with economic improvement and a rise in living standards throughout the 1850s and 1860s, ensured that the artisans, or 'labour aristocracy', would devote themselves to self-improvement rather than political reform (Epstein and Thompson 1982). William Jones summed up this development when he wrote that:

social wrong and the morally degrading causes which have pressed so long and so heavily on working men, especially in manufacturing districts can only have permanent removal in proportion to the growth of the masses in Knowledge, Temperance and Self- Respect.

(1849: 12)

Or, as Rowan McWilliam so neatly puts it, 'where workers once read Tom Paine, they now read Samuel Smiles' (1998: 18). Chartist writing both shaped and reflected this change. The poetry ceased to be a call to action and became a means to ennoble and elevate the masses, while the fiction not only extolled the virtues of self-help but began to converge with the values found in Dickens and Mrs Gaskell: class analysis was eschewed in favour of emphasising the underlying similarity of all people, rich or poor (Keating 1971: 22).

THE 'HUMAN' AND CLASS: *NORTH AND SOUTH*

This is a tactic Mrs Gaskell (1810–65) uses in *North and South* (1855) to resolve the industrial dispute between the factory owner, John Thornton, and his workers. Her belief is that 'the individuals of the different classes' should be brought 'into actual personal contact' so that they can 'recognise that "we have all of us one human heart"' (1855 & 1993: 422, 435). The values of commerce and the values of humanity thus seem to be radically opposed to one another. Commerce is seen in terms of a 'battle' between the classes, whereas humanity stresses that the classes were 'dependent on each other in every way' (ibid.: 81, 133, 116). In fact this opposition is illusory and not just because a 'man to man' (ibid.: 42) relation ensures industrial harmony, but because the very idea of the 'human' is an abstraction which derives from the exchange relation. The human is an abstraction to the extent that it represses precisely those economic and social relations which constitute a person's being (Marx 1859 & 1968: 181). Mrs Gaskell can only bring her characters into 'human' contact if she disregards these relations between them.

We have already discussed, in previous chapters, the abstract nature of exchange which resides in the capacity of first commodities and then money to 'embod[y] abstract, undifferentiated and therefore equal human labour' (Marx 1867 & 1995: 55). Marx hints at a connection between exchange and reason when he links the development of money to the development of abstract thought (1846 & 1996: 142). He does not elaborate on the nature of this connection, but the relevant point for our purpose is the suggestion that the exchange relation is implicated in the very nature of thought itself. The abstraction of exchange, we may say, is the ground for the universality of the 'human'. If this is the case, then the 'human' cannot simply be opposed to the 'inhumanity' of capitalism. Instead we must see the 'human' as representative of the very condition it claims to transcend.

The 'human' also has an ideological function in *North and South*. This is inseparable from its source in the exchange relation. The main exchange relation of capitalism is the one between employer and employee. Abstract labour power, in the form of money, is exchanged for actual labour power, the worker's concrete capacity to produce commodities. However, this is an unequal exchange, since, as we saw earlier, its essence is the extraction of surplus value. Exchange, in short, reflects the dominance of the bourgeoisie. According to Marx, '[t]he ruling ideas of each age [are] the ideas of its ruling class' (Marx and Engels 1848 & 1968: 51). It is this that makes these ideas ideological, though it by no means exhausts the concept of ideology (Eagleton 1991). The ruling class disguises the ideological character of its ideas by claiming that they are based on 'human nature', which is eternal, rather than theories which are ephemeral. In Lukács's words, bourgeois thought 'abolishes the process of history and regard[s] the institutions of the present as eternal laws of nature'

(1968 & 1990: 180). The 'human' in *North and South* is a good illustration of these claims. We have already seen how 'the one human heart' effaces specific economic and social relations and we must now look briefly at how the 'human' is defined relative to the bourgeoisie.

The chief bourgeois characteristic against which the working class, and indeed the gentry, are judged to be 'human' or 'non human' in *North and South* is self-mastery. This is understood principally in the context of the market. If the working man, remarks Thornton, 'rules himself to decency and sobriety of conduct, and [pays] attention to his duties ... [he] may raise himself into the position and power of a master' (1855 & 1993: 81). Self-mastery is also a prominent feature of the romantic relation between Thornton and Margaret Hale, the heroine of the novel. Although Thornton is a manufacturer and Margaret is a 'gentlewoman' (ibid.: 59), they both believe that feelings should be restrained not indulged, concealed rather than revealed (ibid.: 124, 190, 213, 333). An economic 'virtue' becomes the regulatory principle of emotional life, highlighting Lukács' point that 'capitalism is the first system of production to achieve a total penetration of society' (1968 & 1990: 62). Lacking the virtue of self-discipline, the working class are judged in the novel to be 'ignorant' and 'improvident', 'sensual and self-indulgent' (Gaskell 1855 & 1993: 81–2). They are therefore in need of reform – hence Margaret's strictures to Higgins, the one working-class character in the novel, about his drinking (ibid.: 222). She is successful in her undertaking for not only does Higgins later show 'a sober judgement and a regulated method of thinking' in contrast to 'his former more eccentric jerks of action' but he also takes 'an interest in sacred things which he had previously scouted' (ibid.: 340, 348).

Margaret's mission to 'civilise' Higgins corresponds to middle-class attempts throughout the nineteenth century to control working-class leisure whose excesses – drunkenness, feasting and brawling – were 'offensive to [the middle-class] sense of station and social order' (Bailey 1978 & 1987: 34, 48). Reformers wanted to replace the diversions of popular leisure with rational recreation whose purpose was to educate the working class into the values of middle-class orthodoxy, thus ensuring social stability. The public library was to be promoted above the public house. This programme had some appeal to the 'labour aristocracy', partly because it was consonant with their own traditions of the importance of education and partly because it was a means of class advancement. The Chartist William Lovett recalled with distaste the crude amusements of his youth and urged the working class to 'study with recreation' and to 'share in rational amusements' (1876: 56) but his enthusiasm was not shared by the many who resented middle-class interference in their pastimes (Bailey 1978 & 1987: 63).

The leisure activities of the working class were seen to diminish their 'human' status because they stimulated the body rather than the mind. Bailey summarises the conventional view when he writes that:

> it was frankly incomprehensible, in an age of progress, that people should amuse themselves by eating scalding porridge with their fingers or by stripping the wicks from a pound of candles with their teeth, all for the sake of a wager and the applause of an audience of like-minded boobies.
>
> (1978 & 1987: 34)

The 'human' status of the working class was even less in evidence in the factory than outside it. Thornton refers to his workers as 'hands' (Gaskell 1855 & 1993: 117) reducing them not just to the body but to that part of it which is significant only in relation to production. Margaret unwittingly draws attention to the non-'human' status of the workers when she pleads with Thornton, during the strike, to speak to them 'as if they were human beings' (ibid.: 177 my emphasis). By going on strike, however, workers become 'animals' or 'wild beasts' (ibid.: 175–6), thus forfeiting what little human status they have. In sum, *North and South* implies that workers can only be regarded as 'human beings' so long as they dutifully fulfil their economic function and aspire to middle-class values.

Although the term 'human' gets part of its meaning from the bourgeois ethic of 'self-mastery' it is also rooted in the social relations of feudalism since it is Margaret, the 'gentlewoman', who invokes it as a standard in the novel. The 'human' is a function of the property relations of feudalism, whose inequalities are justified as the natural expression of differences in 'human' nature. Hence Dixon, the Hales' servant, 'obeyed and respected Margaret [because she] as do many others, liked to feel herself ruled by a powerful and decided nature' (Gaskell 1855 & 1993: 45). Disraeli (1804–81) echoes this belief in a natural ascendancy when he writes that 'the superiority of the animal man is an essential quality of aristocracy' (1845 & 1985: 141). As we have already seen, this 'superiority' entailed certain obligations on the part of the ruling class to care for those below them. Margaret believes that the conflict between masters and men is directly due to the failure to apply this principle to industrial relations (Gaskell 1855 & 1993: 115–16). Master Nixon, a minor character in Disraeli's *Sybil: or, The Two Nations*, would agree. 'Atween the poor man and the gentleman there [is] no connection, and that's the wital mischief of this country', he remarks sadly (1845 & 1985: 183).

Thornton rejects the principle that one class is responsible for another. The masters, he observes would be 'trenching on the independence of the hands ... if we interfered with the life they lead out of the mills' (Gaskell 1855 & 1993: 119). He expresses a similar view when he distinguishes between the idea of a 'gentleman' and the idea of a 'man'. The term 'gentleman', he says, 'only describes a person in relation to others' whereas 'we consider [a man] not merely with regard to his fellow men, but in relation to himself, – to life – to time – to eternity' (ibid.: 164). This distinction is part of a wider debate on the meaning of the term 'gentleman' in the middle decades of the century, prompted by such developments as the extension of the franchise and the growth of the professions (Mason 1982 & 1993). It is clear from Thornton's emphasis that he considers the term 'man' to be more relevant to his world than the term 'gentleman'. The shift from the one to the other not only reflects the apparent rise of the industrial middle class, it also shows that, in the modern world, the relation to the self takes precedence over the social bond. We appear to have moved from the integrated individual of feudalism to the isolated individual of capitalism.

I say 'appear' because Thornton aspires to certain gentlemanly accomplishments even as he distances himself from the general notion. For example, he hires Mr Hale to tutor him in the classics, causing Margaret to exclaim 'What in the world do manufacturers want with the classics, or literature, or the accomplishments of a gentleman?' (Gaskell 1855 & 1993: 35). More particularly, Thornton rents his business premises from Mr Bell, whose position as an Oxford scholar enhances the 'gentlemanly' status he already has from the ownership of land. The manufacturer, in other words, is dependent on the gentleman: far from being obsolete, feudal property relations are essential to the success of the manufacturing enterprise in Milton. This point is underlined when Margaret inherits Mr Bell's property, since that enables her to lend Thornton the money he needs to save his factory. *North and South*, in short, subscribes simultaneously to the hierarchy of feudalism and the dynamism of capitalism. It not only shows the conflict between the two systems but also how they complement one another.

THE INDIVIDUAL AND CLASS

It should be clear from the above that the term 'human' cannot simply be understood in terms of 'one common heart' but is, instead, a tense compromise of bourgeois self-mastery and feudal obligation. It is not, in other words, an 'innocent' but an ideological notion which, by defining social stratification in personal terms, disguises the structural determinants of wealth and poverty and so protects the *status quo* from criticism. In this respect, the 'human' is similar to those moral discourses which, by the mid-century, had superseded the language of class. During the 1850s and 1860s writes Crossick:

> [t]here is less talk of 'working class' and 'middle class', and more of 'deserving' and 'undeserving poor', of 'respectable artisans' and 'gentleman', as a good proportion of society (including much of the working class) came to concentrate on divisions which emphasised moral rather than economic criteria.
>
> (1991: 161–2)

These moral discourses are ideological because they suggest personal differences are responsible for social divisions, and that the shortcomings of society therefore lie with individuals and not with the system. The most popular expression of this view was Samuel Smiles' *Self-Help* (1859) sales of which 'far exceeded those of the great nineteenth century novels' (Briggs 1954 & 1977: 126). The ideological character of these discourses means that they had not, in fact, dispensed with the concept of class, only occluded their relationship to it. As in the case of the 'human', they operated on behalf of a complex alliance between the gentry and the bourgeoisie, an alliance which is expressed in *North and South* by the marriage of Margaret and Thornton.

More generally, there is a correlation between the Marxist conception of class and Freud's account of the human psyche. In very schematic terms, Freud's conception of the conscious ego constantly under threat from an anarchic id approximates to bourgeois fears of civilisation being swept away by working-class radicalism. Similarly, the concern in Marxism over how the prole-tariat can become fully conscious of itself and so transcend the divisions of class society echoes Freud's early belief that a patient can be cured and become whole only if he or she is made fully aware of the origin of their illness. These very general parallels between Marx and Freud suggest that the concept of class is not incompatible with that of the individual; indeed, if it is not to push the point too far, we might almost say that a model of class structures the individual psyche. It is as if, during the course of the nineteenth century, class conflict is gradually internalised as a conflict between different parts of the self (Musselwhite 1987).

The emergence of the idea of the individual and its rise to prominence in Victorian England is the result of a long and com-plex process. Simplifying drastically, the focus on the individual is a consequence of the break-up of feudalism and the growth of the free market. The long transition from feudalism to capitalism dissolved the social ties between individuals and put in their place an economic philosophy which viewed them as autonomous agents, each pursuing their own interests independently of oth-ers. The great chain of being, which had offered an idealised model of social integration, gave way to *laissez-faire*. The Victorians, therefore, had no ready means of conceptualising the relations between individuals. Henry Mayhew, for example, declared that even such a small section of society as the London poor were 'so multifarious that the mind is long baffled in its attempts to reduce them to scientific order or classification' (1862 & 1985: 5). Moreover, the fact that the Victorians viewed the individual in economic rather than social terms militated against the development of a cohesive concept of the social order. It was left to Marx to show that individuals *were* related in eco-nomic terms and that this was the basis of class, the engine of change which would eventually lead to the establishment of a *new* society.

The idea of the individual appealed to at least the upper working class, partly because it was consonant with their tradition of liberty and partly because its corollary, self-help, had been the driving force behind such developments as the Cooperative Society, trade unionism and the friendly and mutual improvement societies. However, as Neville Kirk has argued, these organisations 'enjoyed only a limited presence and appeal among the working class' (1998: 60). This was in no small part due to divisions between skilled and unskilled workers, with the former seeking to exclude the latter from membership of trade unions in, for example, building, printing and engineering. These divisions in the workplace were mirrored in social life by the ones between the 'respectable' and the 'rough'. In Arthur Morrison's *A Child of the Jago* the Roper family are disliked:

> because they furnished their own room, and in an obnoxiously complete style; because Roper did not drink, nor brawl, nor beat his wife, nor do anything all day but look for work; because all these things were a matter of scandalous arrogance impudently subversive of Jago custom and precedent.
>
> (1896 & 1996: 44)

The virtues of 'respectability' included 'industry, thrift, sobriety, discipline, restraint, honesty, modesty and courtesy' while the vices of 'roughness' embraced 'excessive drinking, gambling, sexual enthusiasm and general loose living' (ibid.: 115). 'Respectability' was associated with Liberalism while roughness was associated with Toryism (ibid.: 84, 96). The latter 'situated itself within the culture of conviviality and bonhomie, of beer, bacca, billiards and Britannia' in contrast to 'the straitjacketed Liberal domain of moral exhortation and the improving tract' (Kirk 1994: 194–5). The weight given to 'respectability' and 'roughness' in working-class culture was not only the mark of an internally divided class but of one in which status considerations had overtaken political ones. What was at issue was not the workers' consciousness of themselves as a class but their difference as individuals. The upper working class had moved from attempting to reform society to attempting to reform the self. This was to be achieved by imitating the middle class in the same way that the wealthy middle class imitated the aristocracy. In nineteenth-century England, there was conformity as well as conflict between the classes.

POVERTY AND CLASS IN THE LATE NINETEENTH CENTURY

This should not be taken to imply that low wages and job insecurity had ceased to be 'the major economic feature of working-class life' (Kirk 1998: 123), nor that poverty had been eradicated. On the contrary, it was regarded as the social problem in the final decades of the century. From the 1830s to the 1850s, poverty was associated with the industrial North but in the latter part of the century attention was focused on London, particularly the East End where conditions were described as 'unknown' and 'unexplored'. 'As there is a darkest Africa', asked William Booth (1829–1912), leader of the Salvation Army, 'is there not a darkest England?' (1889 & 1978: 145). This assimilation of London to the African continent was a new element in the representation of poverty. Previously, the poor had been presented as colourful street types, or as the undifferentiated 'hands' of industrial fiction. Now '[t]he lot of a Negress in the Equatorial Forest' was needed to understand 'that of an orphan girl in our Christian capital' (ibid.: 147).

The identification of the poor with the inhabitants of Africa did not, however, entirely depart from earlier perceptions. Indeed, the analogy with Africa reinforced the view of the poor as 'savages' or 'barbarians'. Moreover, it was continuous with the assumption that the poor were in need of civilisation when, in fact, it was that very 'civilisation' which had created the poverty that so shocked contemporaries. In an attempt to map the extent of poverty, some investigators, such as Charles Booth (1840–1916), the man credited with the introduction of old age pensions, adopted a systematic approach reminiscent of the fact-gathering surveys of the mid-century. Williams argues that this represented 'an intrinsic reduction of the poor to objects of study, a depersonalization by classification and grading' (1973: 267). There is some truth in this, but it ignores, for example, Booth's admissions that there were 'individuals of every sort' in each of his 'eight classes', and that the lines between them were by no means clear-cut (1889 & 1978: 115, 124). The attempt to categorise the poor yielded to the dominance of the idea of the individual, which made poverty seem a consequence of personality rather than a result of capitalism. The economic classifications intended to sort the poor, whether they were based on income (Booth) or willingness to work (Mayhew), did not address the fundamental fact of capitalism, the extraction of surplus value by the bourgeois from the proletariat.

Himmelfarb claims that the language of class was used to define poverty and describe the poor in the nineteenth century (1984: 288). If so, then the confused medley which characterised the representation of the poor in the 1880s and 1890s – sympathy, nascent sociology and moral exhortation – reflected a complex and contradictory relationship between the classes. In George Gissing's *The Nether World*, for example, there is a strong awareness that a person's faults are not 'characteristics to be condemned ... but the outcome of cruel conditions' (1889 & 1992: 102) but, at the same time, there is a sense that these conditions do not fully explain the nature of the poor. 'Observe the middle aged women; it would be small surprise that their good looks had vanished, but whence comes it they are animal, repulsive and absolutely vicious in ugliness?' (ibid.: 109). This ambiguous attitude towards the poor, that they were at once the product *of* and willing participants *in* their circumstances, was a barrier to building cross-class alliances which might have led to social change. If there was no bourgeois revolution in England because of that class's relationship to the gentry, there was no proletarian revolution because that class appeared too wedded to its own degradation. Instead of fighting for a better world, it preferred entertainments such as watching a chained dwarf on all fours fight a dog 'using no other weapons than his clenched fists' (Greenwood 1876 & 1978: 62).

NEW UNIONISM AND SOCIALISM

This account, however, ignores two major developments of the late nineteenth century, the appearance of the new unions and the growth of socialism. The old unions were generally craft-based, with a strong sense of hierarchy. There was, declared Robert Knight, General Secretary of Boiler Maker's and Iron Ship Builder's Society, a 'cleavage of interest between the unskilled and the skilled workman' (cited in Hobsbawm 1948 & 1974: 4). The new unions, by contrast, reflected the rise of a semi-skilled, machine-operating class, who were seen as vital links in the chain of production. John Burns, an engineer, a mass orator and finally a Liberal minister, declared that the difference between the old and the new unions was that the latter saw 'that labour saving machinery [was] reducing the previously skilled to the level of unskilled labour' and that the former therefore needed to 'be less exclusive than hitherto' (ibid.: 73). This was a recognition that, irrespective of cultural differences between the 'respectable' and the 'rough', the working class were united by a common experience of exploitation. A consciousness of exploitation lay behind another difference between the old and new unions, namely, a concern with social legislation. The old unions emphasised individualism and self-help, whereas the new ones campaigned for change on a range of issues from the introduction of the eight-hour day to welfare benefits for the unemployed, the sick and the aged. Furthermore, declared the socialist Tom Mann, the new unions were to be 'centres of enlightenment', unlike the old ones which, in his view, had merely been 'the meeting place for paying contributions and receiving donations' (ibid.: 98).

The new unions adopted a more hostile approach to industrial relations than their predecessors, and the late 1880s to the mid-1890s saw a number of clashes between capital and labour. There were, for example, prolonged strikes at the Bryant and May Matchworks (1888) and the London Docks (1889). There were also conflicts in coal mining, cotton, slate quarrying and the boot and shoe industry. The employers responded to these strikes by organising themselves into associations with the express purpose of 'rooting out and destroying trade unions' (McIvor 1996: 6). In some cases, this meant the use of state violence, as when two miners were shot dead by troops at Featherstone in 1893. More usually, the employers locked striking workers out of the factory and brought in non-union labour as in the 1897–8 dispute in engineering. These clashes were class-based to the extent that they centred on the antagonism between employer and employee, but the latter's main demands, even in the most militant wave of new unionism from 1910 to 1914, were not for the overthrow of capitalism but for union recognition and improved pay and conditions (Kirk 1994: 108). For all their differences from the old craft unions, the new unions sought to ameliorate the effects of capitalism rather than to abolish it.

The late nineteenth century also saw a revival of socialism in a variety of forms, most notably the Social Democratic Federation, the Fabian Society and the Socialist League. These were manifestations less of a new class consciousness than of an acceptance of the relevance of class analysis for understanding England at the end of the century. The Social Democratic Federation (founded 1884) was the most Marxist of these organisations with its founder, Henry Hyndman, employing Marxist categories and predicting revolution in his *England for All* (1881). The Fabian Society (founded 1884), which numbered among its members George Bernard Shaw, did not believe in revolution but reform. It argued that society should be understood in terms of a community of interests rather than the class struggle, hence its support for a regulated economy and welfare legislation. Despite Fabian help with the formation of the Union of the Women Matchworkers (1889), the Society failed to win working-class support because its bureaucratic character was 'deeply at odds with the spirit of self-activism which animated the proletarian socialist organisations of the period' (Hall and Schwarz 1985: 23).

Where both the Social Democratic Federation and the Fabian Society protested at the economic and social iniquities of capitalism, the Socialist League couched its criticisms in mainly aesthetic terms. Its founder, William Morris, declared that the leading passion of his life was 'the desire to produce beautiful things'; a desire which, he complained, was entirely contrary to the profit-driven character of modern civilisation (1894 & 1981: 233, 239). In many ways, Morris looked back to medieval England for his model of a harmonious society; John Callaghan, for example, speaks of his 'guild socialism' (1990: 24). But although Morris confessed to 'agonies of confusion' (ibid.: 238) when trying to understand Marx's economics, he did agree with the latter's observation that capitalism had 'mutilate[d] the labourer into a fragment of a man' (cited in ibid.: 25). Morris advocated a form of life which restored 'man' to a condition of wholeness and assigned an important role to art in the process. He wrote:

> It is the province of art to set the true ideal of a full and reasonable life before him, a life to which the perception and creation of beauty, the enjoyment of real pleasure that is, shall be felt as necessary to man as his daily bread, and that no man, and no set of men, can be deprived of this except by mere opposition which should be resisted to the utmost.
>
> (1894 & 1981: 241)

CULTURE AND CLASS

The various socialisms of the late nineteenth century differed from the Chartist movement in that they were largely middle-class led. This limited the appeal of socialism, because it seemed to be just one more manifestation of that middle-class tradition of interference in working-class culture which we have already discussed. Working-class culture had, in any case, changed significantly since the failure of Chartism; in particular it had become less political with the concern for individual status replacing the sense of class solidarity. In his detailed analysis of the London working class in the second half of the century, Gareth Stedman Jones claims that a work-centred culture, realised in trade feasts and a distinctive language and dress, was gradually displaced by one based on the home, sport and the pub (1983: 215). This culture, he continues, was both a defensive reaction to middle-class evangelicalism and a conservative one to the erosion of difference between skilled and unskilled workers (ibid.).

In a similar vein, Ross McKibbin argues that the decline of working-class radicalism was facilitated by the small-scale nature of British industry, the associational character of its leisure pursuits and the importance of 'inherited ideologies which emphasised a common citizenship ... and the class neutrality of the major institutions of the state' (McKibbin 1991: 24). The fact that the majority of factories were not large meant that relations between employers and employees were generally direct, 'which probably tended to undermine a collective sense of class' (ibid.: 7). This was further eroded by a working-class preference for associations based on hobbies rather than organisations based on politics, hence potential radicalism was dispersed 'amongst a profusion of activities' such as fishing, pigeon racing and flower growing (ibid.: 14, 16). Finally, working-class attachment to the monarchy, its respect for Parliament, and its pride in Britain's imperial pre-eminence all appealed to a sense of nation rather than class, thereby highlighting social unity instead of economic division which, of course, is precisely the function of ideology.

The music-hall reinforced the conservative nature of this culture by its criticisms of socialism and its acceptance of class divisions as part of the natural order of things. One performer, known as 'little Titch', joked that his brother was in the gas trade, 'in fact he travels on gas, he's a socialist orator' (cited in Stedman Jones 1983: 229). This contempt for socialists was in marked contrast to the affection with which upper-class characters like Burlington Bertie and Champagne Charlie were portrayed. Indeed, to judge from music-hall turns, it seemed as if English society consisted of only two classes, the aristocracy and the workers since, as Stedman Jones has noted, 'the capitalist [was] completely absent as a music-hall stereotype' (1983: 229). The most significant feature in the presentation of the working class was the scorn heaped on those with pretensions to gentility, the most popular expression of which was Bessie Bellwood's 'Wot Cher, Ria' (Vicinus 1974: 263). 'Putting on airs', writes Vicinus, 'was the greatest sin anyone could commit' and hence the bulk of music-hall entertainment reminded the working class 'to keep its place, to enjoy what it has and to stop others from stepping out of line' (ibid.: 262–3).

The music-hall was part of a shift away from a form of entertainment that spoke directly to the working class out of a shared experience, and one that was provided for the 'masses' by those familiar with their experience, but apart from it. Vicinus distinguishes between class and a 'mass' art as follows:

> A class perspective involves the use of characters and characterizations built upon details which speak for the condition and beliefs of an entire class. A mass perspective involves the use of stereotypes in which the behaviour of a particular group or class is portrayed, but the emotions are generalized and acceptable to all classes.
>
> (1974: 266)

The generalized nature of mass entertainment arises from the exchange relation. One of the main arguments of this book is that the exchange relation forms the basis of representation in capitalist society. Money makes all commodities equivalent and the pursuit of profit ensures that the difference between skilled and unskilled workers disappears, making them all interchangeable as 'hands'. Moreover, the exchange relation establishes abstraction as the principle of social life, whether in the form of the study of poverty or the generalized emotion of the music-hall song (ibid.: 257). The exchange relation drives representation from the concrete and the particular to the abstract and the universal.

The same principle of abstraction which Vicinus detects in music-hall is also apparent in other forms of entertainment in this period. Socialists, in particular, were worried that the new leisure industries were 'encourag[ing] homogeneity' and redefining recreation 'as a mere purchasable commodity' (Waters 1990: 29). The contours of class were being blurred by the growth of consumerism. Socialists like Robert Blatchford believed that the effects of the new leisure might be countered by a programme of rational recreation whereby the individual would forego the pleasures of the pub, gambling, the seaside excursion and football, for the uplifting effects of the temperance cafe, the concert and the public lecture. This resort to the rhetoric of self-improvement was, because of its appeal to the individual, at least partly in tune with a working-class culture which endorsed 'the concrete particular, the local view and personal participation' (Joyce 1980: 338). Moreover, a discourse that valued the individual was potentially radical in a society whose representations were increasingly abstract. However, the idea of the individual has, as we have seen, a problematic history, a complicated relation to class and was too deeply implicated in the social order for its potential ever to be realised.

By the end of the century, then, working-class culture was largely conservative and its entertainments, no longer self-generated but commercially provided, reinforced class boundaries which were at the same time disappearing with the advent of consumerism. This was a very different situation to the middle of the century, when Chartism challenged the established order and created its own literature, both as an expression of class consciousness and as part of a programme of social reform. The Chartists, like Morris, believed in the power of art to change people, but, by the end of the century, art was becoming a commodity and 'a commodity can only be consumed; it acts to prevent change' (Vicinus 1974: 279).

The Aesthetic movement can be seen as an abandonment of the social role of art. Walter Pater's claim that art 'comes to you proposing frankly to give nothing but the highest quality to your moments as they pass, and simply for those moments' sake' (1868 & 1986: 153) is a far cry from Mrs Gaskell's belief that the sensuous qualities of art distract from its didactic purpose (1855 & 1993: 409). And yet there is a sense in which Thornton's view of culture prepares the way for Aestheticism since, although he reads the classics, he asserts that they are completely irrelevant to his mode of life (ibid.). It is not such a great step from this to Oscar Wilde's declaration that '[a]ll art is quite useless' (cited in Small 1979: 101).

Although Aestheticism has been accused of elitism (Small 1979: xviii), it had certain affinities with the new leisure industries – for example, in its attachment to the moment and its emphasis on pleasure rather than moral instruction. These points of contact not only testify to the persistence of that link between the top and bottom of the social scale, they also suggest how both were involved in refashioning perception to suit the emerging consumer society. Entrepreneurs of ice rinks and people's palaces thought not in terms of 'the self-disciplined citizen eager for the benefits of rational recreation', but of 'the discerning consumer choosing judiciously between alternative commodities in a marketplace' (Waters 1990: 25), while the fashions of Aestheticism – extravagant dress, ornate wallpaper and blue china – together with the cultivation of the beautiful, had the effect of aestheticising the commodity. Thus, although Wilde (1854–1900), Pater (1834–94), the poet Algernon Swinburne (1837–1909) and the painter James Abbott McNeill Whistler (1834–1903) may have been in social revolt against their class, they served it well in furthering its economic ends. It is in the absence of a social programme for art, paradoxically, that art may be at its most effective.

This raises, yet again, the relation between art and class. We have already discussed the problems of class consciousness and these are similar to those surrounding the relationship of art and class. Of particular relevance here is the point that a common economic experience does not automatically translate into a social unity, as the division between the 'respectable' and the 'roughs' in the working class shows. The focus needs to be shifted from art as the expression of a particular class to how the ambitions of art are constrained by the pervasive influence of the exchange relation. Since this infiltrates all representations it diminishes the possibility of there being a class art with its own distinctive modes of expression.

Marx has shown how the commodity form represses the social relations which brought it into existence (1867 & 1995: 43), which suggests that there is an inherent bias in capitalism against representation. This is evident in a small way in *North and South*. The novel suggests that a representation should correspond to what is represented: 'Is it not like, papa?' asks Margaret showing her father a sketch she has painted (Gaskell 1855 & 1993: 23). However, the novel also shows that truth can never be represented, for Margaret's brother Frederick, who organised a mutiny, is unable to give his account of events because, in his absence, he was condemned to death and is therefore forced to live in exile. His story, which we are led to believe is the true one, remains untold. The point to stress is that this non-representation cannot be divorced from the non-representation at the heart of exchange. The literary revolution which we know as Modernism elevated what is a structural feature of capitalism into an aesthetic creed. And it is to the twentieth century that we now turn.

6

THE TWENTIETH CENTURY

Although this chapter begins with a consideration of the relation between modernism and exchange, its main focus is how the working class represented themselves and how they were represented, particularly during the 1930s and the late 1950s and early 1960s. It concludes by looking at why the concept of class fell into abeyance and whether or not it is still a useful term today.

THE ECONOMY OF MODERNISM

There are two broad ways in which we can look at the relationship between modernism and class. The first is to consider how economically privileged artists, such as the Bloomsbury group, chose to differentiate themselves from the masses and certain sections of the middle class in cultural terms. The second is to situate some aspects of modernism within the context of the exchange whose extension is an example of how the bourgeoisie 'creates a world after its own image' (Marx and Engels 1848 & 1968: 37). The analogies between art and exchange show that, while modernist artists may have criticised the erosion of 'high' culture in mass society, their work nevertheless is complicit in that process.

John Carey argues that 'the principle around which modernist literature and culture fashioned themselves was the exclusion of the masses, the defeat of their power, the removal of their literacy, the denial of their humanity' (1992: 21). Modernist artists, in other words, were reacting to the consequences of the Education Act of 1871 and the Reform Bills of 1867 and 1884–5 which had extended literacy and the franchise respectively. T. S. Eliot (1888–1965) asserted that 'in our headlong rush to educate everybody, we are lowering our standards' (cited in ibid.: 15), while his description of 'apeneck' Sweeney (1920 & 1969: 56) chimes with the claim of the 'gloomy dean' of St Paul's, William Inge (1860–1954), that 'the democratic man is a species of ape' (cited in Carey 1992: 25). This perception of a mass rather than a class society helped to hide rather than eliminate the differences between classes.

It was for that reason that modernist artists asserted what they saw as their cultural superiority to the 'complacent, prejudiced and unthinking mass' (Eliot cited in Carey 1992: 7), whose very existence was an affront to their refined sensibilities. Hence Clarissa Dalloway, in Virginia Woolf's *Mrs Dalloway*, is offended by Doris Kilman who, in addition to being '[h]eavy, ugly, [and] commonplace' is 'so insensitive' as to wear 'a green mackintosh coat' (1925 & 1989: 111, 122). Leonard Bast, the lower-class young clerk in *Howards End*, excites less revulsion but is incapable of truly appreciating the culture he admires, his 'brain' being filled with 'husks of books' (Forster 1910 & 1987: 150) not their kernels, and this makes him gauche in company, a trait captured in his moustache, 'one of those ... that always droop into teacups, more bother than they're worth, surely, and not fashionable either' (ibid.: 144). The use of culture as a tool of social differentiation has a long history. As one anonymous commentator of the fourteenth century remarked, '[t]he comyn people ... without lyterrature and good informacyon ben lyke to brute beestes' (cited *Oxford English Dictionary* 1963). Modernism may have prided itself on being *avant-garde* but, in this respect at least, it was highly traditional.

Although modernist artists segregated people more on the basis of culture rather than economics this does not mean that we can separate the two realms. At a very general level the modernist cry to 'make it new' is the cultural expression of the bourgeois need to 'constantly revolutionise the means of production, and with them the whole relations of society' (Marx and Engels 1848 & 1968: 38). More specifically, there was a perception in a number of modernist novels that money was becoming the sole measure of value. Margaret, in *Howards End*, for example, declares that 'the very soul of the world is economic' (Forster 1910 & 1987: 72). And Ursula in D. H. Lawrence's *The Rainbow* rages:

> I hate it, that anybody is my equal who has the same amount of money as I have. I know I am better than all of them. I hate them. They are not my equals. I hate equality on a money basis. It is the equality of dirt.
>
> (1915 & 1993: 436)

Ursula's remark indicates that the exchange relation, which makes all commodities equivalent by making money their common measure, has now been extended to humans. It was precisely because money threatened to confer a spurious equality on people that modernists were driven to emphasise the cultural differences between them.

Jean-Joseph Goux, however, has suggested that the style of modernism is related to a new conception of money. His argument, in brief, is that the abandonment of the gold standard meant that money was defined in relative terms and this was related to a crisis of representation in literature, manifest in a disregard for plot, a preoccupation with the impressions of things rather than their objective representation, and the promotion of multiple points of view in a bid to capture a reality that was seen to be ever more elusive.

Was it purely by chance that the crisis of realism in the novel and in painting coincided with the end of gold money? Or that the birth of 'abstract' art coincided with the shocking invention of inconvertible money signs? Can we not see in this double crisis of money and language the collapse of guarantees and frames of reference, a rupture between sign and thing, undermining representation and ushering in the age of the floating signifier?

(Goux 1994: 3)

Although Goux's claim can be challenged on the basis that Britain did not abandon the gold standard entirely – Winston Churchill, for example, resumed it in 1925 before it was abandoned again in 1931 – his argument cannot be entirely dismissed. Fredric Jameson, for instance, draws on Marx's account of the circulation of commodities as a means of understanding the difference between realism and modernism. Marx analyses this circulation using two formulae. The first is C–M–C whereby we see 'the transformation of commodities into money, and the change of the money back again into commodities' (Marx 1867 & 1995: 93). The second is M–C–M whereby we see 'the transformation of money into commodities, and the change of commodities back into money' (ibid.).

Jameson relates the first of these formulae to realism. His claim is that the accentuation of exchange in the seventeenth century, which intensified the transformation of the commodity from a concrete use to an abstract value, led to a compensatory and 'more realistic interest in the body of the world and in the new and more lively human relationships developed by trade [as well as] a keener interest in the sensory nature of wares' (1997: 254). The chief expression of this realism, he continues, was the bourgeois novel. By the late nineteenth century, however, there were signs, such as the vast expansion of credit, that more money was being invested in financial transactions than in productive capacity.

This 'abstract flow of money', argues Jameson, 'determined a whole new and more abstract way of thinking' (ibid.: 258) which is the hallmark of modernism with its 'dedication to the abstract, the general and the classified' (McFarlane 1976 & 1991: 74). In artistic terms, this was manifest in the commitment to form over content. 'Form', wrote the novelist Henry James (1843–1916), 'is the absolute citadel and tabernacle of interest' (1912 & 1980: 235). For the art critic Clive Bell (1881–1964) the one quality which every work of art must have to be worthy of the name is 'significant form' (1914 & 1987: 8). It is the contemplation of 'pure form' (ibid.: 68) which characterises the aesthetic experience not, as 'the vulgar imagine, the realisation of an accurate conception of life' (ibid.: 66). Bell's remark anticipates Pierre Bourdieu's distinction (1979 & 1984) between the middle-class and the working-class attitude to art. The former's preference for form over content subverts conventional perception, while the latter's preference for content over form affirms a continuity between art and life and so reinforces conventional perception. The middle-class aesthetic is thus potentially more radical than the working-class one; 'potentially' because there is still the problem of the parallel between form and exchange. However, to insist on that parallel ignores two points. The first is that modernist experiments, whether in art, literature or music, show the richness and flexibility of form whereas the exchange relation is fixed and rigid. The second point is that the modernist emphasis on technique was geared to the expression of a unique subjectivity unlike the exchange relation where 'the individuals, the subjects between whom this process [of exchange] goes on, are simply and only conceived of as exchangers' (Marx 1867 & 1973: 240).

The modernist focus on the self, its 'incalculable chaos of impressions, its random progress of thoughts and feelings, the strange workings of its nerves, the whisper of its blood and the entreaty of its bone' (Knut Hamsen cited in Bradbury and McFarlane 1976 & 1991: 83–4) is at the expense of the lower-class other and reinforces their oppression. T. S Eliot's reference to 'apeneck Sweeney' and E. M. Forster's dismissal of Jacky Bast in *Howards End* as 'bestially stupid' (1910 & 1987: 224), chime with the view of workers as animals. The originator of scientific management, Frederick Winslow Taylor, observed that 'one of the very first requirements for a man who is fit to handle pig iron is that he shall resemble in his mental make-up an ox more than any other type' (1911 & 1964: 59). Modernist artists may have tried to distance themselves from the mass society of capitalism, judging it spiritually impoverished and culturally barren, but their work underwrites its economic form and relations of domination.

The modernist concern with the self also relates to the shift from *laissez-faire* to a collectivist state in the early years of the century. This was accompanied by a decline in the idea of the individual and the development of the concept of the citizen, the former stressing how people differ, the latter what they have in common. The modernist delight in the 'individual', in the self's 'myriad impressions' (Woolf 1919 & 1980: 77), can be seen as a reaction to the 'abstraction of individuality which is the ground of citizenship' (Sayer 1991: 77). However, the 'individual' and the citizen were not entirely antithetical. As David Sutton notes, citizenship is a mechanism 'by which the dominant classes can break up oppositional class forces by "individualizing" them … political institutions are organised in such a way that the dominant forces of representation depend on the individual rather than classes' (1985: 64). The idea of citizenship was thus largely formulated in opposition to class. It was aimed particularly at the skilled and respectable section of the working class who, in return for political rights and social benefits, would be expected to labour for the improvement of the race, the economy and the extension of empire (ibid.). Since it targeted the top end of the working class, the concept of citizenship probably increased rather than reduced social divisions. It was based on the age-old distinction between the 'deserving' and the 'undeserving' poor, but women, children, the insane, prisoners and migrant workers were among a number of groups who fell outside this apparently universal category. Perhaps the most profound impact of the new discourse of citizenship was that it divided the potentially most progressive part of the working class from the rest.

THE RAGGED TROUSERED PHILANTHROPISTS

The relationship between the higher and lower sections of the working class is one of the themes explored in *The Ragged Trousered Philanthropists* by Robert Tressell (1870–1911). The novel was finished in 1910, the year, according to Woolf (1882–1941), that modernism began. However, Tressell's novel differs from modernist ones in a number of ways. The chief difference is that where modernist novels explore the caverns of the mind, Tressell analyses the structure of society; their focus is consciousness, Tressell's is class. The novel's central character, Frank Owen, named after Robert Owen the nineteenth-century socialist, ceaselessly attempts to explain to his fellow workers the nature of capitalism.

'I mean this,' replied Owen, speaking very slowly. 'Everything is produced by the [the working class]. In return for their labour they are given – Money, and the things they have made become the property of the people who do nothing. Then, as the money is of no use, the workers go to the shops and give it away in exchange for the things they themselves have made. They spend – or give back – *All* their wages; but as the money they got as wages is not equal in value to the things they produced, they find that they are only able to buy back a *very small part*. So you see that these little discs of metal – this Money – is a device for enabling those who do not work to rob the workers of the greater part of the fruits of their toil.

(1914 & 1997: 277)

This, in so many words, is Marx's theory of surplus value which we discussed in the previous chapter. Tressell locates the meaning of money in the social relations of production. Forster saw money as the basis of culture: 'cash', he wrote, 'is the warp of civilization' (1910 & 1987: 134). This could not be more different from Tressell, who believed that the pursuit of money retarded the development of civilization. The employers in his novel, the allegorically named Rushton, Didlum and Sweater, had

> given up everything that makes life good and beautiful, in order to carry on a mad struggle to acquire money which they would never be sufficiently cultured to properly enjoy. Deaf and blind to every other consideration, to this end they had degraded their intellects by concentrating them upon the minutest details of expense and profit. ... Devoid of every ennobling thought or aspiration, they grovelled on the filthy ground, tearing up the flowers to get at the worms.
>
> (1914 & 1997: 459)

Forster, in *Howards End*, has little sense of system and therefore he accepts that '[t]here are just rich and poor, as there always have been and always will be' (1910 & 1987: 193). The fact that he sees no relationship between the rich being rich and the poor being poor is ironic in a novel whose epigraph is 'Only connect'. It is Tressell who makes the connection between rich and poor by showing that '[m]oney is the device by which those who are too lazy to work are enabled to rob the workers of the fruits of their labour' (1914 & 1997: 211).

The problem that Owen faces is how to persuade his fellow housepainters, the philanthropists of the title, to substitute the equality of socialism for the exploitation of capitalism. The term 'philanthropists' is ironic because they are unaware that they suppress their own needs to support the system which impoverishes them. They not only 'submitted ... to the existing state of

things, but defended it, and opposed and ridiculed any suggestion to alter it' (1914 & 1997: 45). Their disposition forms the
basis for the fascist revolution predicted in Jack London's *The Iron
Heel* (1908). Owen's attitude to the pastimes of the philanthropists parallels the modernists' attitude to mass or 'popular'
culture. Like them he identifies 'high' culture – 'books, theatres,
pictures [and] music' – with 'civilization' (1914 & 1997: 29) and,
again like them, uses it as a standard against which the 'masses'
are seen either as 'savages' or 'wild beasts' (ibid.: 431, 451). But,
unlike them, Owen argues that 'what we call civilization ... is
not the [privilege] of any separate class ... but the common heritage of all' (ibid.: 29–30). The philanthropists, however, have no
interest in 'high' culture. They regard Owen as 'a bit of a crank'
because he takes no interest in 'racing or football' (ibid.: 18),
while Owen, for his part, despairs that they prefer 'a smutty story,
a game of hooks and rings ... or the doings of some royal person-
age or aristocrat' (ibid.: 267–8) to a lecture on the causes of
poverty. He believes that the 'popular' culture of the philanthropists prevents them from understanding the system which
oppresses them. The true state of affairs is disguised by newspapers such as the *Daily Chloroform* and the *Daily Obscurer*, a
deception reinforced by popular fiction with its fixation on the
romantic intrigues of the upper class (ibid.: 400). Tressell, in
other words, views 'popular' culture as a species of ideology. It
presents a false view of reality and promotes escapism rather than
enquiry. However, we cannot see that ideology purely in terms of
the dominant class promoting their interests, since they, too, are
determined by 'the system' (ibid.: 203–4). Although they benefit
from it at the expense of the philanthropists, they are 'compelled'
(ibid.) to behave in the way they do thus curtailing their opportunities to manipulate 'the system'.

Tressell's portrayal of the working class as conservative seems
in direct contrast to Marx who saw them as revolutionary.
However, this apparent contrast fails to take into account the fact

that Tressell's philanthropists are not Marx's industrial proletariat. Furthermore, Tressell conflates working-class culture with
mass culture. Traditional working-class culture had been closely
related to the experience of work, but new forms of employment,
higher wages, shorter working hours, the Victorian revolution in
public transport and the growth of the commercial leisure meant
that workers were less constrained in their choice of recreation.
Tressell's condemnation of the pub, sport and the popular press
chimed with socialist pronouncements against 'popular' culture
whose 'sensational pleasures' threatened 'their gospel of educa-
tionalism' (Waters 1990: 177). Men like the socialist Robert
Blatchford (1851–1943), who had a strong influence on Tressell,
sought, through his *Clarion* newspaper and his hugely popular
Merrie England (1895), to convince the working class of the
poverty of 'their' culture under capitalism. They had to be made
to realise that they were not just exploited at work but also in
their leisure. Consequently, socialists sought to develop alternative forms of recreation, cycling, literary study and lectures on
socialism, which would draw the working class away from the
frivolity of the ice rink and the music hall towards the serious
business of the transformation of society. But, as C. F. G.
Masterman (1874–1927), the author and liberal politician
remarked, while socialists were convinced that these measures
would 'inaugurate the golden age of the Socialistic millennium
... the people [were] thinking of entertainment' (cited in Waters
1990: 184). Moreover, those who did join the socialist ranks did
so for social rather than political reasons, so that the promised
marriage of pleasure and politics failed to transpire.

Although Tressell is forthright in his condemnation of the
philanthropists because they are only interested in 'beer, football,
betting and – of course – one other subject [sex]' (1914 & 1997:
545), he also shows why this is the case. 'From their infancy they
had been trained to distrust their own intelligence, and to leave
the management of the affairs of the world to their betters; and

now most of them were absolutely incapable of thinking of any abstract subject whatever' (ibid.: 204). His attitude towards the philanthropists therefore veers between contempt for their refusal to challenge the system and an acceptance that they have been conditioned to preserve it. A close reading of the novel, however, suggests that the philanthropists are not as passive as Owen imagines them to be. One of their most frequent refrains is 'we must try to get some of our own back' (ibid.: 108). This takes many forms: Philpot sneaks a quiet smoke (ibid.: 38), Slyme steals some wallpaper (ibid.: 207), and all the philanthropists endorse the practice of fiddling the time sheet (ibid.: 118). These actions constitute resistance to the employers' culture of surveillance and exploitation. Since they are largely based on the body and its pleasures – smoking, drinking, general horseplay – they are continuous with the primarily physical appeal of 'popular' culture. The most striking instance of bodily resistance to the employers' strictures is when Rushton sends a note to the philanthropists warning them that the removal of any materials from the work-place will result in dismissal, and it is returned to him covered in human excrement (ibid.: 424–5).

Tressell does not recognise the potentially oppositional aspects of the philanthropists' behaviour or 'popular' culture because he views both from the perspective of 'high' culture which sees the body as a threat to 'the refinements of life' (1914 & 1997: 29) and to the advancement of socialism. The philanthropists are more interested in 'downward explosions of flatulence' (ibid.: 220) than in proposals for the elimination of poverty. Although Tressell may believe that 'high' culture is an image of a more complete life than is available under capitalism, it is in fact an expression of the division of labour which lies at its heart. The division between 'high' and 'popular' culture is a division between the body and the mind and so corresponds to the most fundamental division of labour in capitalism itself; that between 'the men who work with their hands and the masters who work with their brains' (ibid.: 138). Adam Smith observed that the division of labour breeds dexterity in a particular trade 'at the expense of [a person's] intellectual, social and martial virtues' (1776 & 1986: 134), while Marx noted, that a 'crippling of body and mind is inseparable from the division of labour in society as a whole' (1867 & 1995: 224). Tressell's attachment to 'high' culture means that *The Ragged Trousered Philanthropists* reproduces a fundamental condition of capitalism even as it seeks to transcend it. 'High' culture cannot therefore be opposed to 'popular' culture since both are implicated in the renewal of the capitalist system of production. Each one, for example, is a commodity: the classical concert requires an entrance ticket as much as the football match and so both reproduce the exchange relation more than they promote alternative ways of being. Tressell only recognises the commodity nature of 'popular' culture but, as Ursula observes of 'high' culture in *The Rainbow*, 'one only learned it in order to answer examination questions, in order that one should have a higher commercial value later on'. And, adds Lawrence, '[s]he was sick with this long service at the inner commercial shrine. Yet what else was there?' (1915 & 1993: 412).

The passive representation of the philanthropists in *The Ragged Trousered Philanthropists* contrasts strongly with the development of the working-class movement in the early years of the century: the Independent Labour Party was formed in 1893, the Labour Representation Committee in 1899 and the Labour Party in 1906. In addition, trade union membership rose and strike action increased consistently from 1902 to 1913, culminating in a prolonged railway strike in 1911. Sympathetic stoppage for the seamen's strike in the same year encouraged different groups of workers to unite, leading to the formation of the Triple Alliance of miners, transport workers and railwaymen in 1914. The difference between Tressell's depiction of a passive working class and an actual active one is due to his dealing with casual labourers not the industrial proletariat. His concern is to awaken such people to the reality of their condition. This is the purpose behind Owen's lectures, drawings, and improvised theatre (Tressell 1914 & 1997: 213–15). These parallel the formal experiments of modern art which are based on the assumption that conventional forms of representation cannot capture the complex nature of reality. The difference, generally speaking, is that Tressell attributes the complex nature of reality to the distorting effects of 'popular' culture whereas artists like Eliot and Woolf attribute it to the nature of modernity itself. The result is that Tressell's formal experiments aim to raise consciousness with a view to the transformation of society, whereas those of modernists assert the integrity of consciousness against the fragmentation of modern life; a condition ultimately related to the refinements of the division of labour associated, for example, with scientific management.

THE INTER-WAR YEARS: WHO SPEAKS FOR THE WORKERS?

The First World War ushered in developments which undermined the structure of the traditional working-class community. The use of women and 'dilutees' to operate machinery that had previously been the preserve of skilled tradesman caused the 'awe that many simpler souls had felt before the mystery of craft to evaporate' (Roberts 1971 & 1983: 199). Similarly, the introduction of mass production techniques led to a lowering of the barriers of caste that previously existed between the skilled worker and his family, bearing out Marx's claim that the various gradations within the ranks of the proletariat are 'equalised in proportion as machinery obliterates all distinctions of labour' (Marx and Engels 1848 & 1968: 43). Those returning from the war contributed to this general dissolution of the working-class hierarchy, not only because they had experienced a greater social mix in the army, but also because the management of the war had taught them to distrust authority. From henceforth, Robert Roberts declares, 'old deference died; no longer did the lower orders believe en masse that class came as natural as knots in the wood' (1971 & 1983: 220).

The years following the First World War were marked by industrial unrest which Cherry (1981) believes was potentially revolutionary, an interpretation Cannadine rejects, claiming that, for all the rhetoric of a polarised society, 'most people continued to believe that Britain was still very finely graded into discrete social layers' (1998: 136). There were a series of strikes in 1919 in Glasgow, Liverpool and London and, in September of that year, railway workers struck for a 48-hour week and won. The British working class were also sympathetic to the Russian Revolution, with delegates attending a 'Hands off Russia' conference in 1920. The Trades Union Council (TUC) even warned that it would organise a general strike unless the government withdrew military support for the counter-revolutionary forces in Russia. The government backed down, but showed greater resolve in the General Strike of 1926 because it had prepared for such an emergency by stockpiling coal and by drawing upon the services of anti-union bodies such as the Organisation for the Maintenance of Supplies. The spark for the strike was the miners' protest at the coal-owners plans for drastic pay cuts, supported by government claims that these were necessary to make industry more competitive. The miners appealed to the TUC who called for selective sympathy strikes mainly in iron, steel, transport, building, electricity and printing. But after nine days the TUC, worried by outbreaks of violence, called upon its members to return to work. Thereafter, the trade unions 'turned away from industrial action in favour of reform through Parliament' (Childs 1995: 7).

Despite confrontations between the working class and government there was, then, no real attempt to overthrow the existing order. The General Strike was about wages not socialism. Furthermore, divisions within the working class prevented any truly concerted action. The majority of workers did not support the General Strike and fewer than half were members of trade unions. These differences were apparent in working-class institutions and writing of the 1920s. The Plebs League was formed in 1908, in opposition to the Workers' Educational Association (1903) which was based, according to its founder, Albert Mansbridge, on Matthew Arnold's view of criticism as the 'disinterested endeavour to learn and propagate the best that is known and thought in the world' (1865 & 1981: 210). Arnold believed that criticism could only achieve this goal by detaching itself from 'the sphere of practical life' (ibid.: 202). The Plebs League, however, believed that 'the best' was an expression of ruling-class interest and that criticism should have a practical application. Its motto was 'I can promise to be candid but not impartial.' True to this principle, the Plebs League demanded that literature promote the proletarian standpoint and propound the laws of historical materialism (Fox 1994: 51).

Many writers, however, found this dictatorial attitude offensive and letters to the organisation's journal, *Plebs*, were keen to point out that working people were perfectly capable of making up their own minds on the issues of the day (Fox 1994: 52). Joe Tarrant, the hero of Harold Heslop's *The Gate of a Strange Field* (1929), objects to the Plebs League proclaiming what the workers ought to think. 'Karl Marx is its lord and King', he snipes, 'not Marx in the spirit, not the theoretical head, but the figurehead, the bogeyman to frighten others' (1929: 111). A similar attitude can be found in Ellen Wilkinson's *Strike* (1929), which adheres to the ordinary miner's view of the General Strike and is dismissive of propaganda for the working class. Both novels, according to Pamela Fox, valorise rank-and-file resistance above the revolutionary transformation preached by the self-appointed guardians of historical materialism (1994: 90). They thus represent a departure from the socialism of *The Ragged Trousered Philanthropists* and a return to the pragmatic and anti-intellectual tradition of the working-class movement.

In the 1920s, working-class writing covered a variety of subjects from industrial strife to tramps, the home and recreation (Klaus 1982 & 1993). However, it is in the 1930s that working-class writing comes to prominence, evident in such novels as *Love on the Dole* (Greenwood 1933 & 1993), *Means Test Man* (1937) and *Cwmardy* (1937). There are at least two reasons for this development: the first is that the decline of modernism favoured a revival of realism, and the second is that unemployment in the early 1930s brought the plight of a section of the working class to the nation's attention. 'Realism' in this context does not mean a Lukácsian representation of a person in the totality of their relations, but rather a respect for the texture of lived experience. It is difficult to say whether this idiom is the property of a particular class or whether it is a shared quality. As we saw in the last chapter, the middle class is hostile to the idea of totality and so its characteristic approach to problems is empirical. Similarly, as Richard Hoggart has pointed out, the 'core' of working-class sensibility 'is a sense of the personal, the concrete, the local' (1957 & 1992: 33), hence it too has little interest in 'general ideas' (ibid.: 102). While it is possible that the middle class has imposed its ideology on the working class, it is also possible that both classes give a different inflection to the common culture of capitalism which, as we have seen, leads to a reified perception of things rather than of the relations between them.

The leap in unemployment following the Wall Street Crash of 1929 and the British financial crisis of 1931 seemed to indicate that capitalism was near to collapse. The parlous state of the capitalist economy was perceived to be a factor in the battle between communism and fascism in the Spanish Civil War (1936–9). The class war suddenly acquired an international dimension and various voices, such as that of Geoffrey Grigson (1905–85), the editor of *New Verse* (1933–9), called upon interested parties to declare their allegiance. The crisis of capitalism had a bearing on attitudes to literary representation. At its simplest, the modernist concern with the self seemed inappropriate in an age of unemployment, poverty and conflict. These had to be confronted and that required a concentration on external events not internal processes. 'Facts', wrote the religious broadcaster Malcolm Muggeridge, 'were wanted about everyone and everything' (cited in Stevenson 1984: 320).

This tendency was particularly apparent in Mass Observation (1937) and the Documentary Film Unit (1928–40). The former recruited observers to report on different aspects of daily life while the latter, under John Grierson, aimed to convince people that a society based on cooperation was better than one based on competition. Both were committed to making people more aware of their world. A crucial part of this process was to challenge conventional representations of the working class as 'the comedy relief, the buffoons, the idiots or the servants' (Baxendale & Pawling 1996: 32). Films such as *Industrial Britain* (1932) and *Coalface* (1935) therefore celebrated the worker as someone who performed an essential service for society. However, this well-intentioned recuperation of the working class also performed an ideological function. It was an attempt to reduce class tension by showing that each person had their part to play in the national community. These films did not therefore aim to change the class system, merely the way it was perceived. In some respects, indeed, they reinforced it since, by idealising the physical nature of work, they perpetuated the hierarchy of mental and manual labour. A similar ambiguity pervades what Lez Cooke (1997) has termed the 'working-class comedies' of the period such as *Sally in Our Alley* (1933). The confrontation in this film between the working-class Sally and the upper-class socialites highlights class differences in contrast to films such as *In Which We Serve* (1942), where they are accepted as part of the natural order. However, as Cooke notes, the final message of 'working-class comedies' is that each class must remain in its own place (1997: 167).

The middle class may have appreciated that the working class were physically active but they deemed them mentally passive. 'Most are accepters', wrote Louis MacNeice (1907–63) in 'Autumn Journal', 'born and bred to harness / And take things as they come' (1939 in Skelton 1977: 45). It was this assumption that justified the middle class speaking for the working class rather than listening to what they had to say. 'We know', W. H. Auden (1907–73) intones in 'A Communist to Others', 'the terrifying brink / From which in dreams you nightly shrink / "I shall be sacked without", you think / "A testimonial"' (1933 in Skelton 1977: 54). The belief in working-class passivity, which preferred the 'dream house' of the cinema to 'weld[ing] a new world' (Day Lewis, 'The Magnetic Mountain' 1933 & 1938 in Skelton 1977: 50, 70), meant that the middle class took the political initiative. 'Come then companions', urged Rex Warner, '[t]his is the spring of the blood, / heart's hey-day, movement of masses, beginning of good' ('Hymn' 1939 in Skelton 1977: 59).

The working class as imagined by the 1930s' poets was very different to the one described by George Orwell (1903–50) in *The Road to Wigan Pier* (1937). This book was included in the Left Book Club series founded by Victor Gollancz in 1938. One of the aims of the Club 'was to provide the indispensable basis of knowledge' which would help create 'a better social and economic order' (Gollancz cited in Reid 1979: 194). Orwell's book fulfilled this aim by its detailed account of working-class life and its analysis of the relations between the classes. He gives a vivid portrayal of poverty and its effects. He sees a woman, 'her sacking apron, her clumsy clogs, her arms reddened by the cold' and notes her face, 'the usual exhausted face of the slum girl who is twenty-five and looks forty thanks to miscarriages and drudgery' (1937 & 1989: 15). Unlike some of his contemporaries, Orwell does not condemn working-class passivity but places it in the context of 'labyrinthine slums' and an 'endless muddle of slovened jobs' (ibid.: 14). 'A thousand influences', he writes, 'constantly press a working man down into a passive role ... he feels himself the slave of mysterious authority and has a firm conviction that "they" will never allow him to do this, that and the other' (ibid.: 44).

Again in contrast to other writers of the period, Orwell appreciates how the differences between the middle and working class prohibit any real alliance between them. These differences are not just to do with money (1937 & 1989: 114) but with 'notions of good and evil, of pleasant and unpleasant, of funny and serious, of beautiful and ugly ... of taste in books and food and clothes, table manners, turns of speech, accent and movements of [the] body' (ibid.: 149). Since these manifest themselves as individual characteristics, class distinctions cannot be discarded merely by an appeal to common humanity but only by 'abolishing a part of yourself' (ibid.: 149) which, Orwell asserts, is a point middle-class socialists have yet to grasp (ibid.: 151). The chief obstacle to the lowering of class barriers is, however, the middle-class view that 'the lower classes smell' (ibid.: 119). The middle-class sensibility finds 'something subtly repulsive about the working-class body' (ibid.: 120), a reaction we have already encountered in Tressell. In social terms, this translates into a fear that the working class will 'sweep all culture and decency out of existence' (ibid.: 123); a fear fuelled by the growing prosperity among certain sections of the working class which were 'ton[ing] down the surface differences between class and class' (ibid.).

Orwell's attachment to the concrete rather than the abstract makes him impatient with the political poetry of the 1930s. Hence he dismisses Auden's famous line in 'Spain' about 'the conscious acceptance of the necessary murder' (1937 in Skelton 1977: 136) as having been 'written by a person to whom murder [was] at most a word' (1940 & 1988: 37). The relationship between the middle-class poets and the working class was rhetorical; it was not the alliance of bourgeois intellectuals and the proletariat predicted by Marx (Marx and Engels 1848 & 1968: 44). But although there is a certain justice in Orwell's remark, it takes too little account of the climate of the 1930s, when the writer's role was 'to express the inarticulate feelings and forces that make for change' (Slater cited in Clark *et al.* 1979: 106) and 'when the brotherhood of man was not only believed in but seemed capable of practical achievement' (Fuller 1973: 137).

While the political poetry of the 1930s may have had a contrived and awkward air, may even have been absurdly naïve in its expression of class conflict – 'you fat man! / You don't want your watch-chain. / But don't interfere with us, because we know you too well. / If you do that you will lose your top hat / and be knocked on the head until you are dead' (Warner 1933 in Skelton 1977: 59–60) – it did at least recognise the existence of class differences and the need to do something about them. It therefore contrasts with other writing of the period, such as Elizabeth Bowen's *The Death of the Heart*, where the sense of class is so deeply embedded it can barely be expressed: 'They want a girl who is someone, if you know what I mean. A girl who – well, I don't quite know how to express it – a girl who did not come from a nice home would not do at all, here' (1938 & 1966: 156). However, the implicit nature of class in Bowen's novel is balanced by the explicit treatment of commodification which is absent in 1930s' poetry. The novel shows how the affections of the heart must give place to the 'self-interest' (ibid.: 90) of society because human beings have been turned into commodities. 'Makes of men date, like makes of cars; Major Brutt was a 1914–18 model: there was now no market for that make' (ibid.).

It is curious that, in these examples, an awareness of commodification seems to exclude an appreciation of class, while an awareness of class seems to exclude an appreciation of commodification; curious because commodification is an expression of the dominance of exchange and hence of the bourgeoisie. The commodification of social life, in other words, is a class relation. However, there is a sense in which commodification suppresses this relation because it institutes a common system of representation and a common measure of value that applies equally to all classes, even though not all classes have equal access to it. To focus on the class struggle ignores the problem of commodification while to focus on commodification is to ignore class. A poet like Randall Swingler (1909–63?) and a novelist like Bowen (1899–1973) shared the same desire for the expression of affections stifled under capitalism. Swingler wanted to 'unloose / The girdle of the heart' (1933 in Skelton 1977: 78) while Bowen shows her characters trying to escape 'from the shut-in room, the turned-in heart' (1938 & 1966: 60). However, because each emphasises either class or commodification, neither can realise their goal. Moreover, they are both trapped in an affective idiom that precludes any rigorous analysis of either class or commodification. In 'September 1, 1939' Auden declared that he wanted to unfold 'the romantic lie in the brain' (1939 in Skelton 1977: 283) but it is his earlier pronouncement in 'Spain' that serves as an epithet for 1930s' writing: 'Tomorrow the rediscovery of romantic love' (1937 in Skelton 1977: 136). The failure to think together class and commodification seems to result in the reproduction of the very conditions against which very different types of writers protest.

LOVE ON THE DOLE

We have seen in the above paragraphs how realism promotes consensus and then shades into romance. A similar conjunction of realism and romance can be found in Walter Greenwood's *Love on the Dole*. Greenwood (1903–74) conveys in compelling prose the poverty endured by the residents of Hanky Park. '[A] bow-legged rickety child just able to walk, came out of the house clad only in his shirt. He toddled to the kerb, and sucking his dirty fingers, made water down the sough then returned to the house' (1933 & 1993: 64). One of the central characters, Larry Meath, attempts, like Frank Owen, to explain the meaning of exchange value to his work colleagues. Money 'is no use in itself. You can't eat it or wear it. If there weren't any things to buy with your money, it wouldn't be any use ... Money means commodities and commodities mean raw material and labour power' (ibid.: 182, 184). Like Owen, he also tries to awaken people to the fact that '[s]ociety has the means, the skill, and the knowledge to afford [everyone] the opportunity to become Men and Women in the fullest sense of those terms' (ibid.: 86) and, like Owen, he meets with scepticism and derision. However, Larry is different to Owen in that he is primarily a romantic figure whose relationship with Sally Hardcastle forms one of the main interests of the story. The effect of Larry's involvement with Sally is to weaken his importance as a socialist. Once he decides to marry her, he takes little further part in politics. When he does, it is to try and prevent the riot in which he is killed (ibid.: 205). His death can be seen as a tragedy in terms of the love interest or as a sign that the working-class intellectual no longer has a part to play in working-class culture.

Romance colours the traditional conception of work as the expression of masculinity. Harry, Sally's younger brother, is painfully conscious of the contrast between himself and the employees of the local engineering firm, Marlowe's. 'He felt ashamed of himself. All these men and boys wore overalls; they weren't clerks, *they* were Men engaged in men's work' (1933 & 1993: 19). Accordingly, Harry applies for an apprenticeship but he soon realises that tending a machine is not, as he thought, 'proper man's work' but 'child's play' (ibid.: 45, 70). Indeed, far from endowing him with masculinity, the lathe reduces Harry to a mere 'cog in the great organisation' (ibid.: 20). Worse still, these 'beautiful, marvellous, wonderful contraptions' (ibid.: 70) that had filled Harry with such pride, are responsible for putting him on the dole. His romantic view of work vanishes with the reality: 'what had been tinged with glamour crumbled to stark and fearful reality' (ibid.: 76). Harry's perception of a gap between romance and reality represents an advance on the philanthropists' understanding of capitalism, but it does not lead to political action. On the contrary, he is as passive as Tressell's philanthropists, seeing himself as a prisoner with 'walls and doors everywhere closing in on him' (ibid.: 172). Harry's only solace is Helen '[o]nly she could assuage this fear of the future', only she makes him feel 'safe and secure' (ibid.: 78, 80).

Both Harry and Larry find a refuge in the personal relationship, the one from the disillusion of work and the other from despair at working-class apathy. They 'won't think for themselves, won't do anything to help themselves … it makes you want to chuck up the whole sponge' (1933 & 1993: 186–7). The romantic union between man and woman is one new locus of identity; another is consumerism. This transforms the traditional appearance of working-class culture: cheap fashionable clothes, for example, mean an end to 'the picturesque clogs and shawls of yesterday' (ibid.: 42). Consumerism and romance are, of course, connected, since Harry and Helen go shopping for furniture when they decide to get married (ibid.: 129–30). However, they cannot afford what they would like, an experience which is intensified by unemployment. Harry 'read the movie play-bills [and] groaned inwardly that he lacked the necessary threepence each for Helen and he' (ibid.: 171). Similarly, Larry is painfully aware that, as a single person, his wages barely cover the necessities of life, a situation marriage can only aggravate (ibid.: 150–2).

It is clear that the identities and pleasures of these characters are centred upon the emerging consumer society. The desire to be part of this society shows a fundamental acceptance of capitalism which complements the circular structure of the novel: it begins and ends with a description of early morning drizzle, a policeman, Blind Joe waking the residents of Hankinson Street, and the 'melancholy hoot of a ship's siren' (1933 & 1993: 13–14, 255–6). This suggests that nothing can change, but in fact the novel is a record of subtle alterations in the composition of the working class in the inter-war years. It is beginning to define itself in terms of consumerism rather than production, which means a greater focus on the individual rather than the class. This is underlined by the respective fates of Larry and Ned Narkey; the one stands for class politics the other for self-seeking individualism. Both are made redundant but Larry dies and Ned becomes a policeman. In contrast to Larry who 'ain't of the strongest' (ibid.: 164), Ned is a 'beefy, hulking brute [who] repelled one' (ibid.: 22). He is a key figure in the suppression of the march protesting at the cut in benefits, and he relishes the prospect of a confrontation: 'Ah hope t' Christ the bastards start summat' (ibid.: 198). The death of Larry in the ensuing riot, in which 'Narkey's great bulk was conspicuous as he laid about him, right and left, recklessly indiscriminate' (ibid.: 205) means that the working class are implicated in the destruction of their own radicalism. Moreover, the emphasis Greenwood gives to Ned's physique in this episode indicates that the body has ceased to be a potential mode of resistance, as it was in Tressell, and has become an instrument of repression.

Although Greenwood may be pessimistic about the possibility of change, other sections of the working class were more hopeful. The Workers' Theatre Movement (1929–33) dramatised *The Ragged Trousered Philanthropists* in 1927, but it mainly concentrated on agitprop, that is, a form of theatre aimed at agitation and propaganda. Agitation referred to 'political activity in relation to day to day campaign demands, issues and struggles'; propaganda to 'the long-term aim of winning the people to the general aims of the labour movement, to education on the underlying reasons and purpose for the fight against capitalism and for socialism' (Clark 1979: 222). Its stage was the street, its style was didactic and its idiom was the slogan. The limitations of this form of theatre led to the establishment of Unity Theatre (1936–9), whose name announced a break from the more sectarian goals of the Workers' Theatre Movement. Its most famous production *Waiting for Lefty*, by the American dramatist Clifford Odets (1906–63), was performed over 300 times between 1936 and 1939. The play concerns a decision by a trade union whether or not to strike. They hope that Lefty will arrive and lead them in their protest. However, as one of the characters remarks, 'What are we waiting for ... Don't wait for Lefty! He might never come' (1937: 45). The point is that the working class must take responsibility for their own destiny and not rely on others, a view we have already encountered in Harold Heslop's *The Gate of a Strange Field* and Ellen Wilkinson's *Strike*. Samuel Beckett (1906–89) used the central idea of *Waiting for Lefty*, of people anticipating the arrival of someone who will solve their problems but who in fact never appears, as the basis for *Waiting for Godot* (1953). This chapter began by noting that modernist artists disdained mass culture, but here one appropriates a genuinely popular play for the purpose of 'high' art and, in the process, transforms progressive class politics into a pessimistic metaphysics of existence.

POST-WAR: AFFLUENCE AND CLASS

Both the middle and working class underwent a series of changes in the inter-war period, whose effects only became clear in the late 1950s. The middle class increased in size and 'drastically changed its composition' (McKibbin 1998: 46). It expanded due to the growth of new occupations, particularly those based in science and engineering, which gave it a more technical character than when it had been dominated by the Church, the law, medicine and the armed forces. The middle class, like the working class, was by no means homogeneous. It covered a variety of professions from lawyers to librarians and contained owner-occupiers as well as those who could only afford rented accommodation. There were also important differences between the urban and the provincial middle class which were further aggravated by religious divisions (ibid.: 70–102). The middle class resolved these tensions within its ranks by developing a style of sociability which frowned on political or religious enthusiasms – the very things which first defined it – and which emphasised personal qualities 'such as niceness and humour' (ibid.: 98). This 'depoliti-cization of relationships' (ibid.: 96) enabled the middle class to see itself as the public; a public, moreover, which was 'directly opposed to the working class' whom they saw as either overpaid or else living comfortably on the dole (ibid.: 58). Indeed, McKibbin claims that this hostility to the working class was the defining quality of the middle class (ibid.: 50).

The working class, too, underwent profound changes during this period. They declined as a proportion of the total population and the skilled component shrank faster than the semi-skilled and unskilled (McKibbin 1998: 106). These changes were related to developments in the economy whereby there was a shift from heavy industry such as coal and shipbuilding to the light indus-tries such as automobiles and electrical goods. Although manual workers' pay rose 241 per cent in the period from 1937 to 1949 (ibid.: 128), the move from heavy to light industry meant the loss of traditional work cultures. The horseplay, talk and gossip which characterised work in the forge or mine were entirely absent from the new factories where the speed of work, and its individual nature, prevented contact with colleagues. The Peek Frean biscuit factory, for example, permitted no talking or 'lark-ing about' and stringently enforced its rules. This management style was in contrast to that of the old industries, where many workers enjoyed a degree of autonomy that was distinctly absent in the new factories. In these, they were subject to the rigours of the 'Bedaux' system – the setting of the assembly line at an opti-mally fast pace – and the constant monitoring of the time-and-motion man.

The 'rate checker' at the bicycle factory where Arthur Seaton, the anti-hero of Alan Sillitoe's *Saturday Night and Sunday Morning,* works 'is public enemy number one' (1958 & 1994: 32). And although Arthur has little control over his working conditions, he does have some autonomy in determining how fast he will work, which in turn determines his earnings. By achieving his quota in the morning he is able to 'dawdle through the afternoon' (ibid.: 31). This gives him the opportunity to play practical jokes such as scaring a woman with a half-stunned mouse (ibid.). His pleasure in the incident comes from aggravating the rate checker, who cannot discover who is responsible for the prank (ibid.). This is in the tradition of the philanthropists 'getting some of their own back'. In general terms, however, there was little room for such behaviour. The power of the 'rate checkers' was a source of aggravation to the workers and was as much a cause of strikes as the need to protect wages and jobs.

The art of the late 1950s and early 1960s focused more on the working class than the middle class. In particular, attention was directed to working-class *culture*, thereby eclipsing its political and economic *relations* with the middle class. The language of citizenship, based on the political consensus over the mixed economy, full employment and the welfare state, seemed to leave culture as the sole marker of class difference (Perkin 1989: 332–3). The growth of white-collar work prompts Charles Lumley, the hero of John Wain's *Hurry on Down,* to observe that with these 'new kinds of jobs ... you couldn't rightly say whether a fella was a workman or a manager' (1953 & 1977: 99). It is only his belief that the working class do not take pride in 'a good job well done' (ibid.: 33, 73), that allows him to separate them from the middle class. The focus on culture as a form of class differentiation is also apparent in films like *A Taste of Honey* (1961) and *A Kind of Loving* (1962) which, while faithfully reproducing the surface of working-class life, refuse to set it in any larger context. The characters are placed in working-class settings but their problems are seen in personal terms rather than as a consequence of structural inequalities. Representations of the working class thus suppressed the issue of class in the very act of staging it.

They also addressed a number of anxieties about post-war Britain, one of which was the nature of British identity in a post-imperial age. The empire had provided an image, however inadequate, of national community. Its loss provoked a need for alternatives which were provided by certain idealised images of the working class. One such was the TV soap opera, *Coronation Street* (1960), whose very name connects a national symbol with a particular locality to create a fantasy of social unity. This unity, however, is premised on the absence of a middle class, and relies on an association between the top and bottom of society more relevant to feudalism than to mid-twentieth-century capitalism. It is an interesting reversal that in the nineteenth century the working class were regarded as a threat to society but in the mid-twentieth were seen as its cohesive force. Ironically, the very moment when the working class were perceived in this manner was the very moment when their communities were being destroyed by redevelopment.

Michael Young and Peter Willmott examined the effects of this dispersal in their classic study *Family and Kinship in East London* (1957). Those who moved from Bethnal Green to Greenleigh may have gained a 'spacious modern home' (1957 & 1970: 132) but they lost a dense network of family and friends with 'mum' as the pivotal figure. The distance from the old neighbourhood and the lack of amenities meant a change from 'a people-centred existence to a house-centred existence' (ibid.: 154). Since there were few opportunities to socialise in Greenleigh, people could not be judged by their personal characteristics but by their appearance and their possessions (ibid.: 154–61). Consequently, life on the new estate was characterised by a competition for status between the inhabitants. This was very different to Bethnal Green, where 'the first thing they think about [someone] is not whether he has a fridge or a car' but whether he is 'bad-tempered, or a real good sport, or the man with a way with women, or one of the best boxers of the Repton Club, or the person who got married to Ada last year' (ibid.: 161). The break-up of traditional communities thus reinforced the trend, which we noticed in *Love on the Dole*, for working-class identity to be expressed through consumerism.

In *Saturday Night and Sunday Morning* Arthur rejects the values of his community, for example, 'settling down'; does not believe in 'sharing'; and regards his expensive clothes as his 'riches' because they 'made him feel good as well as look good' (Sillitoe 1958 & 1994: 47, 66, 168). On a more general note, consumerism is the ally of exchange, since the perception of people in terms of their possessions parallels the perception of commodities in terms of money. In both cases human qualities, either of sociability or labour, exist in an alienated form. Hence the spread of consumerism strengthens the abstract system of representation which lies at the heart of capitalism, making it difficult to develop alternative forms of viewing the social order.

Richard Hoggart examines this, among other issues, in *The Uses of Literacy*. He is interested in the relationship between working-class art and the newer mass art. His argument is that there are elements of working-class art which resist the 'depredations' of the new sort, while others facilitate it (1957 & 1992: 14, 24). Hoggart identifies the main characteristics of working-class culture as a preference for the concrete, a deep attachment to home and family, and a strong sense of group membership based on the perception of the world as divided into 'us' and 'them' (ibid.: 81, 83, 104). Other characteristics include 'tolerance', 'keeping cheerful' and a relish for the small pleasures which break the routine of life such as a 'fish and chips for supper in midweek' (ibid.: 93, 140, 143). These various affiliations and attitudes provide the context for working-class art whose 'overriding interest is in the close detail of the human condition' (ibid.: 120).

Hoggart gives as an example of such art *Peg's Paper*, which consists of advertisements for cosmetics, cures for constipation, beauty hints, horoscopes, stories, and advice on problems. Hoggart notes that the new magazines offer a similar fare but claims that *Peg's Paper* has a 'felt sense for the texture of life in the group it cater[s] for', which the slickly marketed 'glossies' lack (1957 & 1992: 121). It is the same with traditional singing and the new style 'crooning' (ibid.: 154). The former assumes that 'deep emotions about personal experience are something all experience and in a certain sense share' whereas the latter promotes 'a sentimental attitude towards the self' by stressing the incommunicable uniqueness of a feeling (ibid.: 154, 228). In addition, the old-style songs confront the harshness of existence, encouraging people to 'all be cheerful together' whereas the 'more recent ones invite us simply to "dream" or "wish" when in trouble' (ibid.: 226). The difference between working-class art and the new mass art, in short, is that the concrete particularity of the former is replaced by the abstract generality of the latter. The new mass art is 'almost entirely sensational and fantasy-producing [and] cut off from any serious suggestion of responsibility and commitment' (ibid.: 232). A similar view is expressed by Beatie, a character in Arnold Wesker's play, *Roots*, who claims that the 'workers' are responsible for the quality of the art that is presented to them.

> 'We know where the money lies', they say. 'The workers've got it so let's give them what they want. If they want slop songs and film idols we'll give 'em that. If they want words of one syllable, we'll give 'em that then. If they want the third-rate, *blust*! We'll give 'em *that* then. Anything's good enough for them 'cos they don't ask for more!'
>
> (1959 & 1972: 148)

Beatie's reference to the workers having money picks up the idea that high wages were making the working class more middle class. This was known as the *embourgeoisement* thesis and was investigated in some detail by John Goldethorpe and David Lockwood in their study of car workers in Luton. They concluded that 'the idea of appreciable numbers of manual workers and their wives "turning middle class" [was] a highly questionable one' (Goldethorpe *et al.* 1969: 161). This was partly to do with the fact that, despite increased earnings and improved working conditions, the working class still sold their labour. So too did large sections of the middle class, but they received a salary rather than wages and enjoyed better pension and health schemes as well as superior holiday entitlements. The real difference, however, was not so much in earnings as in outlook. The participants in Goldethorpe's and Lockwood's study neither shared nor aspired to the middle-class view of the social structure. Broadly speaking, the middle class saw society as a relatively open hierarchy in which individuals could improve their position by hard work. The working class, by contrast, saw society in terms of an immutable division between 'us' and 'them'. Consequently, there was an emphasis on 'putting up' with things and on helping each other in the face of the vicissitudes of life (ibid.: 118–21). This acceptance of a polarised society encouraged the working class to live in the present, fostering a 'mild hedonism' that the sensationalism of the new mass art ruthlessly exploited (Hoggart 1957 & 1992: 91–6). It also meant that the working class did not demand anything more than was offered, an attitude Beatie berates in her passionate outburst at the end of *Roots*:

> 'Anything's good enough for them 'cos they don't ask for no more!' The whole stinkin' commercial world insults us and we don't care a damn. Well, Ronnie's right – it's our own bloody fault. We want the third rate – we got it.
>
> (Wesker 1959 & 1972: 148)

Beatie's reference to the working class first as 'them' and then as 'us' shows that she is both apart from and a part of that class. Arthur Seaton is in a similar position; he too is inside and outside the working class. However, Beatie's relationship to her class is expressed in mainly cultural terms, Arthur's in mainly economic ones. Wesker uses Beatie to explore the relationship between the cultural aspirations of the working class and the potential of mass art, while Sillitoe uses Arthur to examine the effects of the new consumerism on the traditional working-class sensibility. In both cases the focus is on the individual struggle against that 'extensive and sometimes harsh pressure to conform' which the working class 'imposes on its members' (Hoggart 1957 & 1992: 84). At the end of *Roots*, Beatie finds her own voice, whereas at the end of *Saturday Night and Sunday Morning* Arthur is compelled to submit to the community he has fought against for so long. The relationship between the individual and society, which was a major theme of the nineteenth-century novel, has become the relationship between the individual and his or her class; specifically the struggle to escape it.

Joe Lampton, the hero of John Braine's novel *Room at the Top,* sees the difference between working class and middle class purely in economic terms. 'The ownership of the Aston-Martin automatically placed the young man in a social class far above mine; but that ownership was simply a question of money [and] I was going to enjoy all the luxuries which that young man enjoyed' (1957 & 1991: 28–9). Joe wants to be middle class because he will be able to afford more things. Jimmy Porter, the protagonist of John Osborne's play *Look Back in Anger*, is different to Joe in that he is a reluctant entrant to the middle class through his marriage to Alison, the daughter of a diplomat. His famous outburst, 'There aren't any good brave causes left' (1957 & 1983: 84) is an indictment of a class that seems to have lost its sense of direction. Jimmy, says his wife, Alison, is an 'eminent Victorian' (ibid.: 90) and it is from that perspective that he excoriates the timid, cliché-ridden middle class of his day with its obsessive concern for respectability. The energy and vitality of Joe and Jimmy stand in sharp contrast to that middle-class 'style of sociability' which, as we noted earlier, prohibited discussion of important issues. The passion banished by the middle class returns as upwardly mobile members of the working class enter its ranks; its precise effect, however, remains a moot point.

The migration from one class to another suggested that class barriers were crumbling and, in the 1960s, commentators believed that Britain was making great progress towards becoming a classless society. As evidence for their claim, they cited the popularity of northern pop groups such as the Beatles and the lionising of figures like the actor Michael Caine, the model Twiggy and the photographer David Bailey. However, as Francis Wheen points out, 'entertainment had always been a profession in which working-class or lower-middle-class people could rise [and] as the industry expanded to incorporate television, fashion photography and modelling, it inevitably allowed a few more working-class talents to reach the top' (1982: 114). The spread of mass culture had convinced commentators that Britain was a unified society. People dressed in a similar fashion, watched the same television programmes and aspired to the same consumer goods. Class seemed to be fading away and those who sought to maintain the old divisions were heavily criticised, as in the film *I'm Alright Jack* (1959). The appearance, however, was very much at odds with the reality. For example, Brian Abel-Smith and Peter Townsend found in their study *The Poor and the Poorest* (1965) that the number of people living in poverty had doubled between 1953 and 1960. Similarly, John Westergaard and Henrietta Resler showed that there had been little change in the proportion who owned private property. In 1911 the richest 10 per cent owned 92 per cent of the nation's wealth and in 1960 they owned 83 per cent: despite rising standards of living, there was a marked persistence of economic inequality (1975: 112, 119).

We can see evidence of this in Barry Hines' novel *A Kestrel for a Knave* (1968). Billy Casper lives with his mother and older brother, Jud, on a new council estate where the houses are already damp and where prams rust in the front gardens. Billy can be seen as a symbol of all those on the outside of the affluent society. On his paper round he looks into a house and sees that the 'hall and stairs were carpeted' and that there is a 'radiator with a glass shelf

along one wall' (1968: 16). This is in direct contrast to Billy's
home which has lino and no central heating (ibid.: 9). The
poverty of his physical environment is matched by the poverty
and, indeed, brutality of his emotional one. His mother takes no
interest in him, merely pausing to give him money as she rushes
to the pub '[h]ere, there's two bob for you, go and buy yourself
some pop or crisps or summat', while his brother's vicious bully-
ing climaxes in his killing Billy's beloved hawk (ibid.: 39, 149).
The world Billy inhabits is very different to the one described by
Hoggart. Here there is no attachment to home and family, neither does Billy think in traditional terms of 'us' and 'them';
rather, he sees himself as alone and in conflict with the world.
Billy's hawk symbolises his spirit: '[i]t's fierce an' it's wild, an' it's
not bothered about anybody, not even about me, right. And that's
why it's great' (ibid.: 118). He is the heir to Arthur Seaton whose
motto, 'don't let the bastards grind you down' (Sillitoe 1958 &
1994: 40), could serve as Billy's own. Billy is like Arthur in
another respect; he too is trapped in his class. He does not want
to follow his brother down the mine (Hines 1968: 139) but his
poor education means that he has little idea of what he does want
to do. He receives no help from his careers officer who 'printed
MANUAL on the form' and then dismissed him with the remark
' I haven't got all day you know, I've other lads to see before 4 o'
clock' (ibid.). Billy differs from Arthur, however, in his poverty.
He is a symbol not so much of the working class as of an emerging underclass.

This ideologically loaded term was widely used in the 1980s
and the 1990s as economic recession, de-industrialization and
cuts in welfare increased the number of poor in Britain and the
United States. The term 'underclass' combines concerns about
delinquency, dependency and unemployment. Those on the right
use the term to refer to 'those unwilling to take jobs' and to the
rise in the number of single mothers, particularly, in the USA,
black ones (Pilling 1996: 31). Those on the left argue that the

underclass is an integral part of the class system, since it means that those in work can be replaced by those out of work should the former agitate for higher wages or better conditions. What this analysis does not take into account is the alienation that members of the underclass feel in relation to mainstream society. Renton, the narrator of Irvine Welsh's *Trainspotting* positively rejects the accoutrements of a 'normal' life: 'the fact is that ye jist simply choose tae reject what they have to offer. Choose us. Choose life. Choose mortgage payments; choose washing machines; choose cars ... Well, ah choose no tae choose life' (1993: 187–8). He chooses 'smack' instead (ibid.).

THE CLASSLESS SOCIETY?

We have seen that, during the course of the century, class was increasingly perceived in cultural rather than economic terms. The main reason for this shift of emphasis was the decline of manufacturing industry and the growth of the service economy, which blurred the old class boundary between manual and non-manual labour. The measurement of class according to occupation, therefore, becomes more of a problem, and other factors, such as social attitudes, cultural aspirations and lifestyle, have to be taken into account. This explains the focus on culture that was characteristic of writing about the working class in the late 1950s and early 1960s. However, the development of the consumer society dissolved the traditional links between class and culture by appropriating elements associated with different groups and combining them in a commodified form. One example of this process was the use of 'Nessun dorma' for the 1990 Football World Cup: the aria 'elevated' football which, in turn, 'popularised' opera. The message of mass culture seemed to be – and indeed still is – that we live in a classless society.

There are two main objections to this assertion. The first is that inequality still exists and the second is that mass culture is the means by which the dominant class universalises its values. We have already alluded to the continued existence of inequality but it is worth repeating the point. Pat Barker's novel, *Liza's England*, tells the story of Liza Jarrett from her childhood to her death. She is born into poverty and dies in poverty. 'I haven't got any money', she tells the boys who rob her, '[a]ll I've got's me pension' (1986 & 1999: 267). Barker's novel draws clear parallels between the past and the present to underline the point that the working class continue to suffer under capitalism. She shows, for example, how unemployment runs like a scar through the century. Liza's husband loses his job at the steelworks in the 1930s, while the father of the other main character in the book, Stephen, is made redundant in the 1980s from the engineering firm where he had worked for thirty years (ibid.: 40, 144). The youths who attack and kill Liza, however, have never worked since there are no jobs for them. They are part of the underclass who spend their time vandalising the estate and sniffing glue (ibid.: 7–15). Billy Casper could have been their father.

There are many reasons for the levels of unemployment on Britain's run-down estates. They include new technology, the deregulation of finance, the use of cheap foreign labour and the stripping away of union power. These developments are examples of how the capitalist class dominates the working class in its pursuit of profit. The terms 'capitalist class' and 'working class' are problematic at this point in history, when there is so much discussion about what constitutes a class. John Scott, in his investigation of whether there is a 'capitalist class' in Britain, concludes that there is, though it is now based more on investments in 'direct-ownership stakes, membership of partnerships and trusts or shareholdings' than on active participation in business (1991: 67). Similarly, Ralph Milliband claims that the working class not only still exists, but that the term should be expanded to include all white-collar employees since they too produce surplus value for the capitalist (1991: 38). Although it is possible to argue about the exact composition of these classes, the evidence seems to suggest that there exists a dominant class with the capacity 'to create and maintain conditions under which it is able to appropriate surplus labour' from a subordinate class (ibid.: 8). It is this relation which, in Marxist terms, is the source of the poverty and inequality so graphically documented by Nick Davies in his book *Dark Heart* (1997).

In the tradition of, among others, Henry Mayhew and George Orwell, this work is concerned to highlight the causes as well as the culture of poverty. Davies notes that between 1979 and 1992 the wages of the highest paid grew by 50 per cent while those of the lowest paid actually fell below what they had been in 1975 (1997: 174–5). During Mrs Thatcher's first term of office (1979–83) the unemployed had their benefits cut, as did pensioners, pregnant women and the disabled. More was to follow. Housing benefit and the rate support grant were cut, while council house rents were raised. Young people under 18 lost their general right to receive any benefit, which was a contributory factor in the growth of homelessness among that age group. Income Support, which had replaced Supplementary Benefit, was itself replaced by the Jobseeker's Allowance, which would be withheld if claimants did not accept offers of work regardless of its suitability. A loan, known as the Social Fund, replaced the exceptional hardship grant that the poor were previously entitled to if they ran into a crisis, and the cost of repaying the loans left many without enough money for proper food or adequate clothing (ibid.: 291). The cuts in welfare benefit saved £12 billion, £8 billion of which funded tax cuts for the rich (ibid.: 293): a stark example of how the dominant class was able to use its power to consolidate its wealth.

The combined effect of unemployment and welfare cuts was to impoverish a third of the British people (Davies 1997: 144). There are significant differences, however, between poverty today and poverty in the early and middle years of the century. The privations that Liza endures in Barker's novel are the direct consequences of class relations. There is a clear connection between 'people who work their guts out and people who get the profit' (1986 & 1999: 56). Poverty is part of the lived relations of class: Liza's mother, for example, cleans for the factory-owning Wynyards, and her father works for them, every night bringing home 'the smell of iron' (ibid.: 27). The experience of poverty thus occurs within an immediate class context which has largely disappeared from British life: where Liza encountered the bourgeoisie, the unemployed encounter the police, the social workers and the probation officers, a whole army of officials who act as a buffer between the top and bottom of British society.

The sense of community was also a key component in the traditional working-class experience of poverty. 'We were a lot poorer [and] it was a physically gruelling life but people shared the burden. Everyone helped out' (cited in Danziger 1997: 109). Liza makes a similar point.

> We had a way of life, a way of treating people. You didn't just go to church one day a week and jabber on about loving your neighbour. You got stuck in seven days a week and bloody did it, because you knew if you didn't you wouldn't survive.
>
> (Barker 1986 & 1999: 218)

This contrasts with the present where, according to Stephen, people 'chaf[e] against each other without intimacy, without community' (ibid.: 64). Davies gives a real life example of the deterioration of a community in his account of Hyde Park, a housing estate in Leeds. The community centre was the first place to close, then the churches. Those who took advantage of the 'right to buy' legislation sold their council houses to professional landlords 'who divided the houses into small flats and rented them out on short lets to anyone who would take them' (1997: 47–8). There was violence on the street and people were frightened to go out. Jean Ashford, who had lived on the estate from the beginning, told Davies that it had changed from one where people believed 'in living in peace and harmony in a community to which everyone belonged' to one where people 'believed in nothing' (ibid.: 51). This estate, like many others that house the 'underclass', is riddled with subcultures of crime, drugs and prostitution (ibid.: 236). Although these subcultures stand outside the law, their values of money, power and excitement are those of mainstream society. Working-class culture, by contrast, was governed by values quite different to those holding sway in capitalism; for example, cooperation rather than competition. Its disintegration into subcultures is at once a sign of increased inequality and the triumph of capitalist ideology, albeit in its most anarchic form.

I said above that there were two objections to the idea that we are now living in a classless society. The first, the continued existence of inequality, we have just considered, and it is now time to look at the second, the claim that mass culture is an expression of bourgeois values. Marx declared that, in capitalist society, 'culture ... is a mere training to act as a machine' (Marx and Engels 1848 & 1968: 49). Adorno's analysis of what he calls the 'culture industry' can be taken as an interpretation of Marx's claim. The 'culture industry' refers first of all to a fusion of work and leisure. The very nature of amusements, such as the video game, is further training in the use of technology which is essential to the continued development of capitalism. Moreover, just as a car is made from standard parts so is a film made of standard components of plot and character (Adorno and Horkheimer 1944 & 1992: 137). Both work and leisure reinforce one another to promote the values of capitalism. Industry 'is interested in people merely as customers and employees', and has in fact 'reduced mankind as a whole and each of its elements to this all-embracing formula' (ibid.: 147). 'The individual', writes Adorno, 'is tolerated only so long as his [her] complete identification with the generality is unquestioned' (ibid.: 154). Consequently, it is possible for any one individual to replace any other, just as a machine receives a new part when the old one no longer works. Although all individuals are equal to the extent that they are identified with the general, they are identified with it in different ways. Differences between cultural products, for example a Keats poem and a pop song, exist to classify, organise and label consumers. 'Something must be provided for all so that none may escape; the distinctions are emphasised and extended' (ibid.: 123). The differences between one consumer good and another not only classify 'individuals' but also confer on them a 'pseudo individuality' which makes them appear unique when in fact they are mere variations of the 'totality' (ibid.: 154–5).

The 'culture industry' can thus be said to take the value of individualism from the middle class and the value of the group from the working class, abolishing the tension between them so that each becomes a mirror of the other. To the extent that the 'culture industry' is an artificial synthesis of middle- and working-class values, it appears to transcend class. However, because in the manner of exchange it replaces what is individual with what is general, the 'culture industry' represents the triumph of the bourgeoisie; but it is a hollow triumph since for them, too, 'personality scarcely signifies anything more than shining white teeth and freedom from body odour and emotions' (Adorno and Horkheimer 1944 & 1992: 167). Nor does there seem to be any possibility of altering this state of affairs because 'the rhythm of mechanical production and reproduction promises that nothing changes' (ibid.: 134). With the 'culture industry', we come to the end of history.

The work of the Centre for Contemporary Cultural Studies at Birmingham (CCCS), founded by Hoggart in 1964 and later run by Stuart Hall, was a reaction against this account of mass culture (Harris 1992). In the first place, it acknowledged the existence of class and, in the second, it argued that the working class did not

simply accept the messages of the mass media but actively negotiated them within the context of their own experience.
Meanings, in other words, are not passively consumed but
actively produced. Of particular importance here was Gramsci's
concept of hegemony, which describes how the dominant class
seeks to maintain its position by persuading subordinate ones
that its values are in the interests of all, a process which involves
constant struggle, negotiation and compromise. More specifically,
hegemony works through ideology, not primarily as a system of
false ideas about the social order, but by 'inserting the subordinate class into the key institutions and structures which support
the power and social authority of the dominant order. It is, above
all, in these structures and relations that a subordinate class lives
its subordination' (Clarke *et al.* 1976: 39).

An example of the work of the CCCS is their study of youth
culture in *Resistance through Rituals* which tested the claim that
class had been eroded by the advent of affluence, mass culture and
spread of education. (Clarke *et al.* 1976). In hegemonic terms,
these developments functioned to dismantle working-class resistance and 'deliver the spontaneous consent of that class to the
authority of the dominant one' (ibid.: 40). However, as hegemony
involves resistance as well as dominance, the aim of the CCCS
was to show how the various youth cultures were able to create
their own meanings out of the resources offered to them. Hence
the bootlace tie of the teddy boy, appropriated from the slick city
gambler in Westerns, was at once an expression of his social reality, his status as an outsider, and his social aspiration, to win status for his ability to live by his wits (Jefferson 1976: 8).
Skinheads 'struggled' against the decline of the working-class
community by re-creating it through gang membership (Clarke
1976: 99). Mods 'negotiated' consumer culture by first appropriating the commodity, then by redefining its use and value before
finally relocating its meaning within a totally different context.
'Thus the scooter, a formerly ultra-respectable means of transport

was appropriated and converted into a symbol of solidarity' (Hebdige 1976: 93). Although these examples showed that hegemony could not absolutely absorb the working class into the dominant order, there was also a strong sense that the economic relations of class were decisive, since they condemned the members of subcultures to 'educational disadvantage, dead-end jobs and low pay', which no amount of 'ritual' can remove (ibid.: 47).

There were problems in trying to maintain this dual perspective, as was apparent in the mismatch between the prominence given to class in the long introduction to *Resistance through Rituals* and its low profile in the individual chapters. Consequently, it was not always clear how the 'rituals' described related to class. The case of the teddy boy suggests the replacement of working-class solidarity by the desire for upward mobility, but this was not brought out in the analysis. The account of the skinheads is also questionable, since gangs have been a factor in the behaviour of young men long before the disappearance of working-class communities. Furthermore, as Hebdige himself suggests, the mods do not really resist the system so much as retreat from it, seeking compensation for their low status in an amphetamine-fuelled hedonism (1976: 91). A related problem was that, while the contributors assumed a class context to the rituals they described, there was no discernible class consciousness among the youths themselves.

As the work of the CCCS diversified in the 1970s and 1980s, the concept of class was replaced by that of discourse. 'Discourse', declares Dave Morley, 'cannot be explained by or reduced to classes' (1980: 172). There is no single meaning to 'discourse' but in cultural studies it is generally taken to refer to the work of the French philosopher Michel Foucault (1926–84) who used the term to describe how specific institutions, such as law and medicine, produced and organised forms of authoritative knowledge which regulated the behaviour of everyone in society. Each 'discipline' has its own specialist discourse which has the power to name, account for and process those who come into contact with it. An important concern, therefore, is to analyse the institutional base of discourse, asking questions such as who is permitted to speak, to whom and under what conditions? Discourse is also seen as a site and object of struggle, where different groups strive for the right to determine meaning. Although discourse theory is closely related to Gramsci's concept of hegemony, it is not, as is the latter, ultimately grounded in a theory of class. Foucault rejects the binary model of bourgeois and proletariat, calling instead 'for a plurality of autonomous struggles, waged throughout the micro-levels of society, in the prisons, asylums, hospitals and schools' (Best & Kellner 1991: 56). It is this notion of 'micro-struggle' rather than 'macro-struggle' that inspired the ethnic and feminist and sexual identity politics of the 1980s and the 1990s, as groups attempted 'to contest the hegemonic discourses that position individuals within the straitjacket of normal identities in order to liberate the free play of difference' (ibid.: 57). The idea that identity is constructed and that it can be contested gave rise to a politics of subjectivity which 'celebrates fragmented and libidinal states of being over personal and social identity' (ibid.: 290). While discourse theory is certainly a useful corrective to a Marxist model which reduces the complexity of social reality and its multiplicity of identities to the uniformity of class, it nevertheless overlooks the profound connections between the economic base and the superstructure whereby what is celebrated as freedom may in fact be an oppression. For example, is it not possible to see the postmodern delight in fragmentation as the culmination of that process of the separation of body and mind which we traced to the nature of the commodity?

The work of John Fiske brings a number of these issues into sharp relief. 'Popular culture', he writes, 'is made by subordinated peoples in their own interests out of resources that also, contradictorily, serve the economic interests of the dominant' (1989a: 2); and he uses this paradigm to account for a range of phenomena from shopping to rock music. In his view, the aim of 'evading' or 'resisting' the dominant culture is 'pleasure'. People evade the dominant culture when they engage in certain activities, such as video games or fairground rides, which release the body 'from its social definition and control [in] a moment of carnivalesque freedom closely related to Barthes's *jouissance*' (1989b: 83). People resist the dominant order when they alter the meaning of commodities, for example, by tearing a pair of jeans, to suit their own purposes rather than those of the system (ibid.: 14–15). The meaning of commodities, Fiske concludes, lies not in 'their condition of production but by the way they are consumed' (1989a: 28).

Fiske's account of popular culture both draws on and denies the concept of class. It draws on class by re-working Marx's account of the antagonistic relations between the bourgeoisie and the proletariat as a generalised relation between the dominant and subordinate groups, but it denies class by shifting attention away from production to consumption, thereby suppressing problems of inequality and exploitation. Fiske, therefore, fails to provide a context for understanding the struggle between the dominant and subordinate groups: he forgets that though people make meanings, they do so under conditions not of their own choosing. He barely acknowledges the economic forces or political and ideological relations which limit consumers' ability to produce meanings, preferring instead to concentrate on the bodily pleasures of opposition (ibid.: 6). This represents the triumph of the philanthropists' improvisation over Owen's socialist vision since they too prize the physical sensations of 'getting some of their own back' over expositions of the social structure. The most serious criticism of Fiske's model, however, is that he offers no evidence for his view that consumers are engaged in acts of 'semiotic resistance' (1989a: 10) against commodity culture: that is how he sees them, not how they see themselves. Consequently, he has no basis for claiming that shoppers are really subverting the values of the market. Fiske, like many before him, speaks for others rather than allowing them to speak for themselves, thus underlining the continued exclusion of a large majority from the organs of opinion-formation. Moreover, what Fiske fails to appreciate, and what Adorno understood, is that consumption has now become the instrument of social classification. We noted earlier that people were increasingly identified in terms of their possessions; now this process has been refined by niche marketing, which ensures that all sections of society are ranked in terms of commodities. This implies a return to a more status-based society but with this difference: in the medieval period a person's status was related to their function in society but this connection has now disappeared.

CLASS AND POST-STRUCTURALISM

The fate of class in cultural studies is paralleled by its fortunes in post-structuralist literary theory, a broad body of writing inspired by the work of, among others, Foucault, Lacan and Derrida. There was a tension in traditional literary criticism between valuing a work and placing it in it historical context. F. R. Leavis, a dominant figure in traditional criticism, argued that while the work was 'indubitably there' its context could only ever be a 'construction' (1953 & 1986: 197). Furthermore, he believed that only literature could respect the 'complexity [of] cultural values' which received scant attention 'in the doctrine, strategy and tactics of the Class War' (ibid.: 33). Leavis claimed that because Marxism used an abstract language it could not appreciate human autonomy, whereas literary criticism could because of its 'vigilan[ce] and scrupulous[ness] about the relation between words and the concrete' (ibid.: 43). Tony Bennett, however, claims that this 'reinforce[d] class differentiation at the level of language' (1979: 161), thereby giving the lie to Leavis' view that 'there [was] a point of view above classes' (ibid.: 35). Although Leavis was frequently criticised for being elitist it was not until the late

1970s, with the advent of French 'theory', that his work was effectively challenged.

The first wave of 'theory' included the work of the French Marxists Louis Althusser and Pierre Macherey. They argued that literature was not so much an expression of a class's 'collective consciousness' (Goldmann 1964 & 1975: 9) as an exposure of the ideological contradictions of capitalism. Althusser, for example, describes the ability of art to 'make us see ... the ideology from which it is born, in which it bathes [and] from which it detaches itself as art' (1966 & 1996: 270). This view of the relationship between literature and ideology depended on a distinction between art that was 'authentic' and art that was 'mediocre' (ibid.). Post-structuralism, particularly that branch of it known as deconstruction, challenged this distinction, claiming that such binary oppositions were untenable and inherently unstable. The concept of 'literature' as a 'superior' form of writing was also under attack from cultural studies, which saw literary value as a mystification 'through which the ruling block exercised its hegemony' (Easthope 1991: 70). The argument was that 'literature' contained no intrinsic merit which set it apart from 'popular' writing and that all texts lent themselves to being discussed in terms of six related concepts: 'institution, sign system, ideology, gender, identification and subject position' (ibid.: 71). This desire to eliminate differences between texts, to impose on them common properties whereby they can be measured against each other, is consistent with the operation of exchange and is therefore not as radical a gesture as it at first seems.

The dissolution of the idea of 'literature' was paralleled by the dissolution of the concept of class. There were many reasons for this development which manifested itself in a shift from a Marxist to a postmodern paradigm, but perhaps the most important was that traditional accounts of class had ignored the issues of race, gender and culture. The subsequent concentration on these problems, however, may have diverted attention from the growth of poverty. Anne Phillips believes this was the case, claiming that 'fights on the race and gender fronts obscured real, persisting and fundamental economic divisions' (*Guardian* 4.9.99). Ultimately, of course, race, gender, sexuality and culture cannot be separated from class. For example, the film *The Full Monty* (1997) shows how a group of steelworkers, after being made redundant, have to abandon a masculinity based on heavy industry and adopt a more 'artistic' one as they train themselves to become strippers. The challenge is to appreciate the difference between the heterogeneity of postmodern identity and the homogeneous one of class, but not to regard them as mutually exclusive. In part this means attending to the question of class more than has been the case in recent years, particularly as inequality has again become a visible and talked-about feature of British society. We have already looked at Davies' *Dark Heart* and David Walker notes that, by the mid-1990s, 'Britain had become more unequal than at any time since the 30s' (*Guardian* 3.11.98). The widening gap between the rich and poor has not resulted in a sharpening of class consciousness but, perversely, in a consensus that 'we are all middle class now' (*Guardian* 29.12.99): four out of the seven bands in the recently revised description of social class issued by the Office of National Statistics (1998) fall into this category.

A closer examination, however, reveals a more complex and uncertain picture. Bert Prescott, the father of John Prescott, the deputy prime minister (March 2000), received a lot of press coverage when he contradicted his son's claim to be middle class by insisting he was working class because that was the class into which he had been born (*Guardian* 16.7.99). Such confusions help to explain the palpable nostalgia for an older order, as witnessed by the enormous popularity of television costume dramas such as *Middlemarch* (1993) and *Pride and Prejudice* (1995). The poetry of Tony Harrison, by contrast, revisited the problems of the scholarship boy and the rift education could cause in working-class families: 'what's still between 's / not the thirty or so years, but books, books, books' (1984: 126). He also, in poems such as 'Them & [uz]' confronted the cultural establishment over its exclusion of the working class from the literary heritage. 'Poetry's the speech of Kings. You're one of those / Shakespeare gives the comic bits to: prose' (ibid.: 122).

John King's *The Football Factory* takes a hard look at what it means to be working class in the 1990s. It is narrated by Tom Johnson, who works in a warehouse during the week and is a soccer hooligan at weekends. He is aware of the nature of society, attacking the free market because 'there's no help for those who can't look after themselves' (1996: 64). He is also class conscious, criticising 'people [who] talked about the working class but didn't have a clue what the working class was all about' (ibid.: 116). However, Tom has no sense of the working-class traditions of self-improvement or social transformation and so his hostility to 'the money men' (ibid.: 149) is diverted into violence against opposing football fans. Tom's viciousness would seem to support Tony Parsons' claim that 'something has died' in the working class, 'a sense of grace, all feelings of community, their intelligence, decency and wit' (1994: 228). However, Parsons fails to appreciate how market forces have devastated working-class communities and brutalised their inhabitants, something Tom understands but to which he still succumbs.

CONCLUSION

The post-structuralist approach to literature has focused on the cultural issues of race, gender and sexuality rather than the economics of class. The concept of class implies an ability to imagine society as a structured whole based on particular economic relations. Post-structuralism, however, is suspicious of the idea of the whole and therefore of class-based analyses. The word 'class', for example, does not even appear in the index of Easthope's otherwise excellent account of the rise of British post-structuralism (1991). Post-structuralism was, in part, a reaction to a view of the literary work as a complex unity where all the parts were subordinated to the expression of a single meaning. Post-structuralists argued that the work could generate many meanings, not just one. They based their claim on Saussure's view that language was a system of concepts for organising reality, not a means of representing its truth. Accordingly, literary works should be viewed as constructs, not as mirror images of a pre-existing reality. These constructs, moreover, served to naturalise the values of the dominant order and hence repressed those which threatened to negate that process. The aim of post-structuralist criticism was to draw attention to the constructed nature of the work, to tease out its repressed meanings, disseminate and multiply them, and to create diversity in place of unity.

Post-structuralism is part of the Marxist tradition to the extent that it saw literature as a branch of the dominant ideology, but is distanced from it by its antipathy to the principle of unity, whether in literary or social terms. Post-structuralism therefore contained a contradiction. On the one hand, it recognised that cultural products were embedded in a wider social context but, on the other, it seemed to imply that their meanings could be endlessly multiplied without any sense of constraint. It is this latter aspect which has been stressed most in the subsequent development of post-structuralism. The result was that, while the cultural context of the work continued to be elaborated, its economic one was progressively ignored. This is a large claim but even a cursory glance at the diverse and complex body of post-structuralist writing supports the view that the economic relations of class have not received the same detailed attention as gender or race. The dislocation between class and culture represents a departure from two traditions: the Marxist tradition which tries to relate culture to the economic base of society, and the English tradition which has used a conception of culture as 'the harmonious development of those qualities and faculties that characterise our humanity' (Coleridge cited in Williams 1958 & 1975: 77) to criticise the purely economic definition of people in capitalism. The Marxist tradition sees culture as an expression of bourgeois capitalism, the English tradition sees it as a corrective of a profit-driven society.

Although these two traditions are distinct, they are also complementary. Tressell was able to combine a Marxist analysis of society with an appeal to 'high' culture. The belief that 'high' culture contains values that are critical of capitalism is not readily acceptable today. In the first place, there is the problem of defining 'high' culture and, in the second, it is hard to dismiss the conventional view that 'high' culture reinforces economic divisions. But 'popular' culture is also difficult to define and it, too, is implicated in the economic arrangements of capitalism. The emphasis on the subversive nature of 'popular' culture has, however, obscured this fact. I have argued that what is conventionally regarded as 'literature' is associated with the rise of the exchange relation and hence the middle class. However, we should not conclude from this that 'literature' always supports the status quo. On the contrary, as Tressell realised, it upholds 'human' against economic values even if it does not always recognise how those values can sometimes be appropriated by the very system they oppose. 'Literature', in short, has the potential to transcend its determinations and offer an image of a fuller, richer life than that which exists under capitalism. At first sight 'popular' culture appears to be classless: it invites everyone to partake of its pleasures, it is based on consumption rather than production, and appeals to individuals rather than groups. However, 'popular' culture is more identified with exchange than 'literature' because it equates human qualities with commodities and identifies the popular with the profitable. As such, it, too, represents the triumph of the middle class.

The traditional aim of class analysis is to understand the

connection between a particular economic arrangement and a particular cultural expression. The problem with that approach, however, is that we can no longer define class in terms of owners and non-owners of the means of production. We have moved from an economy where money was invested in industry to an economy where money is invested in money. The global movement of money means it is hard to give it a local class identity. What we should note instead is how money determines the very coordinates of culture: its structures of representation and means of evaluation. Unless we attend to how money shapes culture, it is unlikely that we can escape being defined by it. There is no part of cultural life which does not speak in the idiom of money. It is for that reason that we are all 'middle class' now. Except, of course, for the poor, whose plight reminds us that class, and what we mean by it, is once more an issue in British society.

GLOSSARY

(Compiled by Joy Dye)

Age of Reason this term refers to the Augustan and Restoration period of the eighteenth century. Reason was associated with order, restraint, balance and harmony.

capitalism social system based on the private ownership of capital and means of production. The goal of capitalism is to maximise productivity.

commodification the process of producing goods for exchange rather than for use.

cultural materialism the analysis of a text within the various contexts of its production and reception and seeing how it both reproduces and finally resists aspects of the dominant order.

discourse traditionally a discussion or treatise, either written or spoken. Now generally refers to how different disciplines, for example law and medicine, produce and organise systems of 'knowledge' about the world. The term usually implies a power relation between those who possess this knowledge and those who lack it.

enclosure system in general, the conversion of land normally used for crops into pasture for grazing. This involved the eviction of tenant farmers from their land and from common land.

estates a system of hierarchical society with individuals categorised according to social rank. In England, the three estates were traditionally spiritual lords, temporal lords and commons.

exchange value the amount of 'socially necessary labour time' needed to produce a commodity. It is this 'socially necessary labour time' which allows commodities to be compared and the difference between them is expressed in terms of money.

feudalism   administrative system introduced into England after the Norman Conquest. Under feudal law, all land belonged to the Crown and lords were placed as tenants over certain areas. Each lord swore loyalty to the one above him all the way to the king. Peasants were legally bound to work the land their lords owned.

great chain of being   the belief that everything has been created and has its divinely ordered place in the natural world.

hegemony   the process of struggle, negotiation and compromise entailed in the attempt by the dominant class to get their ideas and values accepted by the subordinate one.

heroic couplet   decasyllabic lines of poetry arranged in rhyming pairs. Almost always in iambic pentameter.

historical materialism   the basic idea of Marxism that seeks the ultimate cause of all historical events in the economic development of society, in the changes in the mode of production and exchange, and in the consequent division of society into classes and in the struggle of those classes against each other.

humanism   humanism flourished during the Renaissance period with a revival of classical literature. Secular humanism sought to raise the dignity of man by emphasising his potential and by placing him at the head of creation.

ideology   a spontaneously held system of belief and thought which often reflects the interests of the dominant class in society.

laissez-faire   from the French meaning 'leave us alone'. This phrase was used by the free traders who opposed government interference and sought the removal of international trade restrictions.

Marxism   see historical materialism above. In addition, a concern with the precise relation between the economic base and the superstructure, i.e. law, religion, culture and so forth.

picaresque   picaresque literature describes the adventures of a rogue in service to several masters, satirising the society in which it takes place.

post-structuralism   based on Ferdinand de Saussure's distinction between the signifier (the sound or the written form of the word) and the signified (the concept or idea), the two components of the sign. The main idea is that meaning is a function of language rather than a reflection of reality. Consequently, it is possible to change reality by 'describing' it differently. The fact that meaning is not rooted in 'reality' makes it ultimately indeterminate.

proletariat   the working class whose sole value is defined in terms of its labour power. Seen in contrast to the bourgeoisie owning capital and means of production.

Restoration comedy   drama that developed from the restoration of the English monarchy in 1660. Reacting against the puritan age, Restoration comedy presented an elegant, fashionable society with elements of sexual intrigue and flirtation.

romance form   having its roots in chivalric adventure, romance is usually removed from everyday life, with elements of love and gallantry.

serfdom   state of servitude in the Middle Ages whereby serfs were forced to work for their lord for free at given times or else donate a portion of their harvest to him.

socialism   socio-political system of organisation based on state ownership of the means of production. Rooted in the desire for collective benefit over the pursuit of self-interest.

tropes   figurative or rhetorical use of language which subverts the standard meaning of a word.

use value   measuring the value an object has in terms of its usefulness to the owner.

BIBLIOGRAPHY

Marx is in a separate category because his works are cited throughout and it is therefore simpler for the reader to refer to them in one place.

MARX

Bottomore, T. B. and Rubel, M. (eds) (1956 & 1961) *Karl Marx: Selected Writings in Sociology and Social Philosophy*, London: Watts & Co.

Marx, K. (1867 & 1995) *Capital*, an abridged edition: edited with an introduction by David McLellan, Oxford: Oxford University Press.

—— (1867 & 1973) *Grundrisse*, trans. Martin Nicolaus, Harmondsworth: Penguin.

—— (1852 & 1968) 'The Eighteenth Brumaire of Louis Bonaparte' in K. Marx and F. Engels, *Selected Works*, London: Lawrence & Wishart.

—— (1849 & 1968) 'Wage Labour and Capital' in K. Marx and F. Engels, *Selected Works*, London: Lawrence & Wishart.

—— (1859 & 1968) 'Preface to the Critique of Political Economy', in K. Marx and F. Engels, *Selected Works*, London: Lawrence & Wishart.

—— (1844 & 1961) 'Critique of the Philosophy of Hegel' in T. B. Bottomore and M. Rubel (eds) *Karl Marx: Selected Writings in Sociology and Social Philosophy*, London: Watts & Co.

Marx, K. and Engels, F. (1846 & 1996) *The German Ideology*, ed. C. J. Arthur, London: Lawrence & Wishart.

—— (1968) *Selected Works*, London: Lawrence & Wishart.

—— (1848 & 1968) 'Manifesto of the Communist Party', *Selected Works*, London: Lawrence & Wishart.

INTRODUCTION

Adonis, A. and Pollard, S. (1997) *A Class Act: The Myth of Britain's Classless Society*, London: Hamish Hamilton.

Althusser, L. (1966 & 1996) 'A Letter on Art' in T. Eagleton and D. Milne (eds) *Marxist Literary Theory*, Oxford: Basil Blackwell: 269–74.

Aristotle (1962) *The Politics*, trans. T. A. Sinclair, Harmondsworth: Penguin.

Balibar, E. and Macherey, P. (1978) 'On Literature as Ideological Form', *Oxford Literary Review*, 3, 4–12.

Brook, S. (1997) *Class: Knowing your Place in Modern Britain*, London: Victor Gollancz.

Calvert, P. (1982) *The Concept of Class*, London: Hutchinson.

Cannadine, D. (1998) *Class in Britain*, New Haven, CT and London: Yale University Press.

Collini, S. (1994) 'Escape from DWEMsville', *Times Literary Supplement* 27 May.

De. Ste. Croix, G. E. M. (1981) *The Class Struggle in the Ancient Greek World from the Archaic Age to the Arab Conquests*, London: Duckworth.

Demaria, R. (ed.) (1996) *British Literature: An Anthology*, Oxford: Basil Blackwell.

Eagleton, T. and Milne, D. (eds) (1996) *Marxist Literary Theory*, Oxford: Basil Blackwell.

Edgell, S. (1993) *Class*, London: Routledge.

Goldmann, L. (1964 & 1975) *Towards a Sociology of the Novel*, trans. A. Sheridan, London: Tavistock.

Hill, C. (1993) *The English Bible and the Seventeenth Century Revolution*, Harmondsworth: Penguin.

Johnson, S. (1759 & 1996) *The History of Rasselas, Prince of Abyssinia* in Demaria: 863–921.

Lukács, G. (1971) *The Theory of the Novel*, London: Merlin Press.

Milner, A. (1999) *Class*, London: Sage.

Parsons, T. (1994) *Dispatches from the Front Line of Popular Culture*, London: Virgin.

Weber, M. (1948 & 1993) *Essays in Sociology*, edited with an Introduction by H. H. Gerth and C. Wright Mills, London: Routledge.

Williams, R. (1988) *Keywords: A Vocabulary of Culture and Society*, London: Fontana.

—— (1977) *Marxism and Literature*, Oxford: Oxford University Press.

—— (1958) *Culture and Society 1780–1950*, Harmondsworth: Penguin.

Wright, E. Olin (1989) *The Debate on Classes*, London: Verso.

MEDIEVAL

Primary texts

Chaucer, G. (1387 & 1992) *Canterbury Tales*, London: Dent.

Froissart, J. (1388 & 1978) *Chronicles*, trans. G. Brereton, Harmondsworth: Penguin.

Langland, W. (1379 & 1966) *Piers the Ploughman*, Harmondsworth: Penguin.

Malory, T. (1470 & 1998) *Le Morte Darthur*, Oxford: Oxford University Press.

Sir Gawain and the Green Knight (1380 & 1998) K. Harrison (trans.) and H. Cooper (ed.), Oxford: Oxford University Press.

Stockton, E. W. (trans.) (1962) *The Major Latin Works of John Gower, Vox Clamantis and Tripartita Chronicle*, Seattle.

Secondary texts

Aers, D. (1988) *Community, Gender and Individual Identity: English Writing 1360–1430*, London and New York: Routledge.

Anderson, P. (1974 & 1996) *Lineages of the Absolutist State*, London: Verso.

Bloch, M. (1962) *Feudal Society*, trans. L. A. Manyon, London: Routledge.

Bolton, J. L. (1980) *The Medieval English Economy, 1150–1500*, London: Dent.

Coleman, J. (1981) *Medieval Readers and Writers*, London: Hutchinson.

Hilton, R. (1985 & 1990) *Class Conflict and the Crisis of Feudalism*, London and New York: Verso.

Huizinga, J. (1924 & 1968) *The Waning of the Middle Ages*, Harmondsworth: Penguin.

Keen, M. (1990) *English Society in the Later Middle Ages*, Harmondsworth: Penguin.

Medcalf, S. (ed.) 1981) *The Later Middle Ages*, London: Methuen.

Morgan, G. A. (1993) *Medieval Balladry and the Courtly Tradition*, New York: Peter Lang.

Reynolds, S. (1994) *Fiefs and Vassals: The Medieval Experience Reinterpreted*, Oxford: Oxford University Press.

Williams, R. (1988) *Keywords: A Vocabulary of Culture and Society*, London: Fontana.

THE RENAISSANCE

Primary texts

Barnfield, R. (1598 & 1995) 'The Praise of Money' in K. Jackson (ed.) *Money*, Oxford: Oxford University Press.

Beaumont, F. (1613 & 1970) *The Knight of the Burning Pestle* in M. C. Bradbrook (ed.) *Beaumont and Fletcher: Selected Plays*, London: Dent.

Dekker, T. (1599 & 1997) *The Shoemaker's Holiday*, London: Black.

Donne, J. (1971) *The Complete Poems*, Harmondsworth: Penguin.

Hall, J. (1649 & 1953) *The Advancement of Learning*, Liverpool: Liverpool University Press.

Jonson, B. (1607 & 1966) *Volpone* in *Three Comedies*, Harmondsworth: Penguin.

Langland, W. (1379 & 1966) *Piers the Ploughman*, Harmondsworth: Penguin.

Massinger, P. (1632 & 1964) *The City Madam*, London: Edward Arnold.

Middleton, T. (1606 & 1973) *A Trick to Catch the Old One* in R. G. Lawrence (ed.) *Jacobean and Caroline Comedies*, London: Dent.

More, T. (1516 & 1965) *Utopia*, trans. Paul Turner, Harmondsworth: Penguin.

Saintsbury, G. (ed.) (1905) *Minor Poets of the Caroline Period*, Oxford: Oxford University Press.

Shakespeare, William (1988) *The Complete Works*, edited by S. Wells and G. Taylor, Oxford: Clarendon Press.

Spenser, E. (1593 & 1975) *The Shepherd's Calendar and Other Poems*, London: Dent.

Webster, J. (1623 & 1987) *The Duchess of Malfi* in *Three Plays*, Harmondsworth: Penguin.

White, M. (ed.) (1982) *Arden of Faversham*, London: Ernest Benn.

Secondary texts

Armstrong, I. (1989) 'Thatcher's Shakespeare', *Textual Practice*, 3, 1: 1–14.

Barker, F. (1993) *The Culture of Violence: Essays on Tragedy and History*, Manchester: Manchester University Press.

Beier, A. L. (1985) *Masterless Men: The Vagrancy Problem in England 1560–1640*, London: Methuen .

Belsey, C. (1999) *Shakespeare and the Loss of Eden*, Basingstoke: Macmillan.

—— (1992) 'Making Histories' in Holderness: 103–20.

Bourdieu, P. (1979 & 1984) *Distinction: A Social Critique of the Judgement of Taste*, trans. Richard Nice, London: Routledge.

Briggs, J. (1983 & 1997) *This Stage Play World: Texts and Contexts 1580–1625*, Oxford: Oxford University Press.

Danby, J. F. (1948) *Shakespeare's Doctrine of Nature: A Study of King Lear*, London: Faber.

Dollimore, J. (1989) *Radical Tragedy: Religion, Ideology and Power in the Drama of Shakespeare and his Contemporaries*, Hemel Hempstead: Harvester Wheatsheaf.

—— and Sinfield, A. (1992) 'History and Ideology: *Henry V*,' in Holderness: 182–99.

—— and Sinfield, A. (1985) *Political Shakespeare: Essays in Cultural Materialism*, Manchester: Manchester University Press.

Drakakis, J. (ed.) (1985) *Alternative Shakespeares*, London and New York: Methuen.

Frow, J. (1995) *Cultural Studies and Cultural Value*, Oxford: Oxford University Press.

Giddens, A. (1981) *The Class Structure of the Advanced Societies*, London: Hutchinson.

Hawkes, T. (ed.) (1996) *Alternative Shakespeares, Vol. 2*, London: Routledge.

Hill, C. (1996) *Liberty Against the Law: Some Seventeenth-Century Controversies*, Harmondsworth: Penguin.

—— (1972) *The World Turned Upside Down: Radical Ideas During the English Revolution*, Harmondsworth: Penguin.

Holbrook, P. (1994) *Literature and Degree in Renaissance England: Nashe, Bourgeois Tragedy, Shakespeare*, Newark: University of Delaware Press.

Holderness, G. (ed.) (1992) *Shakespeare's History Plays: Richard II to Henry V*, Basingstoke: Macmillan.

Kamen, H. (1971) *The Iron Century: Social Changes in Europe 1550–1660*, London: Weidenfeld & Nicolson.

Kastan, D. (1987) 'Workshop and/as Playhouse: Comedy and Commerce in *The Shoemaker's Holiday*', *Studies in Philology*, 84: 325–37.

Laslett, P. (1965 & 1971) *The World We Have Lost*, London: Routledge.

McLuskie, K. E. (1996) ' "When the Bad Bleed": Renaissance Tragedy and

Dramatic Form' in W. Zunder and S. Trill (eds) *Writing and the English Renaissance*, Harlow: Longman: 69–86.

Newbolt Report (1921) *The Teaching of English in England: Being the Report of the Departmental Committee Appointed by the President of the Board of Education to Inquire into the Position of English in the Education System of England*, London: HMSO.

Scarman, T. (1981) *The Brixton Disorders 10–12 April 1981: Report of an Inquiry by the Rt Hon. Lord Scarman OBE*, London: HMSO.

Sinfield, A. (1992) *Faultlines: Cultural Materialism and the Politics of Dissident Reading*, Oxford: Clarendon Press.

Southall, R. (1973) *Literature and the Rise of Capitalism*, London: Lawrence & Wishart.

Stone, L. (1967) *The Crisis of the Aristocracy: 1558–1641*, Oxford: Oxford University Press.

Tawney, R. H. (1926 & 1990) *Religion and the Rise of Capitalism*, Harmondsworth: Penguin.

Tillyard, E. M. W. (1943 & 1976) *The Elizabethan World Picture*, Harmondsworth: Penguin.

Williams, R. (1988) *Keywords: A Vocabulary of Culture and Society*, London: Fontana.

Wright, L. B. (1935 & 1958) *Middle-Class Culture in Elizabethan England*, Ithaca, NY and London: Cornell University Press.

Wrightson, K. (1991) 'Estates, Degrees and Sorts: Changing Perceptions of Society in Tudor and Stuart England' in P. J. Corfield (ed.) *Language, History and Class*, Oxford and Cambridge, MA: Basil Blackwell: 30–52.

THE CIVIL WAR AND AFTER

Primary texts

Blackmore, R. (1695 & 1963) *Preface to Prince Arthur* in Spingarn, Vol. 3: 11–18.

Davenant, W. (1650 & 1963) *Preface to Gondibert* in Spingarn, Vol. 2: 9–24.

Demaria, R. (1996) (ed.) *British Literature: An Anthology*, Oxford: Basil Blackwell.

Denham, J. (1688 & 1974) 'Cooper's Hill' in Parfitt: 224.

Dillon, W. (1684 & 1963) 'An Essay on Translated Verse' in Spingarn, Vol. 2: 12–16.

Dryden, J. (1668 & 1997) 'Of Dramatic Poesie: An Essay' in *Augustan Critical Writing*, ed. David Womersley, Harmondsworth: Penguin.

Etherege, G. (1676 & 1967) *The Man of Mode*, London: Edward Arnold.

Glanvill, J. (1678 & 1963) 'An Essay Concerning Preaching' in Spingarn, Vol. 2: 67–73.

Hobbes, T. (1651 & 1985) *Leviathan*, Harmondsworth: Penguin.

Marvell, A. (1976) *The Complete Poems*, Harmondsworth: Penguin.

Milton, J. (1977) *Poetical Works*, ed. Douglas Bush, Oxford: Oxford University Press.

Parfitt, G. A. E. (1974) *Silver Poets of the Seventeenth Century*, London: Dent.

Rochester, J. (1680) 'Signior Dildo' in Demaria: 386–9.

Sharp, A. (ed.) (1998) *The English Levellers*, Cambridge: Cambridge University Press.

Sheffield, J. (1682 & 1963) 'An Essay Upon Poetry' in Spingarn, Vol. 2: 16–26.

Spingarn, J. E. (1963) *Critical Essays of the Seventeenth Century*, Vols 2 and 3, Bloomington: Indiana University Press.

Sprat, T. (1667 & 1963) 'From *The History of The Royal Society*,' in Spingarn, vol. 2: 43–9.

Temple, W. (1690 & 1963) 'Of Poetry' in Spingarn, Vol. 3: 36–7.

Wycherley, W. (1675 & 1976) *The Country Wife* and *The Man of Mode* in *Restoration Plays*, London: Dent.

—— (1676 & 1967) *The Plain Dealer*, London: Edward Arnold.

Secondary texts

Ashley, M. (1968) *England in the Seventeenth Century*, Harmondsworth: Penguin.

Buchan, J. (1997) *Frozen Desire: An Inquiry into the Meaning of Money*, London: Picador.

Derrida, J. (1994) *Given Time: I. Counterfeit Money*, trans. Peggy Kamuf, Chicago: University of Chicago Press.

Dimock, W. and Gilmore, M. (eds) (1994) *Re-thinking Class: Literary Studies and Social Formations*, New York: Columbia University Press.

Eliot, T. S. (1932 & 1976) *Selected Essays*, London: Faber .

Greaves, R. (1992) *John Bunyan and English Non-Conformity*, London: Rio Grande.

Guillory, J. (1993) *Cultural Capital: The Problem of Literary Canon Formation*, Chicago: University of Chicago Press.

Gunn, J. A. W. (1969) *Politics and the Public Interest in the Seventeenth Century*, London: Routledge.

Hill, C. (1980 & 1997) *Some Intellectual Consequences of the English Revolution*, London: Phoenix.

—— (1972) *The World Turned Upside Down: Radical Ideas During the English Revolution*, Harmondsworth: Penguin.

Hirschman, A. (1977 & 1997) *The Passions and the Interests: Political Arguments for Capitalism before its Triumph*, Princeton, NJ: Princeton University Press.

Jacob, J. R. (1980) 'Restoration, Reformation and the Origins of the Royal Society' in Owen: 241–52.

Kishlansky, M. (1997) *Monarchy Transformed: Britain, 1603–1714*, Harmondsworth: Penguin.

Lipson, E. (1964) *The Economic History of England, Vol. 3: The Age of Mercantilism*, London: Adam and Charles Black.

MacLachlan, A. (1996) *The Rise and Fall of Revolutionary England: An Essay on the Fabrication of Seventeenth-Century History*, Basingstoke: Macmillan.

Manning, B. (1996) *Aristocrats, Plebeians and Revolution in England*, London: Pluto Press.

McKeon, M. (1988) *The Origins of the English Novel: 1600–1740*, Baltimore, MD: Johns Hopkins University Press.

Morgan, E. Victor (1965) *A History of Money*, Harmondsworth: Penguin.

Owen, W. R. (ed.) (1980) *Seventeenth-Century England: A Changing Culture: Vol. 2: Modern Studies*, Milton Keynes: Open University Press.

Parfitt, G. (1985 & 1992) *English Poetry of the Seventeenth Century*, London and New York: Longman.

Pooley, R. (1992) *English Prose of the Seventeenth Century, 1590–1700*, Harlow: Longman.

Poovey, M. (1994) 'The Social Constitution of "Class": Towards a History of Classificatory Thinking' in Dimock and Gilmore: 16–56.

Roseveare, H. (1991) *The Financial Revolution, 1660–1760*, London: Longman.

Shell, M. (1982) *Money, Language and Thought*, Baltimore, MD: Johns Hopkins University Press.

Smith, N. (1994) *Literature and Revolution in England, 1640–1660*, New Haven, CT and London: Yale University Press.

Tawney, R. H. (1926 & 1990) *Religion and the Rise of Capitalism*, Harmondsworth: Penguin.

Thirsk, J. (1978) *Economic Policy and Projects: The Development of a Consumer Society in Early Modern England*, Oxford: Clarendon Press.

Thompson, J. (1996) *Models of Value: Eighteenth-Century Political Economy and the Novel*, Durham, NC: Duke University Press.

Weber, M. (1930 & 1967) *The Protestant Ethic and the Spirit of Capitalism*, London: Allen & Unwin.

Wilson, C. (1965 & 1996) *England's Apprenticeship, 1603–1763*, Harlow: Longman.

THE EIGHTEENTH CENTURY

Primary texts

Defoe, D. (1719 & 1972) *Robinson Crusoe*, Harmondsworth: Penguin.

Demaria, R. (1996) (ed.) *British Literature: An Anthology*, Oxford: Basil Blackwell.

Fielding, H. (1743 & 1947) *Jonathan Wild*, London: Hamish Hamilton.

—— (1741 & 1960) *Joseph Andrews*, London: Dent.

Johnson, S. (1759 & 1996) *The History of Rasselas, Prince of Abyssinia* in Demaria: 863–921.

—— (1749 & 1996) 'The Vanity of Human Wishes' in Demaria: 843–51.

Kant, I. (1784 & 1995) 'What is Enlightenment?' in I. Kramnick (ed.) *The Portable Enlightenment Reader*, Harmondsworth: Penguin: 1–6.

Locke, J. (1690 & 1995) *An Essay Concerning Human Understanding* in Kramnick: 185–7.

Pope, A. (1978) *Poetical Works*, Oxford: Oxford University Press.

Richardson, S. (1740 & 1962) *Pamela*, London: Dent.

Shakespeare, William (1988) *The Complete Works*, edited by S. Wells and G. Taylor, Oxford: Clarendon Press.

Steele, R. and Addison, J. (1988) *Selections from The Tatler and Spectator*, Harmondsworth: Penguin.

Secondary texts

Armstrong, N. (1987) *Desire and Domestic Fiction: A Political History of the Novel*, Oxford: Oxford University Press.

Barrell, J. (1983) *English Literature in History, 1730–80: An Equal Wide Survey*, London: Hutchinson.

Bush, M. L. (ed.) *Social Orders and Social Classes in Europe Since 1500*, Harlow: Longman.

Cannadine, D. (1998) *Class in Britain*, New Haven, CT and London: Yale University Press.

Cauldwell, C. (1937 & 1977) *Illusion and Reality*, London: Lawrence & Wishart.

Dimock, W. and Gilmore, M. (eds) (1994) *Re-thinking Class: Literary Studies and Social Formations*, New York: Columbia University Press.

Doyle, B. (1989) *English and Englishness*, London: Routledge.

Eagleton, T. (1990) *The Ideology of the Aesthetic*, Oxford: Basil Blackwell.

Gorz, A. (1989) *Critique of Economic Reason*, trans. Gillian Handyside and Chris Turner, London: Verso.

Hay, D. and Rogers, N. (1997) *Eighteenth-Century English Society*, Oxford: Oxford University Press.

Hazard, P. (1965) *European Thought in the Eighteenth Century*, trans. J. Lewis May, Harmondsworth: Penguin.

Klaus, H. Gustav (1985) *The Literature of Labour: 200 Years of Working-Class Writing*, Brighton: Harvester.

Jameson, F. (1988) *The Ideologies of Theory: Essays 1971–1986*, Minneapolis: University of Minneapolis Press.

Langford, P. (1997) 'The Eighteenth Century' in Morgan.

McKeon, M. (1988) *The Origins of the English Novel: 1600–1740*, Baltimore, MD: Johns Hopkins University Press, 317–45.

Morgan, K. O. (ed.) (1997) *The Oxford Illustrated History of Britain*, Oxford: Oxford University Press.

Nicholson, C. (1996) *Writing and the Rise of Finance: Capital Satires of the Early Eighteenth Century*, Cambridge: Cambridge University Press.

Poovey, M. (1994) 'The Social Constitution of "Class": Towards a History of Classificatory Thinking' in Dimock and Gilmore: 16–56.

Porter, R. (1990) *English Society in the Eighteenth Century*, Harmondsworth: Penguin.

Probyn, C. (1994) *English Fiction of the Eighteenth Century, 1700–1789*, Harlow: Longman.

Robbins, B. (1993) *The Servant's Hand: English Fiction from Below*, Durham, NC: Duke University Press.

Roseveare, H. (1991) *The Financial Revolution, 1660–1760*, London: Longman.

Sambrook, J. (1993) *The Eighteenth Century: The Intellectual and Cultural Context of English Literature*, Harlow: Longman .

Seed, J. (1992) 'From "Middling Sort" to Middle Class in Late Eighteenth- and Early Nineteenth-Century England' in Bush: 114–36.

Stone, L. (1977) *Family, Sex and Marriage in England, 1500–1800*, Harmondsworth: Penguin.

Thompson, E. P. (1993) *Customs in Common*, Harmondsworth: Penguin.

Thompson, J. (1996) *Models of Value: Eighteenth-Century Political Economy and the Novel*, Durham, NC: Duke University Press.

Watt, I. (1957) *The Rise of the Novel: Studies in Defoe, Richardson and Fielding*, Harmondsworth: Penguin.

Williams, R. (1988) *Keywords: A Vocabulary of Culture and Society*, London: Fontana.

Žižek, S. (1994) *The Sublime Object of Ideology*, London: Verso.

THE NINETEENTH CENTURY

Primary texts

Anonymous (1847 & 1995) 'The Charter and the Land' in Haywood: 191–4.

—— (1840 & 1995) 'A Simple Story' in Haywood: 41–5.

—— (1838 & 1995) 'Will Harper: A Poor Law Tale' in Haywood: 26–32.

Blake, W. (1975) *William Blake*, introduced and edited by J. Bronowski, Harmondsworth: Penguin.

Booth, C. (1889 & 1978) 'East London: The Eight Classes' in Keating: 112–24.

Booth, W. (1890 & 1978) 'Why Darkest England?' and 'The Way Out' in Keating: 141–51.

Carlyle, T. (1829 & 1981) 'Signs of the Times' in Keating: 43–68.

Cobbett, W. (1830 & 1985) *Rural Rides*, Harmondsworth: Penguin.

Coleridge, S. T. (1817 & 1986) *Coleridge: Poems and Prose*, selected by Kathleen Raine, Harmondsworth: Penguin.

Cooper, T. (1845) '"Merrie England" – No More!' in Haywood: 53–9.

—— (1845) 'Seth Thompson, the Stockinger' in Haywood: 46–52.

Dickens, C. (1841 & 1964) *Barnaby Rudge*, London: Hazel, Watson & Viney.

Disraeli, B. (1845 & 1985) *Sybil: or, The Two Nations*, Harmondsworth: Penguin.

Eliot, G. (1872 & 1965) *Middlemarch*, Harmondsworth: Penguin.

Engels, F. (1845, 1892 & 1958) *The Condition of the Working Class in England*, trans. W. O. Henderson and W. H. Chaloner, Oxford: Oxford University Press.

Gaskell, E. (1855 & 1993) *North and South*, London: Everyman.

Gissing, G. (1889 & 1992) *The Nether World*, Oxford: Oxford World Classics.

Greenwood, J. (1876 & 1978) 'A Man and Dog Fight in Henley' in Keating: 62–71.

Haywood, I. (1995) *The Literature of Struggle: An Anthology of Chartist Fiction*, Aldershot: Scolar Press.

Hutton, M. (1839 & 1995) 'The Poor Man's Wrongs' in Haywood: 186–90.

Jones, E. (1848 & 1995) 'The London Doorstep (A True story)' in Haywood: 195–7.

Jones, W. (1849) *The Spirit; or a Dream in the Woodlands*, Leicester: Joseph Ayer.

Keating, P. (1981) *The Victorian Prophets: A Reader from Carlyle to Wells*, London: Fontana.

—— (1978) (ed.) *Into Unknown England: Selections from the Social Explorers*, London: Fontana.

Lovett, W. (1876) *The Life and Struggles of William Lovett*, London: Chapman Hall.

Mayhew, H. (1862 & 1985) *London Labour and the London Poor*, Harmondsworth: Penguin.

Morris, W. (1894 & 1981) 'How I Became a Socialist' in Keating: 237–41.

Morrison, A. (1896 & 1996) *A Child of the Jago*, London: Everyman.

Owen, R. (1816 & 1972) *A New View of Society*, Basingstoke: Macmillan.

Pater, W. (1868 & 1986) *The Renaissance*, Oxford: Oxford University Press.

Shelley, P. (1821 & 1979) 'The Defence of Poetry' in Clayre: 211–16.

Somerville, A. (1839 & 1995) 'Dissuasive Warnings to the People on Street Warfare' in Haywood: 107–30.

Wordsworth, W. (1989) *Selected Poems*, ed. Walford Davies, London: Dent.

Secondary texts

Ackroyd, P. (1996) *Blake*, London: Minerva.

Altick, R. (1957) *The English Common Reader: A Social History of the Mass Reading Public 1800–1900*, Chicago: University of Chicago Press.

Anderson, P. (1992) *English Questions*, London: Verso.

Bailey, P. (1978 & 1987) *Leisure and Class in Victorian England: Rational Recreation and the Contest for Control*, London: Methuen.

Briggs, A. (1967 & 1983) 'The Language of "Class" in Early Nineteenth-Century England' in Neale: 2–29.

—— (1954 & 1977) *Victorian People*, Harmondsworth: Penguin.

Cannadine, D. (1998) *Class in Britain*, New Haven, CT and London: Yale University Press.

Callaghan, J. (1990) *Socialism in Britain*, Oxford: Basil Blackwell.

Chandler, A. (1971) *A Dream of Order: The Medieval Ideal in Nineteenth-Century English Literature*, London: Routledge.

Clayre, A. (1979) *Nature and Industrialization*, Oxford: Oxford University Press.

Corfield, P. J. (ed.) (1991) *Language, History and Class*, Oxford and Cambridge, MA: Basil Blackwell.

Crossick, G. (1991) 'From Gentleman to the Residuum: Languages of Social Description in Victorian Britain' in Corfield: 150–78.

Eagleton, T. (1991) *Ideology: An Introduction*, London: Verso.

Epstein, J. and Thompson, D. (eds) (1982) *The Chartist Experience: Studies in Working-Class Radicalism and Culture, 1830–1860*, Basingstoke: Macmillan.

Gilmour, R. (1993) *The Victorian Period: The Intellectual and Cultural Context of English Literature, 1830–1890*, Harlow: Longman.

Gorz, A. (1982) *Farewell to the Working Class*, trans. Michael Sonenscher, London: Pluto.

Hall, S. and Schwarz, B. (1985) 'State and Society' in Langan and Schwarz: 7–32.

Hemstedt, G. (1978) 'The Novel' in Lerner: 3–24.

Himmelfarb, G. (1984) *The Idea of Poverty: England in the Early Industrial Age*, London: Faber.

Hobsbawm, E. J. (1964) *Labouring Men: Studies in the History of Labour*, London: Wiedenfeld.

—— (1948 & 1974) *Labour's Turning Point, 1880–1900*, Hassocks: Harvester Press.

Inglis, B. (1972) *Poverty and the Industrial Revolution*, London: Panther.

James, L. (1974) *Fiction for the Working Man*, Harmondsworth: Penguin.

Joyce, P. (1980) *Work, Society and Politics*, Hassocks: Harvester.

Keating, P. (1971) *The Working Class in Victorian Fiction*, London: Routledge.

Kirk, N. (1998) *Change, Continuity and Class: Labour in British Society, 1850–1920*, Manchester: Manchester University Press.

—— (1994) *Labour and Society in Britain and the USA: Challenge and Accommodation, 1850–1939*, Aldershot: Gower.

Langan, M. and Schwarz, B. (eds) (1985) *Crises in the British State, 1880–1930*, London: Hutchinson.

Lebowitz, M. (1992) *Beyond Capital: Marx's Political Economy of the Working Classes*, Basingstoke: Macmillan.

Lerner, L. (ed.) (1978) *The Victorians*, London: Methuen.

Lukács, G. (1968 & 1990) *History and Class Consciousness*, trans. Rodney Livingstone, London: Merlin.

Lyotard, Jean François (1984) *The Postmodern Condition: A Report on Knowledge*, trans. G. Bennington and B. Massumi, Manchester: Manchester University Press.

Mason, P. (1982 & 1993) *The English Gentleman: The Rise and Fall of an Ideal*, London: Pimlico.

McIvor, A. J. (1996) *Organised Capital: Employer's Associations and Industrial Relations in Northern England*, Cambridge: Cambridge University Press.

McKibbin, R. (1991) *The Ideologies of Class: Social Relations in Britain, 1880–1950*, Oxford: Oxford University Press.

McWilliam, R. (1998) *Popular Politics in Nineteenth-Century England*, London and New York: Routledge.

Murphy, P. T. (1994) *Towards a Working-Class Canon: Literary Criticism in British Working-Class Periodicals, 1816–1858*, Columbus: Ohio State University Press.

Musselwhite, D. (1987) *Partings Welded Together: Politics and Desire in the Nineteenth-Century Novel*, London and New York: Methuen.

Neale, R. S. (1983) (ed.) *History and Class: Essential Readings in Theory and Interpretation*, Oxford: Basil Blackwell.

Small, I. (ed.) (1979) *The Aesthetes: A Sourcebook*, London: Routledge.

Stedman Jones, G. (1983) *The Language of Class: Studies in English Working-Class History*, Cambridge: Cambridge University Press.

Thompson, E. P. (1963 & 1988) *The Making of the English Working Class*, Harmondsworth: Penguin.

Vicinus, M. (1974) *The Industrial Muse: A Study of Nineteenth-Century British Working-Class Literature*, London: Croom Helm.

Vincent, D. (1981) *Bread, Knowledge and Freedom: A Study of Working-Class Autobiography*, London: Europa.

Walton, J. (1999) *Chartism*, London and New York: Routledge.

Waters, C. (1990) *British Socialists and the Politics of Popular Culture 1880–1994*, Manchester: Manchester University Press.

Whiteley, J. H. (1938) *Wesley's England*, London: Methuen.

Williams, R. (1958 & 1975) *Culture and Society, 1780–1950*, Harmondsworth: Penguin.

—— (1973) *The Country and the City*, London: Paladin.

THE TWENTIETH CENTURY

Primary texts

Allott, M. (ed.) (1980) *Novelists on the Novel*, London: Routledge.

Arnold, M. (1865 & 1981) 'The Function of Criticism at the Present Time' in Keating: 185–213.

Barker, P. (1986 & 1999) *Liza's England*, London: Virago.

Bell, C. (1914 & 1987) *Art*, Oxford: Oxford University Press.

Bourdieu, P. (1979 & 1984) *Distinction: A Social Critique of the Judgement of Taste*, trans. Richard Nice, London: Routledge.

Bowen, E. (1938 & 1966) *The Death of the Heart*, Harmondsworth: Penguin.

Braine, J. (1957 & 1991) *Room at the Top*, London: Arrow.

Danziger, N. (1997) *Danziger's Britain: A Journey to the Edge*, London: Flamingo.

Davies, N. (1997) *Dark Heart: The Shocking Truth about Hidden Britain*, London: Chatto & Windus.

Eliot, T. S. (1969) *The Complete Poems and Plays of T. S. Eliot*, London: Faber.

Forster, E. M. (1910 & 1987) *Howard's End*, Harmondsworth: Penguin.

Greenwood, W. (1933 & 1993) *Love on the Dole*, London: Vintage.

Harrison, T. (1984) *Selected Poems*, Harmondsworth: Penguin.

Heslop, H (1929) *The Gate of a Strange Field*, London: Bretanos.

Hines, B. (1968) *A Kestrel for a Knave*, London: Michael Joseph.

Hoggart, R. (1957 & 1992) *The Uses of Literacy*, Harmondsworth: Penguin.

James, H. (1912 & 1980) 'Form is Substance' in Allott: 235.

King, J. (1996) *The Football Factory*, London: Jonathan Cape.

Klaus, G. (ed.) (1982 & 1993) *Tramps, Workmates and Revolutionaries: Working-Class Stories of the 1920s*, London: Journeyman.

Lawrence, D. H. (1915 & 1993) *The Rainbow*, London: Dent.

London, J. (1908) *The Iron Heel*, London: Dent.

Odets, C. (1937) *Waiting for Lefty*, London: Victor Gollancz.

Orwell, G. (1937 & 1989) *The Road to Wigan Pier*, Harmondsworth: Penguin.

—— (1940 & 1988) *Inside the Whale and Other Essays*, Harmondsworth: Penguin.

Osborne, J. (1957 & 1983) *Look Back in Anger*, London: Faber.

Roberts, R. (1971 & 1983) *The Classic Slum: Salford Life in the First Quarter of the Century*, Harmondsworth: Penguin.

Sillitoe, A. (1958 & 1994) *Saturday Night and Sunday Morning*, London: Flamingo.

Skelton, R. (ed.) (1977) *Poetry of the Thirties*, Harmondsworth: Penguin.

Smith, A. (1776 & 1986) *The Wealth of Nations*, Harmondsworth: Penguin.

Tressell, R. (1914 & 1997) *The Ragged Trousered Philanthropists*, London: Flamingo.

Wain, J. (1953 & 1977) *Hurry on Down*, Harmondsworth: Penguin.

Welsh, I. (1993) *Trainspotting*, London: Minerva.

Wesker, A. (1959 & 1972) *The Wesker Trilogy*, Harmondsworth: Penguin.

Westergaard, J. and Resler, H. (1975) *Class in a Capitalist Society: A Study of Contemporary Britain*, London: Heinemann.

Wilkinson, E. (1929 & 1989) *Strike*, London: Virago.

Winslow Taylor, F. (1911 & 1964) *Scientific Management*, London: Harper Row.

Woolf, V. (1925 & 1989) *Mrs Dalloway*, London: Grafton.

—— (1919 & 1980) 'Modern Fiction' in Allott: 76–7.

Secondary texts

Abel-Smith, B. and Townsend, P. (1965) *The Poor and the Poorest*, Occasional Papers on Social Administration No. 6, London: HMSO.

Adorno, T. and Horkheimer, M. (1944 & 1992) *Dialectic of Enlightenment*, London: Verso.

Althusser, L. (1966 & 1996) 'A Letter on Art' in Eagleton and Milne: 269–74.

Baxendale, J. and Pawling, P. (1996) *Narrating the Thirties: A Decade in the Making 1930 to the Present*, Basingstoke: Macmillan.

Bennett, T. (1979) *Formalism and Marxism*, London: Methuen.

Best, S. and Kellner, D. (1991) *Postmodern Theory: Critical Interrogations*, Basingstoke: Macmillan.

Bradbury, M. and McFarlane, J. (1976 & 1991) *Modernism: A Guide to European Literature*, Harmondsworth: Penguin.

Cannadine, D. (1998) *Class in Britain*, New Haven, CT and London: Yale University Press.

Carey, J. (1992) *The Intellectuals and the Masses: Pride and Prejudice Among the Literary Intelligentsia, 1880–1939*, London: Faber.

Cherry, S. (1981) *Our History: A Pocket History of the Labour Movement in Britain*, Norwich: University of East Anglia.

Childs, D. (1995) *Britain since 1939: Progress and Decline*, Basingstoke: Macmillan.

Clark, J. (1979) 'Agitprop and Unity Theatre: Socialist Theatre in the Thirties' in Clark *et al.*: 219–39.

Clark, J., Heinemann, M., Margolies, D. and Snee, C. (eds) (1979) *Culture and Crisis in Britain in the 30s*, London: Lawrence & Wishart.

Clarke, J. (1976) 'The Skinheads and the Magical Recovery of Community' in Hall and Jefferson: 99–102.

Clarke, J., Hall, S., Jefferson, T. and Roberts, B. (1976) 'Subcultures, Cultures and Class' in Hall and Jefferson: 9–77.

Cooke, L. (1997) 'British Cinema: Class, Culture and Consensus, 1930–1955' in Day: 163–90.

Day, G. (ed.) *Literature and Culture in Modern Britain, Vol. 2: 1930–1955*, Harlow: Longman.

Eagleton, T. and Milne, D. (eds) (1996) *Marxist Literary Theory*, Oxford: Basil Blackwell.

Easthope, A. (1991) *Literary into Cultural Studies*, London: Routledge.

Fiske, J. (1989a) *Reading the Popular*, London: Unwin Hyman.

—— (1989b) *Understanding Popular Culture*, London: Unwin Hyman.

Fox, P. (1994) *Class Fictions: Shame and Resistance in the British Working-Class Novel, 1890–1945*, Durham, NC: Duke University Press.

Fuller, R. (1973) *Professors and Gods*, London: André Deutsch.

Goldethorpe, J., Lockwood D., Bechofer, F. and Platt, J. (1969) *The Affluent Worker in the Class Structure*, Cambridge: Cambridge University Press.

Goldmann, L. (1964 & 1975) *Towards a Sociology of the Novel*, trans. A. Sheridan, London: Tavistock.

Goux, J. (1994) *The Coiners of Language*, Norman: University of Oklahoma Press.

Hall, S., Hobson, D., Lowe, A. and Willis, P. (eds) (1980) *Culture, Media, Language*, London: Hutchinson.

Hall, S. and Jefferson, T. (eds) (1976) *Resistance through Rituals: Youth Subcultures in Post-war Britain*, London: Hutchinson.

Harris, D. (1992) *From Class Struggle to the Politics of Pleasure: The Effects of Gramscianism on Cultural Studies*, London: Routledge.

Hebdige, D. (1976) 'The Meaning of Mod' in Hall and Jefferson: 87–96.

Jameson, F. (1997) 'Culture and Finance Capital', *Critical Inquiry*, 24, 1: 247–65.

Jefferson, T. (1976) 'Cultural Responses of the Teds' in Hall and Jefferson: 81–6.

Langan, M. and Schwarz, B. (eds) *Crises in the British State, 1880–1930*, London: Hutchinson.

Lea, J. and Pilling, G. (eds) (1996) *The Condition of Britain: Essays on Frederick Engels*, London: Pluto.

Leavis, F. R. (1953 & 1986) *Valuation in Criticism and Other Essays*, ed. G. Singh, Cambridge: Cambridge University Press.

McFarlane, J. (1976 & 1991) 'The Mind of Modernism' in Bradbury and McFarlane: 71–93.

McKibbin, R. (1998) *Class and Cultures: England 1918–1951*, Oxford: Oxford University Press.

Milliband, R. (1991) *Divided Societies: Class Struggle in Contemporary Capitalism*, Oxford: Oxford University Press.

Morley, D. (1980) 'Texts, Readers, Subjects' in Hall *et al.*: 162–73.

Office of National Statistics (1998) *Economic and Social Review of Government Social Classifications*, London: HMSO.

Parsons, T. (1994) *Dispatches from the Front Line of Popular Culture*, London: Virgin.

Perkin, H. (1989) *The Rise of Professional Society: England since 1880*, London: Routledge.

Pilling, D. (1996) 'Engels and the Condition of the Working Class Today' in Lea and Pilling: 84–97.

Reid, B. (1979) 'The Left Book Club in the Thirties' in Clark *et al.*: 193–207.

Sayer, D. (1991) *Capitalism and Modernity: An Excursus on Marx and Weber*, London: Routledge.

Scott, J. (1991) *Who Rules Britain?*, London: Polity.

Stevenson, J. (1984) *British History 1914–1945*, Harmondsworth: Penguin.

Sutton, D. (1985) 'Liberalism, State Collectivism and the Social Relationships of Citizenship' in Langan and Schwarz: 63–79.

Waters, C. (1990) *British Socialists and the Politics of Popular Culture 1880–1994*, Manchester: Manchester University Press.

Wheen, F. (1982) *The Sixties*, London: Century.

Williams, R. (1958 & 1975) *Culture and Society, 1780–1950*, Harmondsworth: Penguin.

Young, M. and Willmott, P. (1957 & 1970) *Family and Kinship in East London*, Harmondsworth: Penguin.

INDEX